MODELLERS
11
DATAFILE

THE BRITISH AEROSPACE
Sea Harrier

A COMPREHENSIVE GUIDE FOR THE MODELLER

'Falklands Fighter'

by Andy Evans

SAM PUBLICATIONS

Modellers Datafile No.11
The British Aerospace Sea Harrier
by Andy Evans

First published in 2007 by SAM Publications
Media House, 21 Kingsway, Bedford, MK42 9BJ, United Kingdom

© 2007 SAM Publications
© Andy Evans – Text
© David Howley – Colour artwork
© David Howley – Scale plans

ISBN 0-9551858-2-3

Typeset by SAM Publications, Media House, 21 Kingsway, Bedford, MK42 9BJ, United Kingdom
Designed by Simon Sugarhood
Printed and bound in the United Kingdom by Printhaüs, United Kingdom

The Modellers Datafile Series
- No.1 – De Havilland Mosquito *
- No.2 – Hawker Hurricane *
- No.3 – Supermarine Spitfire (Part 1: Merlin-Powered) *
- No.4 – Avro Lancaster (Inc Manchester & Lincoln)
- No.5 – Supermarine Spitfire (Part 2: Griffon-Powered)
- No.6 – Bristol Beaufighter
- No.7 – English Electric Lightning
- No.8 – Gloster (& Armstrong-Whitworth) Meteor
- No.9 – Messerschmitt Bf 109 (Part 1 Prototype to E Variants)
- No.10 – Messerschmitt Bf 109 (Part 2 F to K Variants)
* Out of print

Acknowledgments
Thanks are due to the following who have helped in the preparation of this Modellers Datafile.
Firstly to Nick Greenall whose insight, enthusiasm and models were one of the driving factors in the book, and to all members of the IPMS Harrier Special Interest Group for their help and co-operation.

To Gordon Bartley for his support and photographs, and to Barry James of the Midland Air Museum.

Thanks are also due to the following, in no order of preference for use of their images and their help is gratefully recognised:
Karl Branson, Tim Mansfield, Matthew Clements, Chris Lofting. Derek Fergusson, Paul Regan, Robert Trewinard-Boyle, Michael Freer, Joop De, P. Tonna, Dennis J Calvert, Hilary Calvert, Ed Groenendjjk, Tim Beech, Gary Parsons, Tim Beech, Alistair Jones, Lt. Commander David Morgan, Royal Navy Photographic Section and the Fleet Air Arm Museum.

Andy Evans
June 2007

SAM PUBLICATIONS

Contents

Introduction

The Fleet Air Arm surely reached its lowest ebb when it launched its last fixed-wing aircraft, a Phantom FG.1 from HMS Ark Royal's catapult on 27 November 1978. This followed the then Labour government's decision to end the Navy's fixed-wing capability, having already cancelled the P.1154RN and a new carrier destined to replace Ark Royal. The decision makers settled instead for helicopter-based 'commando carriers' or 'through-deck cruisers' (more commonly known as 'see-through cruisers' as they were so obviously designed with the Harrier in mind). The first of these ships was ordered from Vickers in April 1973, to be named HMS Invincible, with a second, Illustrious, being laid down in June 1976. Both were fitted with Harrier 'ski-ramps' in the light of successful shore-based trials. The Harrier had been flying off ships since the early 1960s; Bill Bedford had 'cushioned' P.1127 XP831 on to the Ark's deck on 8 February 1963 while she anchored off Lyme Bay, and the Tri-Partite Kestrel had undertaken deck trails from HMS Bulwark in 1966, ably demonstrating that VSTOL could be used as a 'stand-alone' force or integrated with other assets. The Navy was interested in the supersonic version of the P.1127, the more ambitious P.1154, but when this was cancelled the Senior Services' interest in VSTOL waned. Little did they know that Bill Bedford's Harrier trials of 1963 were the shape of things to come, and that in just a few short years the Navy would loose its fixed wing airpower altogether! In the ensuing years land-based RAF Harriers were operated from the Navy's carriers, GR.1s completed trials aboard HMS Eagle as well as Ark Royal, and the 'Crabs' of No.1(F) Squadron (Navy-speak for anyone not wearing navy blue) received their service clearance to operate from decks in 1970, another clear pointer to the future.

During 1971 a Naval Air Staff requirement was developed for a seagoing aircraft based on the RAF's Harrier GR.3, and Hawker Siddeley were given a contract to study and develop a suitable design. There were two major hurdles for the HSA team to overcome in order to meet the Navy's requirements. Firstly, as the aircraft's primary role was to be that of air defence, it had to be fitted with radar and, secondly, it would be necessary to replace components in the GR.3's make-up that would be prone to salt-water corrosion. Additionally one of the Navy's stipulations was that the aircraft should be able to carry two of the new BAe Sea Eagle missiles. One of the original P.1127(RAF) airframes, XV277, was modified as a trials aircraft to show that the Harrier could carry such a weapon. It was decided that XV277 should initially fire a Martel ASM as a demonstration, and the aircraft gained a new nose section (similar in shape to that of the future Harrier II Plus) as a mock-up of what a seagoing Harrier might look like. Following a successful study, an order for twenty-four 'Sea Harriers' was announced in May 1975 and this was later increased to thirty-five - and the story of the last all-British Fighter had begun, and its chronicle became the stuff of legend.

Andy Evans
June, 2007

ZA193/93 ready for take-off on CAP. From the weather and conditions it is possible this photo was taken on 24th May 1982, so it may show Lt Dave Smith about to take off for the CAP on which he destroyed an Argentine Dagger
(© Dave Morgan)

Glossary

The flight deck crew need to hunker down as an F/A.2 roars down the deck of HMS Illustrious
(© Royal Navy)

AAA	Anti-Aircraft Artillery
AAM	Air to Air Missile
AEW	Airborne Early Warning
AMRAAM	Advanced Medium Range Air to Air Missile
ASM	Air to Surface Missile
ASRAAM	Advanced Short-Range Air to Air Missile
CBLS	Carrier Bomb Light Stores
CBU.	Cluster Bomb Units
Cndr	Commander
CO	Commanding Officer
ECM	Electronic Conter Measures
EDSG	Extra Dark Sea Grey
FAA	Fleet Air Arm
FAC	Forward Air Controller
FDO.	Flight Deck Officer
FLIR	Forward Looking Infra-Red
Flt.Lt	Flight Leiutenant
FRS	Fighter Reconnaisance Strike
GPS	Global Positioning System
HOTAS	Hands On Throttle And Stick
HUD	Head Up Display
IFF.	Indentification Friend or Foe
IFR	In-Flight Refuelling
IFTU	Intensive Flying Trials Unit
INAS	Integrated Nav/Attack System
INS	Inertial Navigation System
JSF	Joint Strike Fighter
LAU.	Launcher Unit
Low-Vis	Low Visibility (colours)
LOX	Liquid Oxygen

LRMTS	Laser Ranging and Market Target Seeker
Lt	Lieutenant
Lt.Cndr	Lieutenant Commander
MADGE	Microwave Aircraft Digital Guideance Equipment
MDC	Miniature Detonation Chord
MFD	Multi-Function Display
MLU	Mid Life Update
MoD	Ministry Of Defence (UK)
MSG	Medium Sea Grey
NAS.	Naval Air Service
NVG	Night Vision Goggles
OBOGS	On Board Oxygen Generating System
OCU	Operational Conversion Unit
OEU.	Operational Evaluation Unit
RAE.	Royal Aircraft Establishment (Farnborough)
RCV	Reaction Control Valve
RNAS	Royal Naval Air Station
RWR	Radar Warning Receiver
SA	Situational Awareness
SHAR	Sea Harrier
SHOFTU.	Sea Harrier Operational Flying Training Unit
SPLOT.	Senior Pilot
Sqn	Squadron Leader
Sqn Ldr.	Squadron Leader
TACAN	Tactical Aid to Navigation
TEZ	Total Exclusion Zone
VSTOL	Vertical and/or Short Take-Off and Landing
WAC	Weapon Aiming Computer

The Sea Harrier FRS.1

The 'FRS' designation stood for Fighter, Reconnaissance and Strike, the latter referring to the aircraft's ability to carry nuclear weapons or nuclear depth charges should the need ever arise. To save costs, the Sea Harrier was to be what was later frequently referred to as a 'minimum change' derivative of the RAF's GR.3. However, the FRS.1 introduced a number of new and key features. Firstly the cockpit floor was raised by 10 inches to provide more equipment space thus allowing, for the first time in a Harrier, some semblance of a decent downward view over the massive intakes, and this revision was further enhanced with the fitting of a 'bubble' canopy, which gave the pilot a better all-round view. The radar was a miniature masterpiece called Blue Fox, developed by Ferranti; it was a version of their ARI.5979 Sea Spray set already in service with the Royal Navy's Lynx helicopter fleet. This I-band pulse modulated set was designed for air-to-air interception, air-to-surface search and strike with ground-mapping abilities. This little set was then fitted into a pointed radome that folded sideways for easy access and space saving aboard the smaller UK carriers.

To avoid the problems of setting up the inertial platform on a moving deck, the GR.3's FE.541 INS was replaced by a twin-gyro platform and a Decca 72 Doppler, giving a very small navigational error after a typical 50-min sortie. In the cockpit a

Factory fresh! XZ450 is towed out. Note the high gloss paintwork
(© Andy Evans Collection)

The first Sea Harrier XZ450 minus any markings
(© Hilary Calvert)

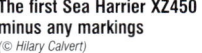

XZ450 in the early flamboyant markings of No.801 Squadron, with their gold trident and cross swords on a red background edged in white. Note the 'N' tailcode
(© Don Gilham)

XV451 showing the short-lived tail markings of No.700A Squadron, the Sea Harrier Intensive Flying Trials Unit (IFTU)
(© Don Gilham)

Preserved at the Fleet Air Arm Museum as XZ493 showing the early markings style of No.800 Squadron
(© Andy Evans Collection)

Four No.899 Squadron Harriers pre-Falklands, showing their high colour markings and glossy paint schemes
(© Martin Freer)

XZ458 showing the detail of its tail markings
(© Dennis Calvert)

A pair of Sea Harriers. Of note here is the Winged Fist in red triangle logo on the nose and the Rolls Royce badge on the intake. The pilot's name is Flt Lt A Penfold, soon to find fame in the Falklands War
(© Ed Groenendijk)

A superb line-up of No.801 Squadron jets pre-Falklands, nearest the camera is the personal mount of Lt Commander Tim Gedge the unit's OC
(© Martin Freer)

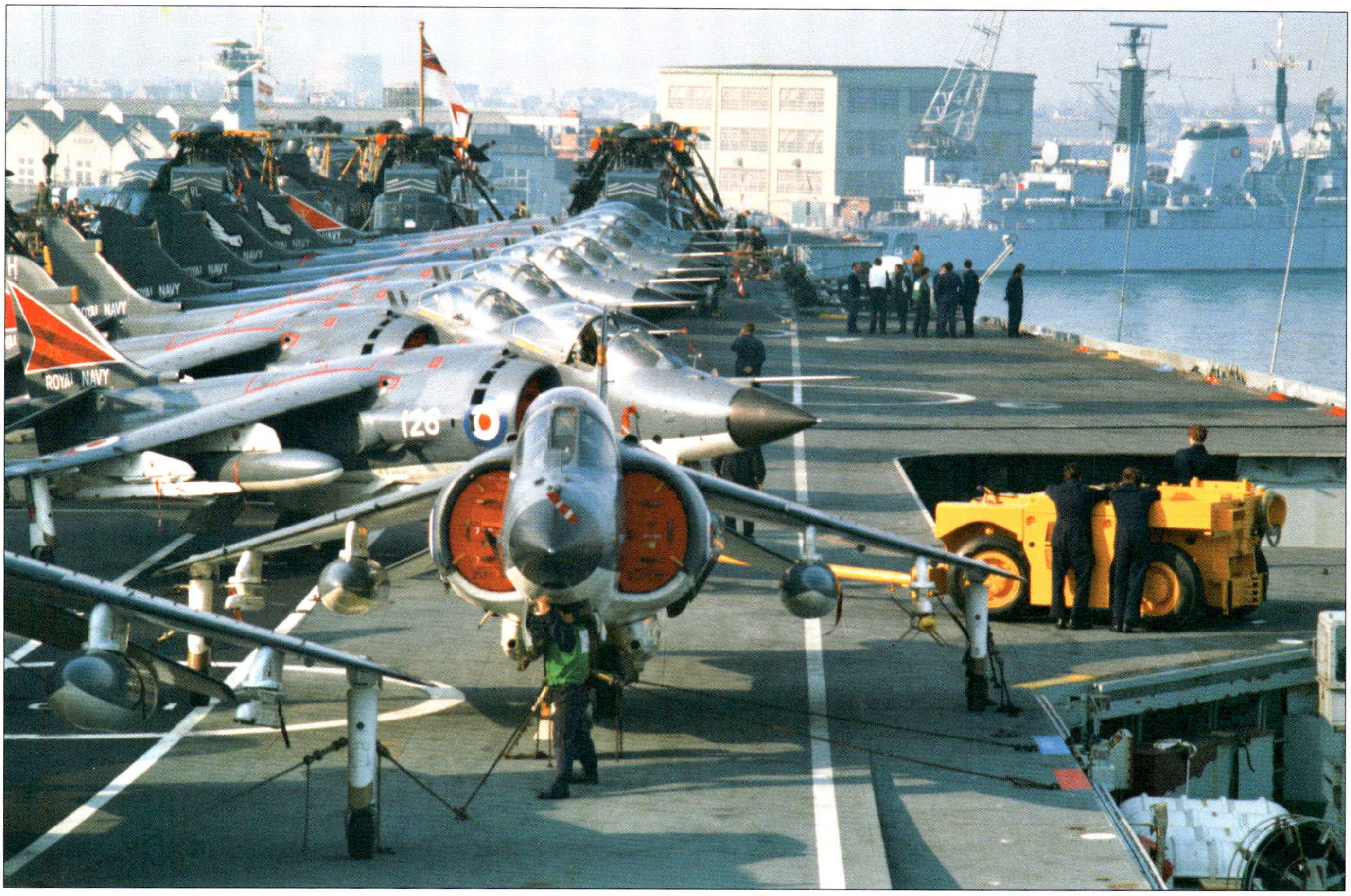

new Smiths Industries HUD was fitted, driven by a 20,000-word digital computer; and as well as displaying its symbology it also served as a weapon aiming computer (WAC) for air-to-air and air-to-surface deliveries. Tie-down lugs were fitted to the main wheels and outriggers, and an enhanced water-injection system to aid carrier recovery was added. The ejector seat was replaced by a Martin-Baker Mk.10 and a revised RWR was also fitted, as was a radio altimeter and starboard F.95 oblique camera in the side of the nose, and the moving map display of the GR.3 was deleted. Because of its primary role, from the outset the Sea Harrier was outfitted to carry Sidewinder AAMs fitted to LAU-7A/5 launch rails on the outer pylons. The aircraft also retained the Aden cannon on their under-fuselage stations. The engine was a Pegasus Mk 104, an especially developed and 'navalised' version of the Mk 103, eliminating the major magnesium components and having a similarly rated thrust as the Mk 103 at 21,5001b.

The first production Sea Harrier FRS.1, XZ450, made its

Ranged on the deck of HMS Hermes as she prepares to leave Portsmouth are her precious cargo of Sea Harriers, bound for the South Atlantic in 1982. The high visibility peacetime colours would soon be replaced by drab warpaint
(© David Morgan)

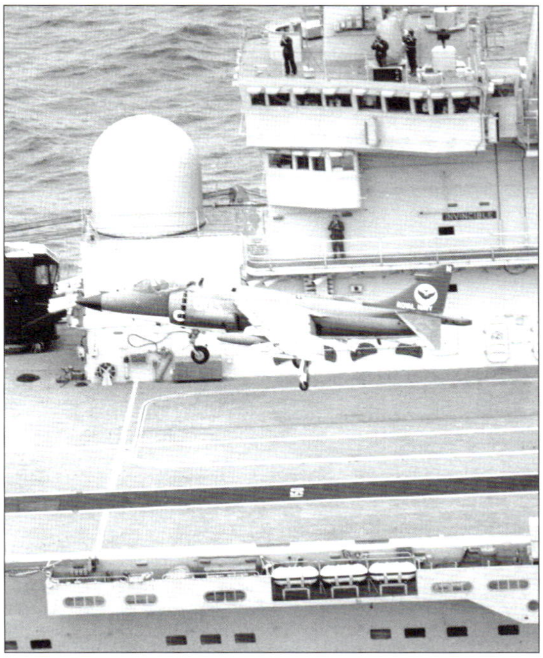

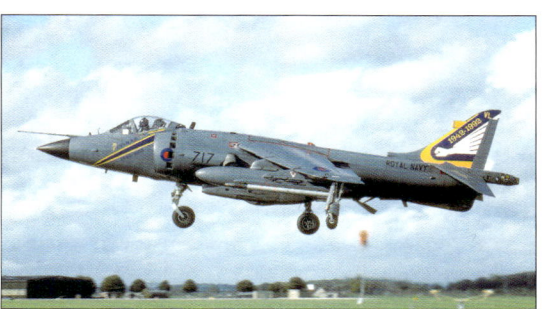

A No.800 Squadron aircraft prepares to alight aboard HMS Invincible
(© Denis Calvert)

ZA175 of No.899 Squadron resplendent in its 50th Anniversary livery
(© Chris Lofting)

maiden flight from Dunsfold on 20 August 1978 with test pilot John Farley at the controls, and within two weeks it was ready to make a spectacular debut at the Farnborough Airshow. Three development aircraft came a little later, XZ438 on 30 December 1978, XZ439 on 30 March 1979 and XZ440 on 6 June 1979. The first Sea Harrier handed over to the Royal Navy was XZ451, which was delivered to RNAS Yeovilton on 18 June 1979, and the initial unit to form on the new aircraft was No.700A Intensive Flying Trials Unit (IFTU) during May 1979, in anticipation of the arrival of their first aircraft. At its zenith, 700A flew five Sea Harriers, and developed the operational techniques required for safe VSTOL operations at sea, embarking aboard HMS Hermes in October of that year.

The workhorse that was XZ450, carrying Sea Eagle missiles. The shooting down of this aircraft in the Falklands War may have convinced the Argentineans that all Sea Harriers could carry the missile, therefore making them unwilling to commit their ships
(© BAe)

Subsequently, its work completed, in March of 1980, 700A disbanded to become No.899 Squadron, the Headquarters and Training Unit for all naval Sea Harriers and their pilots. The 899 Squadron 'Mailed Fist' emblem, which had last adorned their Sea Vixens, was reinstated on the Harriers' tails and their camouflage scheme of extra dark sea grey and white was firmly re-established in the Navy's tradition. When 700A first received its Sea Harriers the radars were not fitted, hence the aircraft were fitted with concrete ballast, giving rise to the 'Blue Circle' radar nickname (Blue Circle being a well known brand of cement)

The Royal Navy planned for three Invincible Class carriers to be produced and the first, HMS Invincible, was commissioned in 1980. However to accommodate the shortfall of available carriers from which to operate the new Sea Harriers, the aging Commando carrier HMS Hermes went through a refit program in 1979-80, adding a 12-degree ski-jump to her bow in order to fill the gap created by the second of the new carriers, HMS Illustrious, not being available until 1982, and the third, HMS Ark Royal, still a number of years away. Plans were laid to equip three front-line squadrons, Nos 800, 801 and 802, each having five Sea Harriers, and a Harrier OCU. In the event, only No.s 800 and 801 were commissioned, however, No.809 Squadron saw a brief return to duty during the Falklands conflict. In April 1980 the first front-line unit

The shortest lived Harrier unit was No.809 Squadron, reactivated during the Falklands War. Here we see their aircraft drawn from many sources, and painted in the lighter grey scheme with pale pink and pale blue colours used for their markings
(© Royal Navy)

XZ453 in the early markings of No.899 Squadron
(© Gordon Bartley)

was commissioned, No.800 Squadron, under Lt Cdr Tim Gedge, with some extremely flamboyant tail markings which sadly were short-lived. Meanwhile, 899's aircraft had made the first ski-jump launches at sea in November 1980, and 800 Squadron embarked on HMS Invincible in January 1981. The Squadron did sterling work in developing the Sea Harrier's tactics, and on 16 June 1981 Invincible was declared 'operationally ready'. Her first cruise, which included an Operational Readiness Inspection, took place later in June, and by this time the second of the Sea Harrier Squadrons, No.801, with its traditional 'Winged Trident' motif on their tails had been commissioned with Lt Cdr 'Sharkey' Ward at the helm. During the second half of 1981 HMS Invincible and her Harriers took part in Ocean Venture and Ocean Safari, followed

XZ454/250 taxies out to the main runway
(© Ian Robertson)

The FRS.1, and F/A.2 both carried the same bolt-on IFR probe
(© Michael Baldock)

XZ455 captured at an airshow in Prestwick in 1981. Note the No.899 logo inside a triangle on the nose
(© Derek Ferguson)

XZ457 showing the code applied inside the airbrake. This also gives a good view of the fuselage contours of the Sea Harrier
(© Andy Evans Collection)

A No.801 Squadron FRS.1 seen here on a goodwill visit to Australia. Of note is all black tail markings and lack of gun-pods
(© via Nick Greenall)

The white on the tail chequer boards has been removed here, and also note the touching up on the wing tanks and airframe
(© P Tonna)

XZ451 in the hover
(© Martin Freer)

A good undersides view here showing the yellow Doppler under the nose, and the undercarriage arrangement
(© Tim Beech)

No.899 Squadron, the Sea Harrier OCU, similarly adopted low-vis markings
(© Andy Evans Collection)

A pair of No.899 Squadron Harriers taxi out for ski-jump practice
(© Joop De Groot)

XZ460 (253) taxies out wearing its high visibility pre-Falklands colour scheme
(© Andy Evans Collection)

A good topside view of XZ498 in pre-Falklands colours. Note the shape of the '5' inside the airbrake
(© via Nick Greenall)

by Alloy Express in early 1982. Her refit and sea trials over, HMS Hermes embarked No.800 Squadron as her first air group with five Sea Harriers. The intention had been for the Royal Navy to have two operational carriers, commissioning Ark Royal in 1985, selling Invincible to the Australian Navy (on the understanding that it would go hand-in-hand with an order for Sea Harriers), and doing a similar deal with the Indian Navy selling them HMS Hermes also with a complement of Sea Harriers. Following the Falklands War the Australian deal fell by the wayside, and it became prudent to maintain a three-carrier force. The Indian Navy deal went thorough successfully, making that service the only other user of the Sea Harrier.

XZ450 seen here at the Paris Air Show wearing its appearance number 241
(© Andy Evans Collection)

XZ458 (125). Note the forward cold nozzle painted in the Dark Sea Grey colour of the upper fuselage
(© Martin Freer)

A typical weapons load as laid out in front of a twin-Sidewinder armed FRS.1
(© Gordon Bartley)

On a misty March Morning in 1983, a post-Falklands line-up of No.899 Squadron Sea Harriers on the ramp at Yeovilton, a sight never to be repeated
(© Andy Evans)

The No.801 Squadron post-Falkland's tail emblem
(© Gordon Bartley)

BAe's test Harrier carrying Sea Eagle missiles visits the Yeovilton ramp
(© Andy Evans)

A pilot prepares his SHAR for a sortie. Note the dark grey around the intakes
(© Andy Evans Collection)

T.4N – Sea Harrier FRS.1 Training

Following the order for 24 Sea Harriers, initial VSTOL training was undertaken by the RAF at Wittering and the Royal Navy had one T.4A two-seat trainer XZ445 on strength as part of 223 OCU. Once this first phase had been passed the fledgling aviators moved to RNAS Yeovilton where they would pick up the Sea Harrier route on one of three Harrier T.4Ns, navalised versions of the standard T.4, with the Pegasus 104 engine and assigned to No.899 Squadron. The dual-base training continued until 1989 when No.899 Squadron undertook sole responsibility for Sea Harrier training. To duplicate the Sea Harrier's cockpit and systems three T.4Ns – ZB604, ZB605 and ZB606 had their front cockpits outfitted with the Sea Harrier FRS.1's avionics (less the radar) thereby making conversion training easier. As the T.4Ns lacked the Blue Fox radar of the FRS.1, the Royal Navy also obtained three Hawker Hunter T.8Ms fitted with the Blue Fox as radar trainers. Some of the T.4Ns had their noses painted to represent a 'radar nose', and colour schemes included overall Light Grey and the more usual overall Extra Dark Sea Gray.

A good view of the larger tail boom of XZ445. The two-seat Harrier has a longer rear fuselage to counterbalance the larger cockpit section
(© Derek Fergusson)

ZE696 showing open panel detail
(© Andy Evans)

Close in on the cockpit section of the N.899 Squadron 50th Anniversary two-seat Harrier
(© Andy Evans)

Technicians get the aircraft ready for the next student
(© Andy Evans)

Externally the same as the RAF's Harrier T.4
(© Andy Evans)

T.4N with a replacement nose section
(© Andy Evans)

Unusually, this T.4 has a black nose simulating a radar, which it did not carry
(© Gordon Bartley)

A T.4 gets prepares to take flight
(© Derek Fergusson)

The Anniversary jet – stripped and scrapped!
(© TZ Aviation)

One of the unique Sea Harrier radar-equipped Hunter T.8Ns
(© Derek Fergusson)

No.899 Squadron decorated both a single-seat and two-seat Harrier for their 50th Anniversary
(© Andy Evans)

Sea Harriers in the Falklands War

When Argentina invaded the Falkland Islands on 2 April 1982, the Royal Navy had just thirty-one Sea Harrier FRS.1s on strength, with seven in storage and four engaged in trials work. A Task Force was assembled under the aegis of Operation Corporate to recapture the Islands, and included in the flotilla of warships were the two carriers HMS Hermes, the flagship, and (on the verge of being sold to Australia) HMS Invincible, both of which embarked Harrier Air Groups. When the Task Force sailed on 14 April it took with it twenty Sea Harrier FRS.1s drawn from the two operational units, Nos.800 and 801 Squadrons, and the shore-based training establishment No.899 Squadron. HMS Hermes carried twelve Harriers from No.800 Squadron, commanded by Lt Cdr Andy Auld, augmented by pilots from No.899 Squadron. HMS Invincible sailed with six Harriers to be joined by a further two as she sailed down the English Channel; these aircraft were from No.801 Squadron, led by Lt Cdr Nigel 'Sharkey' Ward, again augmented by No.899 Squadron. Additionally a further Sea Harrier unit was hastily formed, bringing together all the airframes that remained in the UK, except for four that were to stay at RNAS Yeovilton for training purposes. The Harriers that remained in the UK were XZ440, XZ438 (which later crashed testing long-range tanks), XZ439 and XZ497. The new Harrier unit saw the reformation of No.809 Squadron under the leadership of Lt Cdr Tim Gedge, and it took its eight aircraft to the South Atlantic aboard the containership Atlantic Conveyor.

As they left the UK the aircraft of Nos.800, 801 and 899 Squadrons all wore the 'standard' scheme of the day, Dark Sea Grey upper surfaces and white lower surfaces, with full-colour unit markings and national insignia. En route the on-board paint shops worked overtime to produce an all-over, single-colour finish, which gave each aircraft initially deployed on the two carriers a 'war paint camouflage scheme of glossy Extra Dark Sea Grey, with toned down red and blue type 'B' roundels and black code numbers. All of the unit markings were obliterated as were the Royal Navy legends; the only visible markings were those for the emergency escape systems. No.809's aircraft were all resprayed at Dunsfold in a much lighter (and as it turned out far more visible) scheme of Medium Sea Grey upper surfaces and Barley Grey under the wings and tailplanes. They also wore a pale pink and pale blue phoenix badge on their tails, pale blue Royal Navy tiles on the tail-fin (these were overpainted on reaching the war zone), and pale pink and pale blue roundels on the forward fuselage and wings. The first six aircraft flew out from the UK on 30 April, refuelled by Victor tankers to Ascension Island. This small British outpost was the only 'friendly' base in the area roughly halfway between the UK and the Falklands. Two more aircraft followed on 3rd May. The

Sea Harriers and RAF GR.3s are covered against the elements as they sit aboard Atlantic Conveyor for the final leg of their trip to the Falklands. Note the Alert Bird carrying AIM-9G Sidewinders
(© BAE Systems)

Navy Sea Harrier and RAF GR.3s are prepared aboard Atlantic Conveyor for the journey south
(© BAE Systems)

Safe return as a SHAR comes home
(© BAE Systems)

aircraft then embarked aboard the Atlantic Conveyor which took them on the final leg to meet up with the Task Force. One Sea Harrier was kept on alert, fully fuelled and armed on a purpose-built landing pad at the prow of the ship, in case it was necessary to provide air defence.

The Sea Harriers received several modifications for their war role; the attack system was altered to allow for loft bombing from an IP (initial point) offset, and to permit blind delivery against ground targets. The aircraft were also cleared for higher take-off weights using the larger 330 gallon ferry tanks. Some aircraft also received a Tracor AN/ALE-40 chaff/flare dispenser fit behind the airbrake. Those not so fortunate rammed as much chaff into the air-brake well as possible, allowing for a 'one-shot? dump; smaller amounts of chaff were also liberally stuffed between weapon and pylon on the wings and centreline. The Harriers had an intensive work-up on their way south, making live firings against towed targets and Lepus flares. First contact by the Task Force with Argentine aircraft was made on 21st April, when XZ460 from 801 Squadron flown by Lt Simon Hargreaves was dispatched to 'Hack the Shad' – a FAA 707-320B surveillance aircraft, known colloquially as 'The Burglar'. It was not fired upon, but it was made known through diplomatic channels that other incursions into the Task Force's zone would lead to a more aggressive response. Once within the Falklands area the Task Force set up a TEZ (Total Exclusion Zone) around the islands and prepared to use whatever means were necessary to enforce it. The air war began on the 1st May with a night-time 'Black Buck' bombing raid by an RAF Vulcan. This was followed by a dawn strike against Port Stanley airfield by nine 800 Squadron aircraft, eight each armed with three BL.755 CBUs and one with three l,000lb bombs, and a three-ship attack on Goose Green, ably supported by nine air-defence configured Harriers from 801Squadron. ZA192, flown by Flt Lt Dave Morgan, took a shell hit in the tailfin, which was quickly repaired once it was back on the carrier. No aircraft had been lost in the attack, much to the relief of the commanders, who had expected to lose at least three. The Sea Harriers took up CAP (combat air patrol) stations, flying at 15,000ft where the performance of the expected Mirage fighters would be degraded if they engaged in air combat. Flt Lt Paul Barton and Lt Cdr John Eyton-Jones were soon vectored to intercept two 'bandits' detected by one of the radar piquet ships. The high flying Mirages seemed reluctant to come down from their 34,500ft altitude, as they obviously wanted to tempt the Sea Harriers into a high altitude fight, but the experienced SHAR pilots would have none of it. Eventually fuel became critical and the enemy turned away. Later that afternoon Lt Cdr Sharkey Ward, and Lt Mike Watson from No.801 Squadron were vectored to intercept three Beech T-34C Turbo-Mentors which were about to make an attack on British warships. The Argentine aircraft soon departed for the protection of the Port Stanley defences on first sight of the Sea Harriers. Returning to their CAP station, the pair were again vectored to another threat; Ward thought that he had spotted contrails from Argentinean aircraft and tried to lock up one of his Sidewinders; however, they turned out to be smoke trails from missiles fired at them – the attack was ineffective and Ward reported seeing one of the missiles fall harmlessly into the sea.

The first air-to-air kill of the war fell to Flt Lt Paul Barton of 801 Squadron flying XZ452. Barton splashed a Mirage III from Grupo 8, which exploded in a brilliant blue fireball, and a few minutes later his wingman Flt Lt Steve Thomas in XZ453 damaged another Mirage, which attempted an emergency landing at Port Stanley only to be shot down by very nervous AAA gunners, a classic 'own goal'. The third kill of the day was that of a Dagger from Grupo 6, 'shredded' by Flt Lt Bertie

Sea Harriers and RAF GR.3s arranged on the deck of HMS Hermes
(© BAE Systems)

Penfold's AIM-9L while flying in XZ455, followed shortly afterwards by Lt Al Curtiss from 801 Squadron dispatching one of three Canberra bombers from Grupo 2. For their air defence role the Sea Harriers were armed with two AIM-9 'Lima' Sidewinders, two wing tanks and twin 30mm Aden cannon. Two SHARS also attacked and disabled the trawler Narimi with bombs and cannon fire. On 21st May the Task Force went ashore at San Carlos, which provoked the Argentineans into a concerted attack pattern. However the Sea Harriers were more than a match for them. Lt Cdr Ward started the most successful day for the SHARs, destroying a Grupo 3 Pucara with 30mm cannon fire, while flying XZ451, and 800 Squadron's Lt Cdr Mike Blissitt in XZ496 and Lt Cdr Neil Thomas in XZ492 each downed an A-4Q Skyhawk, and Rod Fredriksen took out a Dagger from Grupo 6. These were followed in short order by a further two Daggers from the same unit dispatched by 801 Squadron's Steve Thomas in ZA190 and a third by Sharkey Ward in ZA175

May also saw the first Sea Harrier loss of the conflict when Lt Nick Taylor, flying XZ450 whilst making a low-level attack on Goose Green, was hit by radar-directed Oerlikon AAA fire reportedly hitting his wing tank, totally destroying the aircraft. This loss led to a rethinking of tactics, and from that point the Sea Harriers would no longer overfly heavily defended targets and their operations would be from 18,000-20,000ft, making wings-level bomb deliveries or 'toss bombing' from outside the Argentine defensive envelope. The Sea Harrier Force was also dealt a double blow when 801 Squadron's Lt Cdr Eyton-Jones in XZ452 and Lt Curtiss in XZ453 collided in thick fog, both pilots being killed. For good measure, Lt Clive Morrell caused an A-4Q from 3 Escuadrilla to break in half and severely damaged a

The calm before the storm above and below deck
(© BAE Systems)

An atmospheric photograph illustrating a swarm of activity over the crowded flight deck of HMS Hermes in the latter days of the Falklands War
(© Dave Morgan)

ZA191/718 of 899 NAS lands on HMS Hermes; note the lack of Squadron badge and base letters on her fin
(© Dave Morgan)

second with cannon fire while flying XZ457; his wing-man, Flt Lt John Leeming, 'cannonised' a third, bringing the day's total to an impressive ten for no losses. The Force lost a further two Sea Harriers in non-combat accidents: Lt Cdr Gordon Batt of 800 Squadron was killed when ZA192 exploded and hit the water following a night launch, and on 29 May Lt Cdr Mike Broadwater's ZA174 slid off Invincible's deck, Broadwater ejecting safely. 'Bomb-alley', as San Carlos water had become known, continued to come under Argentine air attack, but 23rd May brought more successes: Rod Fredriksen and Martin Hale strafed and beached the patrol vessel Rio Iguanez, and 800 Squadron's Dave Morgan in ZA192 and John Leeming in ZA191 attacked and destroyed an A109 helicopter on the ground with cannon fire and also spiralled a Puma into the dirt in their wake. A second Puma was damaged by Morgan and was subsequently finished off by Tim Gedge of 801 Squadron flying ZA494, ably assisted by Mike Braithwaite in ZA190. Later in the day Lt Hale from 800 Squadron shot down a Dagger from Grupo 6 in ZA194 and Lt Cdr Andy Auld m XZ457 took out two more Daggers, whilst his wingman Dave Morgan in ZA193 hit a third. The Argentine night-time Hercules resupply effort was a constant irritation to the Task Force, so it was with some pleasure that in daylight on 1 June Sharkey Ward shot down a C-130, with two Sidewinders and 200 rounds of cannon fire. Later that same day Flt Lt Ian Mortimer in XZ456 was hit by a Roland SAM; Mortimer ejected to be picked up by a No 820 Squadron Sea King. The final air engagements of the war took place on 8th June, when Dave Morgan, flying ZA177, shot down two A-4Bs from Grupo 5 and Lt Dave Smith in XZ499 got a third.

Aircraft In Detail

HMS Hermes Air Group

HMS Hermes sailed from Portsmouth for the Falkland Islands on 05-Apr-82 with five Sea Harriers of 800 NAS plus four SHARs from 899 NAS, which had in effect been absorbed into 800 NAS on 02-Apr-82. The original 800 NAS pilots were Lt Commanders Andy Auld (CO), Mike Blissett and Rod 'Fred' Fredriksen, Lts Mike Hale, Simon Hargreaves, Andy McHarg, Clive 'Spag' Morrell, Dave Smith and Nick Taylor and Flt Lt Ted Ball. The 899 NAS pilots who joined them were Lt Cdrs Neill Thomas (CO), Tony Ogilvy and Gordon Batt, S/Lt Andy George, Flt Lts David 'Mog' Morgan and Robert 'Bertie' Penfold.

Departure Colours

The 800 NAS aircraft were in their original gloss Extra Dark Sea

Grey (EDSG) and white scheme, with the following squadron markings being carried:- 'Royal Navy' at the base of the fin, the ship code H (Hermes) at the tip of the fin in white 7" high letters – the three-digit aircraft side code in white 12" high standard RN style numbers on the panel ahead of the forward nozzle, with the last digit inside the airbrake as a 12" high black numeral – the 800 NAS fin emblem of two crossed swords and a trident in gold with black detail on a red pennant outlined in white. The 899 NAS SHARs were similarly finished though with the white outlined in black winged-fist Squadron badge and base code VL (Yeovilton) on the fin. Their side codes, again in 12" high standard white numerals, were underneath the cockpit. Intake interiors of all aircraft were EDSG except where the white undersurface colour overlapped by about 6" into the intakes.

Low-vis colours Introduced

On 10th April a low-visibility scheme was given to all the aircraft. The white undersurfaces were overpainted by brush with EDSG as were the first digit – 1 for 800 NAS or 7 for 899 NAS – of the side codes- the pilot's names under the windscreens – the underwing serial numbers of all aircraft except XZ459, and some undersurface stencilling- all fin markings, except the sling stencils – gunpods, pylons, and many of the AIM-9L launch rails. However photo references show that some launch rails remained white whilst others were toned-down with a bright blue colour. The difference in the quality and tone of the brush painted areas compared to the original spray-painted EDSG is evident in many black and white photos of the

aircraft – the new paint often looking lighter, though sometimes darker! Photographs also show a strip of white left unpainted on either side of the u/c doors, this strip having been masked by the dropped doors during the painting. Some of the undersurface stencilling, especially the fuselage and wing trestle markings and the underfin 4" high serial numbers were reinstated in black in their original locations. The underfin rear IFF aerial remained black and the two radar altimeter aerials on the underfin varied in colour being either black or tan. The white portions of all roundels were overpainted by brush in Roundel Blue (BS381C:538) to give an out of proportion B-type roundel, however for some reason ZA193 retained its original D-

The light grey scheme survived for a short while after the aircraft returned to the UK
(© BAE Systems)

type underwing roundels. The remaining two digits of the side codes were overpainted either in black or Roundel Blue, and some sources note that the original 800 and 899 SHARs had the last digit of their side code painted inside the airbrake.

'Kill' markings

Images of XZ455/12 taken on 13th June aboard HMS Fearless some days after it had destroyed 2 Daggers show that no kill markings had been applied by this date, at least to this SHAR. This may indicate that the Mirage /Dagger (4" long) and Skyhawk (5" long) kill marking silhouette stencils were only applied to 800/899 SHARs after the war ended and prior to their return to the UK.

The Airbrake Chaff fit

As the Sea Harriers carried no dedicated chaff launchers at the time of the Falklands War Lt Phil Hunt devised a combination of welding rods, split pins and string to hold in place and release

A Sea Harrier ski-jumps into the South Atlantic skies
(© BAE Systems)

up to six bundles of chaff fixed in the SHAR's airbrake, the release happening when the airbrake was fully deployed past the usual 25° – the string being tied to a drilled-out rivet hole in the airbrake's rear edge. The effect of dumping this much chaff gave the SHAR a radar image the size of a frigate! Invincible used the same system for its SHARs.

Sea Harriers as yet unpainted en-route to the Falklands. Note the non-standard engine access panels on the aircraft nearest the camera
(© David Morgan)

A Harrier GR.3 in the company of both light and dark grey coloured Sea Harriers
(© BAE Systems)

Painting over the white of the roundels
(© David Morgan)

A crowded deck scene as aircraft are prepared for more action
(© BAE Systems)

AIM-9 colours

AIM-9Gs were used by 809's VTOL alert SHAR on Atlantic Conveyor and these had white bodies and fins. AIM-9Ls as used by the squadrons on Hermes and Invincible during the fighting had U S 'Ghost' Grey FS.36375 (a pale blue/grey) bodies and fins. The front fins and heads of the both variants were a dark green / gunmetal shade, the seeker heads being various metallic shades.

800 Squadron Sea Harrier FRS.1s

XZ492

H/123 of 800 NAS. Side code – black 23, airbrake code – black 3.
1st May	Lt Clive Morrell, as 'Red 4' carried 3x Variable Time (VT) 1,000lb bombs and toss-bombed for the first attack on Stanley Airport.
21st May	Lt Cdr Neill Thomas destroyed an A-4C Skyhawk, either C-309 or C325 of Grupo 4, with an AIM-9L Sidewinder.
21st July	Returned to Portsmouth on Hermes with the addition of a white Skyhawk stencil below the cockpit on the port side. The area of the port side code 23 was now overpainted with a roundel blue rectangle and it carried white Sidewinder rails.

XZ459

H/125 of 800 NAS. Side code – black 25, airbrake code black 5 (later roundel blue). Underwing serial numbers not overpainted.
1st May	Lt Cdr Gordon Batt, nominal 'Red Leader' with 3x VT 1,000lb bombs, toss-bombed Stanley Airport.
16th May	Lt Cdr 'Gordy' Batt bombed and strafed the supply vessel Rio Carcarana in Falkland Sound near Port King, causing it to be abandoned.
21st July	Returned to Portsmouth on Hermes. The side codes were now in roundel blue with the numeral 5 of the port side code, now on a Dark Green panel.

XZ460

H/126 of 800 NAS. Side code – black 26, airbrake code – black 6.
21st April	Lt Simon Hargreaves intercepted an Argentinean Air Force Boeing 707 surveillance aircraft.
1st May	Lt Mike Hale, 'Tartan 2 may have destroyed Pucara A-527 of Grupo 3 with a 600lb CBU during the raid on the airstrip at Goose Green.
9th May	Lt Cdr Gordy Batt hit the intelligence trawler Narwal but his bomb failed to explode.
31st May	Equipped with 1,000lb bombs, flown by Lt Cdr Rod Frederiksen with the similarly armed XZ455/12 flown by Lt Andy McHarg, ZA191/18 armed with 2x 1,000lb LGBs flown by Lt Clive Morrell and Harrier GR.3 XZ989/07 flown by Squadron Leader Peter Harris, attacked Mount Usbourne.
21st July	Returned to Portsmouth on Hermes. The numeral 2 of the port side code was now partly covered by a small roundel blue and white patch.

XZ496

H/127 of 800 NAS. Side code black 27, airbrake code black 7. Of note was the yellow strip marking carried by this SHAR near its upper wing roundels.
1st May	Lt Cdr Neill Thomas, 'Red 3' with 3x VT 1,000lb bombs, toss-bombed Stanley Airport.
21st May	Lt Cdr Mike Blissett destroyed an A-4C Skyhawk, either C-309 or C325 of Grupo 4, with an AIM-9L fired from the starboard rail.
21st July	Returned to Portsmouth on Hermes with the addition of a white Skyhawk stencil below the cockpit on the port side. The rudder and forward port nozzle were now Medium Sea Grey replacements and the Sidewinder rails were painted bright blue.

XZ500

H/130 of 800 NAS. Side code roundel blue 30, airbrake code not known.
1st May	Lt Cdr Tony Ogilvy, Red 2 dropped 3x Delayed Action (DA) 1,000lb retard bombs, onto Stanley Airport. Ogilvy took over as Red Leader when Batt's NAVHARS went unserviceable shortly after take-off.
16th May	Lt Cdr Andy Auld strafed the supply vessel Bahia Buen Suceso
21st May	Flt Lt John Leeming destroyed A-4Q Skyhawk 0667/3-A-314 of 3 Escuadrilla with cannon fire.
19th July	Returned to Portsmouth on Hermes but flown off to Yeovilton on this date before the ship docked at Portsmouth. Noted with one white Skyhawk stencil below the cockpit on the port side.

The Sea Harriers being toned down for their war roles
(© David Morgan)

XZ450

Of note is that this was a famous trials aircraft and in the rush to get it prepared for departure its Sea Eagle firing unit in the cockpit was not removed, just disconnected and carried its 'BAe markings' – a 12" high white 50 in the centre of its fin above the ROYAL NAVY title. In its low-vis EDSG scheme a side code of 50 was painted in black in the usual 800 NAS position, but in a fairly rough style, and no airbrake code is known.

1st May   Flt Lt Ted Ball, 'Black 4' carried 3x 600lb CBUs for the attack on Stanley Airport.

4th May   While being flown by Lt Nick Taylor during a CBU attack on Goose Green it was hit by 35mm Oerlikon AAA and crashed, killing Lt Taylor; the first SHAR and pilot to be lost. In the wreckage the Argentineans would have found Sea Eagle fittings, which may have led them to believe that all SHARs were so fitted. With the loss of the General Belgrano this may have been a factor in their Navy's reluctance to emerge from port.

ZA192

3rd April moved to RNAS Yeovilton from storage at St Athan. In its low-vis EDSG scheme, side code 92 was painted in black in the usual 800 NAS position in the standard RN numerical style. No airbrake code visible.

1st May   Flt Lt David Morgan, 'Black 2' carried 3x 600lb CBUs for the attack on Stanley Airport. Hit by a 20mm AAA shell in the fin Morgan gave his famous thumbs-up to the cameras when he landed back on Hermes. The area around the exit hole on the starboard fin was cut out – and later presented to Morgan by Hermes' AEOs. A large patch which repaired the damage and stringers were painted roundel blue. A smaller patch was fitted over the entry hole and other blue shrapnel patches added to the starboard.

23rd May   Flt Lt David Morgan strafed and damaged Puma AE-500 of CAB601 with cannon fire; the Puma subsequently crashed, probably due to being caught in the SHAR's turbulent wake.

23rd May   Aircraft was lost when it exploded after take-off, killing the pilot Lt Cdr 'Gordy' Batt.

ZA193

3rd April moved to RNAS Yeovilton from storage at St Athan. In its low-vis EDSG scheme, side code 93 was painted in roundel blue in the usual 800 NAS position in the standard RN numerical style. 93's underwing roundels remained red/white/blue. Airbrake code not known.

1st May   Lt Cdr Mike Blissett, 'Black 3' carried 3x 600lb CBUs for the attack on Stanley Airport.

24th May   Lt Dave Smith destroyed a Dagger, probably C-410 of Grupo 6, with an AIM-9L.

19th July   Returned on Hermes but flown off to Yeovilton on this date before the ship docked at Portsmouth. One white Mirage stencil noted below the cockpit on the port side.

A typical scene aboard Hermes as she sails into the danger area
(© David Morgan)

Sea Harriers from No.809 Squadron, now minus their tail badges
(© David Morgan)

The crude airbrake chaff dispenser as described in the text
(© David Morgan)

899 NAS Sea Harriers – integrated into 800 NAS on 2nd April 1982

XZ455

VL/712 of 899 NAS.

5th April	Flt Lt Robert Penfold – the last SHAR flown to Hermes as she sailed down the English Channel. Side code – black 12. Airbrake code – black 2. The yellow strip marking was carried by this SHAR near its upper wing roundels.
1st May	Flt Lt Robert Penfold, 'Black 5' carried 3x DA 1,000lb bombs for the attack on Stanley Airport.
1st May	Flt Lt Robert Penfold destroyed Dagger C-433 of Grupo 6 with an AIM-9L.
21st May	Lt Cdr Rod Frederiksen destroyed Dagger C-409 of Grupo 6 with an AIM-9L.
31st May	Equipped with 1,000lb bombs, flown by Lt Andy McHarg with the similarly armed XZ460/26 flown by Lt Cdr Rod Frederiksen, ZA191/18 armed with 2 1,000lb LGBs flown by Lt Clive Morrell and Harrier GR.3 XZ989/07 flown by Sqn Ldr Peter Harris for an attack on Mount Usbourne.
13th June	Lt Cdr Neill Thomas diverted to HMS Fearless when the Port San Carlos Forward Operating Base (FOB) – HMS Sheathbill, was damaged by downwash from Chinook HC.1 ZA718. This aircraft was also noted with a white starboard AIM-9L rail and white inboard lower outrigger 'boot' on the starboard side.
2 July	Transferred to 801 NAS aboard HMS Invincible and resprayed EDSG and coded 000 in roundel blue by 801 NAS to replace XZ456. The 000 was in 801's usual high position on the engine compartment. A white 0 was painted on the starboard outrigger cover and a roundel blue 0 inside the airbrake.
17 Sept	Returned to Portsmouth on Invincible as 000.

XZ457

VL/714 of 899 NAS. Side code black 14, airbrake code – black 4. The upper wing RCV warning markings were on two white rectangles with 'Danger' on the inboard one, the rest of the stencil in the outboard one.

1st May	Lt Andy McHarg, 'Tartan 3 carried 3x DA 1,000lb bombs dropped during the raid on the airstrip at Goose Green.
21 May	Lt Clive Morrell destroyed A-4Q Skyhawk 0660/3-A-307 of 3 Escuadrilla with an AIM-9L and damaged A-4Q Skyhawk 0665/3-A-312 of 3 Escuadrilla with cannon fire, this A-4 being lost while attempting an emergency landing.
24th May	Lt Cdr Andy Auld destroyed 2 Daggers – C419 and, probably, C-430 of Grupo 6 with 2 AIM-9Ls.
21st July	Returned to Portsmouth on Hermes with the addition of two white Mirage stencils above a white Skyhawk stencil below the cockpit on the port side. Both gun pods were overall Dark Green replacements from GR.3s. The camera panel was a MSG painted replacement with a diagonal strip of possibly silver duct tape over the aperture.

XZ494

VL/716 of 899 NAS. Side code black 16. Airbrake code – black 6

1st May	Lt Cdr Andy Auld 'Black Leader', 3x 600lb CBUs, led the first attack on Stanley Airport.
21st May	Lt Alan McHarg bombed and strafed the supply vessel Rio Carcarana in Falkland Sound near Port King, causing it to be abandoned.
2nd July	Transferred to 801 NAS and HMS Invincible. Resprayed EDSG and coded 008 in roundel blue by 801 NAS to replace ZA174. A white 8 was painted on the starboard outrigger cover and a roundel blue 8 inside the airbrake.
17 Sept	Returned to Portsmouth on Invincible as 008.

Three 1000lb bombs fitted to this SHAR, as they were carried for the attack on Stanley Airfield
(© David Morgan)

ZA191

VL/718 of 899 NAS. Side code black 18, airbrake code – black 8.

1st May	Lt Cdr Rod Frederiksen may have destroyed Pucara A-527 with a CBU during the attack on Goose Green.
9th May	Flt Lt David Morgan strafed the intelligence trawler Narwal.
16th May	Lt Simon Hargreaves strafed the supply vessel Bahia Buen Suceso, the aircraft being damaged by AAA in the starboard tailplane, and repaired with a roundel blue patch.
31st May	Lt Clive Morrell flew this aircraft armed with 2x 1,000lb Paveway Laser Guided Bombs with Harrier GR.3 XZ989/07 flown by Sqn Ldr Peter Harris being used as the target designator. XZ455/12 flown by Lt Andy McHarg and XZ460/26 flown by Lt Cdr Rod Frederiksen, both aircraft equipped with 1,000lb bombs accompanied them. The target on Mount Usbourne was too close to British positions so a target in Port Stanley was selected. The results of the attack are not known but indications are that it was decided that a Forward Air Controller (FAC) with a designator needed to be in place before the few valuable LGBs available could be used to best effect.
19th July	Returned on Hermes but flown off to Yeovilton on this date before the ship docked at Portsmouth. No kill markings.

809 NAS Sea Harriers – integrated into 800 NAS on 18th May 1982

These were resprayed during 809's work up at Yeovilton in the 'Medium Greys' scheme devised by Mr P J Barley of the RAE Farnborough to match the requirements of the expected weather conditions and combat altitudes in the South Atlantic. In the event the pilots found that at low and mid-levels over land and sea, where many of the engagements took place, these aircraft were much more visible then their EDSG counterparts. Details of the Medium Sea Grey colours denote that on or around 21st and 22nd of April the whole fuselage, wings and tailplane upper surfaces were resprayed Satin Medium Sea Grey (MSG) (BS381C:637) with this colour overlapping the wing and

tailplane leading edges by 4" at the wing roots, tapering to 2" at the wing tips and a constant 2" on the tailplane. The MSG also overlapped some 3" around the intake lips. The intake interiors were finished in Satin White, which soon discoloured. The undersurfaces of the wings and tailplane were in 'Barley' Grey BS4800:18B.21 with 12" correctly proportioned B-type roundels on the fuselage only; under the cockpit these were in Pale Blue and Pale Red to RDM28A specifications. The only stencils carried were: Pale Blue canopy release lever instructions on the port side of the fuselage, the black and yellow areas either side of the word 'Rescue' being replaced with a Pale Blue outline on the canopy rescue arrow, however the word 'Rescue' remained in black on a yellow ground with the arrow's original black outlines above and below it. The canopy release black and yellow stripes remained as did the release illustration on an EDSG panel below the canopy. Pale Red ejection seat triangles and fire access markings on the forward engine cover were reduced as were the black and white tail incidence markings, the black wing/fuselage trestle and nozzle angle markings. Pale Blue 'Royal Navy' lettering was applied to the base of the fin in an 8" high square stencilled style. The 809 NAS badge of a Phoenix rising from the ashes was also applied to both sides of the fin, with Pale Blue for the bird with Pale Pink for the flames, the bird's tongue and eye. The serial numbers for the aircraft were applied in black in two different styles and places, either: 4" high in the usual location on the underfin, or 3" high on the lower fuselage above the underfin, approximately 24" up from the base of the underfin. The aircraft were fitted with IFR probes and 100 gallon tanks, as these SHARs transitioned to Wideawake Island via Banjul in The Gambia between the 30th and 1st May arriving on Ascension the day after. They flew out to Atlantic Conveyor just

off the island on the 6th May, the ship departing for the Falklands on the following day. One SHAR, armed with AIM-9G Sidewinders, was kept on VTOL alert on the bow of the ship, with Victor tankers providing IFR support until 13th May if needed. The 'alert' pilots were 809's CO, Lt Cdr Tim Gedge and SPLOT (Senior Pilot) Lt Cdr Dave Braithwaite. On the 18th May the aircraft allocated to Hermes were flown off to the carrier and integrated into 800 NAS. The 809 NAS pilots who joined 800

were Lt Cdr Hugh Slade, Lt Bill Covington, Flt Lts Steve Brown and John Leeming. After arrival on Hermes the 'Royal Navy' and 809 badges on the fin were overpainted in the nearest approximation of MSG available on the ship; in some photos traces of the badge and lettering can be seen after the overpainting. Side codes were applied in black in the usual 800 NAS location using the last two digits of the aircraft's serial in a rectangular, non-standard style. References also show that the

The light grey scheme survived for a short while after the aircraft returned to the UK
(© David Morgan)

Lt Dave Smith landing ZA193/93 back on Hermes after destroying Dagger (C410 of Grupo 6) on with his port AIM-9L Sidewinder on 24th May 1982
(© David Morgan)

The Harriers flew practice intercepts on the way down
(© David Morgan)

The light colour came under the name of 'Barley Grey'
(© Denis Clavert)

The fin and shrapnel damaged tail surfaces of ZA192/92 after the port side of its fin was hit by a 30mm AAA shell during the first SHAR attack on Stanley Airport on 1st May 1982; pilot Flt Lt D H S Morgan
(© David Morgan)

SHARs finished in the 'Medium Greys' scheme weathered more heavily than their EDSG counterparts.

XZ499

8th April was seen operating with 809 but in 801 NAS colours as N/000, it had been left in the UK when 801 sailed on Invincible as it was unserviceable at that time

1st May	Flown from Yeovilton to Banjul in The Gambia then to Wideawake on 2nd May by Lt Alasdair Craig.
6th May	Embarked Atlantic Conveyor off Ascension, sailing for the TEZ on 07-May-82.
14th May	Flown off to Hermes piloted by Flt Lt John Leeming.
16th May	Lt Mike Hale strafed the patrol vessel Rio Iguazu causing it to be abandoned; top cover was provided by Lt Cdr Rod Frederiksen in XZ460/26.
8th June	Lt Dave Smith destroyed A-4B Skyhawk C204 of Grupo 5 with an AIM-9L.
3rd July	Aircraft is noted with a replacement EDSG rudder, excluding the strake on the rudder which is MSG, an EDSG port Sidewinder rail and a white tip section to the port outer pylon.
19th July	Returned on Hermes but flown off to Yeovilton on this date before the ship docked at Portsmouth. One white Skyhawk stencil noted below the port windscreen

ZA176

6th April	Moved to RNAS Yeovilton from storage at St Athan, side code – black 76.
30th April	Flown from Yeovilton to Banjul in The Gambia then to Wideawake, Ascension on 1st May by Lt Dave Austin.
6th May	Embarked Atlantic Conveyor off Ascension.
18th May	Flown off to Hermes piloted by Lt Bill Covington.
19th July	Returned on Hermes but flown off to Yeovilton on this date before the ship docked at Portsmouth.

XZ494 being 'bombed-up'
(© David Morgan)

ZA177

7th April	Moved to RNAS Yeovilton from storage at St Athan, side code – black 77.
1st May	Flown from Yeovilton to Banjul in The Gambia then to Wideawake, Ascension on 2nd May by Lt Cdr Hugh Slade.
6th May	Embarked Atlantic Conveyor off Ascension.
18th May	Flown off to Hermes piloted by Lt Cdr Hugh Slade.
8th June	Flt Lt David Morgan destroyed two A-4B Skyhawks C226 and C-228 of Grupo 5 with AIM-9Ls during a 'Duskers' sortie. Morgan had seen the A-4s attack landing craft from HMS Fearless operating in Choiseul Sound. Lt Dave Smith in ZA499 was Morgan's wingman.
13th July	Lt Simon Hargreaves diverted to HMS Intrepid when the Port San Carlos FOB was damaged.
21st July	Returned to Portsmouth on Hermes, sitting at the head of the ship's ski-jump. Two white Mirage stencils below the port windscreen – in error for the two Skyhawks – Sidewinder rails white, port 100 gal drop tank Dark Green overall.

ZA194

28th April	Delivered to RNAS Yeovilton after being still under construction at Dunsfold at the end of March. In the Medium Greys scheme (except for roundels) on delivery with serial 4" high and standard underwing serials with side code – black 94.
30th April	Flown from Yeovilton to Banjul in The Gambia then to Wideawake by Flt Lt Steve Brown.
6th May	Embarked Atlantic Conveyor off Ascension.
18th May	Flown off to Hermes piloted by Flt Lt Steve Brown.
23rd May	Lt Mike Hale destroyed a Dagger C-437 of Grupo 6 with an AIM-9L.
19th July	Returned on Hermes but flown off to Yeovilton on this date before the ship docked at Portsmouth. One white Mirage stencil noted below the port windscreen and an EDSG camera port panel

HMS Invincible's Air Group

HMS Invincible sailed from Portsmouth for the Falkland Islands Total Exclusion Zone on 5th April with four Sea Harriers of 801 NAS plus four from 899 NAS. The original 801 NAS pilots were: Lt Cdrs Nigel 'Sharkey' Ward (CO), Doug Hamilton, Lts Charlie Cantan, Alan Curtis, Brian Haigh and Steve Thomas and Flt Lt Ian 'Morts' Mortimer. The 899 NAS pilots who joined them were: Lt Cdrs Robin Kent, John Eyton-Jones and Mike Broadwater, Flt Lt Paul Barton and Lt Mike Watson. Shortly after embarkation Lt Cdr Hamilton suffered a medical condition and was airlifted ashore, so taking no further part in the campaign. The 801 NAS aircraft were similarly finished to their 800 NAS counterparts with these differences: the ship code of N (Invincible) at the tip of the fin was in white 7" high letters, the three-digit aircraft side code in white 16" high standard RN numerical style numbers above the panel ahead of the forward nozzle, with the last digit inside the airbrake as a 16" high black numeral and repeated on the starboard outrigger cover with the 801 NAS fin emblem of a winged trident in roundel blue on a 30" white disc. During the passage south the overall EDSG low-visibility scheme was applied to all the aircraft, this time by respraying of the undersurfaces. At the same time all fin markings and any pilot's names were obliterated. The spray painted EDSG did not weather as well as the brush painted version and later the original demarcation lines could be seen. As with 800's SHARs, some of the undersurface stencilling, especially the fuselage and wing trestle markings and the underfin 4" high serial numbers, were reinstated in black their original locations. The white portions of all roundels were oversprayed in roundel blue; again, this area often appeared lighter in tone than the blue outer ring in black and white photos. The remaining three digits of the side codes were overpainted in roundel blue, the final digit being repeated inside the airbrake 12" high in roundel blue in the standard style, the outrigger code was 8" high in white. Unlike on Hermes, Invincible's 899 NAS SHARs completely lost their identities during the respray process, having their side codes reallocated in the sequence 006 to 009 and repositioned in the location used by 801 NAS. Due to 801's interception capabilities and tactics they tended to provide the air cover sorties during the early days of the war, including for the early attacks undertaken by 800 NAS on Stanley and Goose Green.

801 NAS Sea Harriers

XZ493

N/001 of 801 NAS. The nominal SHAR of the CO – Lt Cdr N D Ward whose rank and name may have been stencilled in white under the starboard windscreen. Side code 001 in roundel blue, airbrake code roundel blue 1, starboard outrigger code, white 1.
17th Sep   Returned to Portsmouth on Invincible.

XZ495

N/003 of 801 NAS. Side code – roundel blue 003, airbrake code, roundel blue 3, starboard outrigger code white 3.
17th Sept   Returned to Portsmouth on Invincible.

ZA175

N/004 of 801 NAS. Side code roundel blue 004, airbrake code roundel blue 4, starboard outrigger code white 4.
1st May   Lt Cdr Mike Broadwater unsuccessfully fired 2 AIM-9Ls at a Canberra.
21st May   Lt Cdr 'Sharkey' Ward destroyed a Dagger C-407 of Grupo 6 with an AIM-9L.
17th Sept   Returned to Portsmouth on Invincible.

XZ498

N/005 of 801 NAS. Side code roundel blue 005, airbrake code roundel blue 5, starboard outrigger code white 5.
17th Sept   Returned to Portsmouth on Invincible, complete with an MSG-coloured replacement canopy.

899 NAS Sea Harriers – integrated into 801 NAS during early April 1982

XZ451

FVL/710 of 899 NAS. Side code roundel blue 006, airbrake code roundel blue 6, starboard outrigger code white 6. The upper wing RCV warning markings were on two white rectangles.
1st May   Lt Cdr 'Sharkey' Ward strafed and damaged a Mentor of 4 Escuadrilla.
1st May   Lt Alan Curtis destroyed Canberra B-110 of Grupo 2 with one of two AIM-9Ls fired. A Canberra kill marking was reportedly stencilled below the port windscreen but removed a few days later.
1st June   Lt Cdr 'Sharkey' Ward destroyed Hercules TC-63 of Grupo 1 with one of two AIM-9Ls and cannon fire.
17th Sept   Returned to Portsmouth on Invincible.

XZ452

VL/711 of 899 NAS. Side code roundel blue ,007 airbrake code roundel blue 7, starboard outrigger code white 7.
1st May   Flt Lt Paul Barton destroyed Mirage IIIEA I-015 of Grupo 8 with an AIM-9L.
6th May   Lost when Lt Cdr John Eyton-Jones was killed, either colliding with Lt Alan Curtis in XZ453/009 or striking the sea.

XZ456

VL/713 of 899 NAS. Side code 008 in roundel blue, airbrake code roundel blue 8, starboard outrigger code white 8.
1st June   Lost when Flt Lt Ian Mortimer was shot down by a Roland missile whilst on armed reconnaissance south of Stanley Airport; 'Morts' being rescued by Sea King HAS.5 XZ574/16.

XZ453

VL/715 of 899 NAS. Both tank tips are weathered back and it had two or three 'zaps' on the starboard panel ahead of the front nozzle, and one looked like a white 899 NAS winged fist over a red equilateral triangle, with the same zap on the starboard nose above the vent ahead of the camera port. Side code roundel blue 009, airbrake code roundel blue 9, outrigger code white 9.
1st May   Lt Steve Thomas damaged Mirage IIIEA I-019 of Grupo 8 with an AIM-9L, the Mirage was then shot down by Argentinean AAA whilst trying to land at Stanley Airport.
6th May   Lost when Lt Alan Curtis was killed, either colliding with Lt Cdr John Eyton-Jones in XZ452/007 or striking the sea.

809 NAS Sea Harriers – integrated into 801 NAS on 18 and 19th May 1982

On 19-May-82 the SHARs allocated to Invincible were flown off Atlantic Conveyor and integrated into 801 NAS. The 809 NAS pilots who joined 801 were Lt Cdr Dave 'Brave' Braithwaite, Lts Dave Austin and Alasdair Craig. As with Hermes' ex-809 aircraft, after arrival on Invincible the 'Royal Navy' and 809 fin badges were overpainted in the nearest approximation of MSG available. 801's side codes were applied in the usual 801 location and standard style with the last digit inside the airbrake in a locally mixed pale blue, which appeared richer in hue than that the roundels; the last digit was also painted in white on the starboard outrigger cover.

ZA174

08-Apr-82 the aircraft was noted operating with 809 but in 801 NAS colours as N/002, it had been left in the UK when 801 sailed on Invincible as it was unserviceable at that time. Side code, in rich pale blue 000, airbrake code rich pale blue 8, starboard outrigger code white 0.
30th April   Flown from Yeovilton to Banjul in The Gambia then to Wideawake by Lt Cdr Dave Braithwaite.
6th May   Embarked Atlantic Conveyor off Ascension.
19th May   Flown off to Invincible by Lt Alasdair Craig.
29th May   Lost while positioning for take-off in a very rough sea, the ship rolled heavily, the aircraft sliding off the deck into the water. Lt Cdr Mike Broadwater ejected safely.

XZ491

14th April   Moved to RNAS Yeovilton from storage at St Athan, still in its ex-801 NAS codes N/004. Side code was a rich pale blue 002, airbrake code rich pale blue 2, starboard outrigger code white 2.
30th April   Flown from Yeovilton to Banjul, then to Wideawake by Lt Bill Covington.
6th May   Embarked Atlantic Conveyor off Ascension.
19th May   Flown off to Invincible piloted by Lt Dave Austin.
26th May   Flown from Invincible direct to Illustrious to join 809 NAS.

XZ458

7th April   Moved to RNAS Yeovilton from storage at St Athan, still in its ex-800 NAS codes H/124. Side code rich pale blue 007. airbrake code rich pale blue 7, starboard outrigger code white 7.
30th April   Flown from Yeovilton to Banjul then to Wideawake by Flt Lt John Leeming.
6th May   Embarked Atlantic Conveyor off Ascension.
18th May   Flown off to Invincible piloted by Lt Cdr Dave Braithwaite.
26th Aug   Flown from Invincible direct to Illustrious to join 809 NAS.

ZA190

07-Apr-82 – moved to RNAS Yeovilton from storage at St Athan and uncoded. Side code in rich pale blue 009, airbrake code rich pale blue 9, starboard outrigger code white 9.
21st May   Lt Steve Thomas as wingman for Lt Cdr 'Sharkey' Ward destroyed two Daggers (C-404 and C403 of Grupo 6) with two AIM-9Ls.
17th Sept   Returned to Portsmouth on Invincible. By this time the inside of the intakes had been repainted MSG and the yellow and black warning arrows on the canopy reinstated.

809 Squadron Sea Harrier FRS.1 HMS Illustrious Falklands Detachment 1982

The Falklands War saw a limited number of kill markings applied to the Sea Harriers, which were swiftly removed on the aircraft's return to the UK. However during No.809 Squadron's return to the South Atlantic from August to December of 1982 the aircraft sported a nice line in names, with pilots and support crews also being added. Sadly, all but one had disappeared on their return to the UK. However the IPMS Harrier Special Interest Group issued a limited edition decal sheet to coincide

A SHAR pilot discusses with his crew
(© FAA Museum)

with their research into this detachment, and their findings are as follows:

ZA176/250
'Hot Lips', Lt Cdr Gedge

ZA194/251
Rosie Lt CDR Thornton, AEM Morse (Pale blue Phoenix and flames)

XZ500/52
Myrtle Lt Austin, AEM Hopper, AEM Horrocks, CPO Mee

ZA191/253
Phyllis Flt Lt Collins, AEM Toman, AEM Bruno, CPO Lovis

ZA193/254
Esmeralda Sqn Ldr West, AEM Reilly, AEM Wilkinson

XZ499/255
Ethel Lt Gilbert, AEM Wadsworth, AEM Price, CPO Jackson

XZ459/256
Emanuelle Sub Lt McLaren

XZ496/257
Mrs Robinson, Lt Robinson, LAEM Boast, AEM Day, CPO Laing

XZ491/258
Cindy-Lou, Lt Hale, AEM Bertouche, AEM Matthews, CPO Copping – direct transfer from Invincible 26/8

XZ458/259
Ermantrude Lt Cdr Frederiksen, AEM Duke, AEM Angus, CPO Elliot – direct transfer from Invincible 26/8

The serials were applied in a stencil style, with odd spacings between the 3" high characters. XZ491 and XZ458's were higher up the fuselage with a continental 4 and XZ458's port serial was noted in white. The pilot's names were carried under the starboard windscreen. The aircraft names were carried on the on the port side of the cockpit, however on their return to the UK all were again erased, except for Ethel, often leaving smudges. Crew names were on both of the front undercarriage doors, one on the left door, the other to the right. The Squadron's traditional Phoenix emblem was missing at the start of the detachment; however on their return to the UK all SHARs had this in pale blue and pale red, both colours having a thin black

The triumphant return to the UK!
(© FAA Museum)

outline. The side, outrigger and airbrake codes were black 12" high on the panel ahead of the front nozzle with last digit low on both outriggers and again repeated inside airbrake.

The known fates of the ex-Falklands War Sea Harrier FRS.1s

XZ492
Converted to Sea Harrier FA.2 in 1994. Privately owned wreck, dump, Faygate, West Sussex.

XZ459
Converted to Sea Harrier FA.2 in 1993. Privately owned wreck, Charlwood Yard, Surrey.

XZ460
9th May 1990 flew into the sea just after takeoff from Invincible, Lt Holmes (800 NAS) killed.

XZ496
16th March 1984 ditched in the North Sea off Norway alongside Illustrious after engine failure, the pilot ejected safely.

XZ500
15th June 1983 as 127, 800 NAS, Lt Simon Hargreaves ejected safely from an inverted spin over the Bay of Biscay.

ZA193
28th May 1992 as 126 of 800 NAS, ditched alongside Invincible off Cyprus when forward pitch nozzle control was lost during landing approach, Lt Wilson ejected safely.

XZ455
Converted to Sea Harrier FA.2 1992. 14th Feb 1996 on approach to HMS Illustrious after a sortie over Bosnia, crashed into the Adriatic 30m off-shore, Lt Phillips ejected safely.

XZ457
Converted to Sea Harrier FA.2 1993. 20th October 1995 as 714 of 899 NAS caught fire while preparing for take-off at Yeovilton. Now in the Boscombe Down Aviation Museum.

XZ494
Converted to Sea Harrier FA.2. Privately owned, Sproughton, Suffolk.

ZA191
4th October 1989 as 004, 801 NAS, hit HMS Ark Royal's mast during a flypast and crashed into sea, Lt Simmonds-Short ejected safely over Lyme Bay.

XZ499
Converted to Sea Harrier FA.2. Now in the Fleet Air Arm Museum Reserve Collection at RNAS Yeovilton.

ZA176
7th June 1983 as 001, 801 NAS Lt Ian 'Soapy' Watson landed on Spanish freighter Alraigo after NAVHARS failure. FRS.2 DB1, converted to Sea Harrier FA.2 1993. Now in Newark Air Museum. This earned him the nickname of the 'Alriago Kid'

ZA177
21st January 1983 as 711, 899 NAS crashed in a spin, Lt Fox ejected but suffered spinal injuries.

ZA194
10th October 1983 as 716, 899 NAS crashed following control restriction, Major O'Hara USMC ejected safely.

XZ493
15th December 1994 as 126, 800 NAS ditched alongside Invincible when yaw control lost in the hover, Lt Kistruck ejected safely. Nose section recovered, restored and fitted to a Harrier GR.3 airframe, XV760. Painted in its pre-Falklands 801 NAS scheme as 001 and now displayed at the Fleet Air Arm Museum Yeovilton.

XZ495
Converted to Sea Harrier FA.2 1992. 5th January 1994 Jan-94 as 713, 899 OEU crashed into the Bristol Channel after engine failure, Lt Wilson ejected safely.

ZA175
Converted to Sea Harrier FA.2 1994. Acquired by the IWM Duxford, it's preserved at the Norfolk & Suffolk Aviation Museum, Flixton, Suffolk.

XZ498
16th April 1994 as 002, 801 NAS shot down by SAM near Gorazde, Bosnia, Lt Nick Richardson ejecting safely and evaded capture.

XZ451
30th November 1989 crashed near Sardinia, Lt Auckland ejected safely.

XZ491
16th April 1986 crashed near Benbecula when out of fuel, Lt Cdr Sinclair ejected safely.

XZ458
1st December 1984 as 125, 800 NAS, crashed after a bird strike caused engine failure near Fort William, Lt Collier ejected with eye injuries.

ZA190
15th October 1987 as 006, 801 NAS and operating from HMS Ark Royal crashed in the Irish Sea after a bird strike, the pilot ejected safely.

Ski Jumps

Carrier operation of the Sea Harrier was greatly enhanced by an elegantly simple idea, devised by Royal Navy Lieutenant Commander Douglas Taylor - the ski-jump take-off ramp. Taylor calculated that simply modifying the deck so that it curved up at the end would throw the fighter up into the air, allowing it to carry a greater warload with a shorter take-off run, as well as giving the pilot more time to eject if it became apparent his aircraft was going to splash. Resistance to the ski-jump concept was so stubborn in some quarters that advocates of the idea collectively referred to the critics as the 'Flat Deck Preservation Society', however the advocates prevailed, and the ski jump was adopted for carrier operations. Both Invincible and Illustrious were originally fitted with a 7-degree ski jump, while the Ark Royal featured a 12-degree ski jump when it was commissioned, however both Invincible and Illustrious were later refitted with a 13-degree ramp.

(© Joop De Groot)

(© Martin Clements)

(© Royal Navy)

(© Martin Clements)

(© Martin Clements)

(© Martin Clements)

Indian Navy Harriers

In 1978, the Indian Government formulated plans for a naval Harrier force operating from a modernised carrier. Subsequently an initial batch of six Sea Harriers together with a pair of two-seat trainers was ordered in 1979, and designated the FRS.51 and T.60, these being delivered between 1982 and 1984. The Indian Government then ordered a further ten Sea Harrier FRS.51s and a single T.60 on 25 November 1985, followed by another batch of seven FRS.51s and another T.60 on 9 October 1986, bringing the total Sea Harrier complement to twenty-seven. A further batch of twenty-one Harriers, seventeen single-seaters and four two-seaters was delivered between 1989 and 1992. In the 1990's attrition replacements for six Harrier trainers were sought, with the Indian Government purchasing

four ex-US Marine Corps TAV-8As from AMARC and a further two ex-RAF T.4s, these having the LRMTS 'Snoopy' noses of the Harrier GR.3. The latter were referred to as T.4(I)s, and were subsequently upgraded to full T.60 standard. To facilitate the arrival of the Sea Harrier, No.300 Squadron, the 'White Tigers', was commissioned at INS Hansa in Goa, and were to serve aboard the INS Vikrant, and later the INS Viraat the former HMS Hermes. Harrier Training was initially undertaken at RNAS Yeovilton before the Indian Navy began its own training courses at Goa and in May 1995 as part of No.551 'B' Squadron, the 'Braves' more commonly known as the SHOFTU, the Sea Harrier Operational Flying Training Unit, was established operating both T.60s, T.4(I)s and FRS.51s.

Pristine, just out of the paintshop at BAe Warton. The full colour roundels on the intake cheeks mirror those of the Royal Navy Sea Harriers of the time
(© BAe Systems)

Damaged beyond economical repair in a landing accident IN-621 is now displayed at the Naval Museum in Goa
(© Callum Dodds)

Four FRS.51s break formation. Note the long range tanks on IN-603 nearest the camera
(© BAe Systems)

A 'Snoopy Nosed' T.4(I) again an ex-RAF machine, unusual in that it retained the LRMTS fairing
(© Indian Navy)

One of the two-seat T.60 trainers acquired by the Indian Navy, basically an ex-RAF T.4 slightly modified for use with the FRS.51
(© Andy Evans Collection)

Close-up of a rather scruffy nose section. Of note is the 'White Tigers' emblem and the heavy staining around the panels
(© Simon Jones)

The Slate Grey Harriers carried only a two-digit fuselage code
(© Simon Jones)

The Indian Navy Sea Harriers are basically the same as those operated by the Royal Navy apart from their LOX system being replaced by an on-board oxygen generating system (OBOGS)
(© BAe Systems)

A good view of four FRS.51s lined on deck showing the contrasting colour schemes
(© Simon Jones)

A good comparison of the two colour schemes applied to the Indian Harriers
(© Simon Jones)

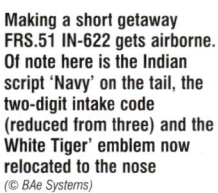

The huge 'elephant ear' intakes are notable here. Also visible is the black edge to the intake lips, the yaw vane and small air scoop with its protective bar across the front. Also of note is the black edging to the wing leading edge
(© Simon Jones)

and the AIM-120 AMRAAM missile, but this was not pursued. However in July 1999, a mid-life upgrade package worth $200 million was reportedly announced by the Indian Navy but this upgrade package was cancelled in favour of purchasing the MiG-29K, and it was planned that the Sea Harriers would retire by 2010 along with the decommissioning of aircraft carrier INS Viraat. Surprisingly then, in March 2005, the Indian Government cleared the way to upgrade of a number of its Sea Harriers. This will involve the fitting of a new multimode fire control radar, the Isreali Elta EL/M-2032, new air-to-air missiles the Rafael Derby DVRAAM. Other improvements also include a combat manoeuvring flight recorder and a digital cockpit voice recorder, and a formal contract was signed in February 2005. One of the latest additions to the Sea Harrier force is the 'Roshini' RWR, a naval variant of the advanced Bharat Electronics (BEL) Tarang Mk II RWR. A few Harriers, including IN-614 and IN-617, have been equipped with this system and these can be identified by the two spiral antennae that protrude out of the tail boom. The forward looking antennas on the tail, however, remain unchanged. IN-604 and IN-613 are still equipped with the conventional ARI.18223 RWR. Currently some sixteen Sea Harriers remain operational with the India Navy.

Originally the Indian Navy Sea Harriers carried the same Dark Sea Grey with white undersides scheme that was originally applied to the Royal Navy's aircraft before the Falklands campaign, with full size orange, white and green national insignia and red engine access panels lines and crosses with the 'white Tigers' emblem on their tails and three-digit codes on the intake sides. During the 1990's the upper surface colour was revised to a Slate Grey with the 'White Tigers' emblem being moved to the nose with the Navy logo written in Indian script on the tailfin and the original three-digit code reduced to two. A further change occurred as a result of dissimilar combat

The Indian Navy Sea Harriers are basically the same as those operated by the Royal Navy apart from their LOX system being replaced by an on-board oxygen generating system (OBOGS). French built Matra R550 Magic AAMs were also acquired as the standard missile because of an embargo placed by the US government on the AIM-9 Sidewinder, and additional armament also included the BAe Sea Eagle anti-shipping missile. Other changes included alterations to the IFF and the radar systems, together with pressure reductions to the water injection system. The T.60s were essentially naval T.4N trainers equipped with the Pegasus Mk 103 engine and cockpit revisions to suit the FRS.51. By the middle of the 1990s the Indian Navy began to explore ways of giving its Harriers a mid-life update (MLU), and possibly replacing the Blue Fox radars with the Blue Vixen set

Making a short getaway FRS.51 IN-622 gets airborne. Of note here is the Indian script 'Navy' on the tail, the two-digit intake code (reduced from three) and the White Tiger' emblem now relocated to the nose
(© BAe Systems)

An excellent top surface view of the Slate Grey derivation of the Indian scheme. Of note are the ferry tanks and the position of the engine access bay warning marks
(© BAe Systems)

Note the marking changes with the Slate Grey and Ghost Grey schemes. The walkway and stencils have changed from red to dark grey
(© Simon Jones)

Note the roundel in pale orange, pale green and the white replaced by the underlying Ghost Grey
(© Simon Jones)

Close in on the nose of a Ghost Grey Harrier. Note the White Tiger logo is now merely an outline
(© Simon Jones)

Shown in its Dark Sea Grey and white delivery scheme on a trial flight with a BAe pilot in his civil international orange flight suit at the controls. Note the civil registration G9-478 on the tail
(© BAe Systems)

Looking up over the wing note the vortex generators, wing fences and light. Also note another variation with the walkway makings, these being pale pink!
(© Simon Jones)

An FRS.51 tied down on deck
(© Simon Jones)

The BAe Sea Eagle missile is still used by the Indian Navy
(© BAe)

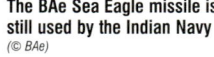

training with some aircraft receiving an overall 'Ghost Grey' colour scheme. The national insignia was also revised to pale orange and pale green removing the white, this being replaced by the background Ghost Grey colour, with all access and panel markings and stencil detail being changed to either Dark Grey, or pale pink and the nose-mounted 'White Tiger' emblem has been reduced to an outline. Once more the three digit intake codes have been returned, and all aircraft have individual names such as IN-613 'Cougar' and IN-603 'Lion'.

IN601 - Mk 51 (05 Oct 1984)   air accident on 04 May 1988
IN602 - Mk 51 (12 July 1984)
IN603 - Mk 51 (13 Dec 1983)
IN604 - Mk 51 (13 Dec 1983)
IN605 - Mk 51 (13 Dec 1983)
IN606 - Mk 51 (12 July 1984)
IN607 - Mk 51 (24 July 1990)
IN608 - Mk 51 (14 Dec 1989)
IN609 - Mk 51 (10 Apr 1990)
IN610 - Mk 51 (14 Dec 1989)
IN611 - Mk 51 (14 Dec 1989) air accident on 30 September 1997
IN612 - Mk 51 (10 Apr 1990) air accident on 09 December 1992

displayed at Goa Museum
IN622 - Mk 51 (14 Jan 1992)
IN623 - Mk 51 (07 Apr 1992)
IN651 - T Mk 60 (15 Mar 1984)
IN652 - T Mk 60 (16 Mar 1984) air accident on 27 June 1988
IN653 - T Mk 60 (10 Apr 1990)
IN654 - T Mk 60 (14 Jan 1992)
IN655 - T Mk 60 (2003) - T Mk 4(I) upgraded to T Mk 60 standard
IN656 - T Mk 60 (2003) - T Mk 4(I) upgraded to T Mk 60 standard

IN613 - Mk 51 (24 July 1990)
IN614 - Mk 51 (24 July 1990)
IN615 - Mk 51 (23 Apr 1991)
IN616 - Mk 51 (17 Sept 1991)
IN617 - Mk 51 (17 Sept 1991)
IN618 - Mk 51 (23 Apr 1991)
IN619 - Mk 51 (23 Apr 1991) air accident on 09 June 1992
IN620 - Mk 51 (17 Sept 1991) air accident on 08 February 1996
IN621 - Mk 51 (17 Sept 1991) beyond economical repair,

Sea Harrier FRS.2 and F/A.2

One of the many consequences of the Falklands conflict of 1982 was the need to have a better equipped Sea Harrier force. Although its performance in the South Atlantic was outstanding, there were many areas where the FRS.1 fell short. The Blue Fox radar had only a limited look-down facility – having great difficulty detecting low-flying targets over the sea – much to the relief no doubt of the nightly C-130 Hercules flights into Port Stanley. The questions of endurance, limited missile armament and self-protection also needed to be addressed. Some shortcomings were corrected by adding twin Sidewinder mounts and larger fuel tanks, the so-called 'Falklands Fit' but what was needed was better radar, linked to missiles with a greater kill range. Plans to accommodate this were to be introduced as part of the Sea Harrier's MLU, and contracts were issued in 1983 for a feasibility study and in 1985 for further studies. In early

December 1988 the MoD awarded BAe a contract to update all existing FRS.1s to a new FRS.2 standard, and in March 1990 announced an order for ten new-build FRS.2s. This new 'standard' incorporated a new radar, the Ferranti Blue Vixen, which was a track-while-scan pulse Doppler set giving an all weather, look-down, shoot-down ability, together with the capability to engage multiple targets simultaneously. The radar data from the Blue Vixen would be presented on the pilot's right-hand Multi Function Display, with the left-hand one being used for navigational data. The left-hand MFD can also be used as a tactical display putting a radar 'slice' on to the screen. The radar set offered a 150km (80nm) range in 40km blocks, and tracks could be established at distances reportedly greater than 85km. The Blue Vixen has already proved its ability to meet the stringent requirements to detect and engage sea-skimming missiles and slow-low targets. The pilot can separate his radar picture on to both MFDs, having

An F/A.2 in the markings of No.800 Squadron
(© Chris Lofting)

Harrier Flyer!
(© Royal Navy)

Harrier – 'break'
(© Royal Navy)

Sea Harrier F/A.2 taxies out
(© Chris Lofting)

pylons, complemented by short-range Sidewinders mounted on the wingtips; however, this was abandoned in favour of having two wing-mounted AIM-120s fitted on BOL/LAU-7 launch rails which would also allow the carrying of the AIM-9, and a further two AIM-120s Weapons are mounted Raytheon LAU-106A ejection-launchers and Varo LAU-7 rail launchers in place of the under-fuselage gun packs. It was also decided to change the designation of the aircraft to reflect its new capabilities, so out went the FRS (Fighter Reconnaissance Strike) and in came the American-sounding F/A – for Fighter Attack – Mk 2, the F/A.2. A new powerplant was also fitted, the Pegasus 106, a 'navalised' 105, and the fuselage as also lengthened by just less than 14" to improve

Everything down as this Sea Harrier makes a vertical drop onto the deck
(© Royal Navy)

Four No.801 Squadron Sea Harriers
(© Royal Navy)

a 'God's-eye' view on the right side and a 'side on' view on the left, which shows the separation and gives him greater SA (situational awareness). The radar's central processor was relocated to the rear of the airframe and the links were established by fibre optic cables. The new radar was also housed in a restyled, bulbous nose radome, being larger and more rounded than of the rather 'sharp' FRS.1, and the latter's nose-mounted pitot tube was relocated to the leading edge of the tailfin. The radar was first trialled aboard ZF433, a BAC-111 and two BAe-125s, XW930 and ZF130, with the latter being outfitted with the full FRS.2 avionics suite.

The missile of choice was the Hughes AIM-120B AMRAAM, which, when combined with the Blue Vixen set, made the new Sea Harrier one of the most potent combat aircraft in the world. The AIM-120, successor to the Sparrow, uses its own inertial mid-course guidance, with updates being given in flight from the aircraft by data link, conferring an excellent BVR ability on the Harrier. The original plans had called for four AIM-120s to be fitted on the outboard

An F/A.2 in the markings of No.800 Squadron
(© Chris Lofting)

Harriers on Invincible
(© Royal Navy)

The enormous intakes and revised nose are evident here
(© Rez Manzoori)

A trio if 801 Squadron SHARS in formation en route to one of the UK ranges, noted by the ACMI pods on the outer wing pylons
(© Chris Lofting)

Joint Force Harrier at work! RAF Harrier GR.7s and Sea Harriers working in tandem
(© Royal Navy)

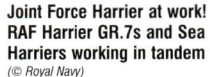

stability and provide space for the extra equipment. This was originally to be a 'plug' just behind the engine, but on new and upgraded aircraft a complete new rear fuselage was added. On the wings the leading edge has been slightly altered, another small fence added and one of the vortex generators has been removed, with wing hardpoints being strengthened to carry up to 1,000lb each. The aircraft has retained its internally mounted F.95 oblique reconnaissance camera and a number of additional air scoops associated with the cooling of the new systems. A Garman 100 GPS was also added as a 'strap-on', mounted on the left side of the cockpit coaming, its data being input by hand. A modern 'office' for the pilot has been designed, with a new HUD and two multi-functional displays added – with the radar's presentation being sited mainly on the right MFD. Later twin white circular GPS antennae were added, one behind the cockpit replacing a blade aerial, and another just in front of the tail fin. The addition of a permanent GPS also resulted in the removal of the undernose. Doppler panel. Also fitted were

improved HOTAS controls, which allow more 'heads-up flying' than in the FRS.1; HOTAS allows the pilot to select the radar and weapons (whether AMRAAM, AIM-9 or guns) without any 'heads-down' time. The FRS.1's ARI 18223 RWR were replaced in the F/A.2 by the Marconi Sky Guardian 2000, and the AN/ALE-40 chaff and flare dispensers were made capable of launching chaff, flares and active expendable GEN-X radar decoys. All the F/A.2's avionics were routed through a 1553B digital databus with the addition of a

Plumes of spray are generated as this Sea Harrier roars off the deck
(© Royal Navy)

Note the lighter radome and dark grey winged fist on this SHAR
(© Andy Evans Collection)

Three SHARS tied down on deck awaiting their next operations
(© Simon Jones)

An F/A.2 prepares for a dusk mission
(© Royal Navy)

Toting a pair of AMRAAM's on the wing pylons, a No.801 Squadron jet comes in for a closer look!
(© Royal Navy)

1979) in March 1989. BAe began to convert the FRS.1 airframes to FRS.2 standard in the early part of 1991, and the first aircraft completed, ZE695, was handed back to the Royal Navy in April 1993. Initial sea-going trials were carried out with both ZA195 and XZ439 on board Ark Royal in November 1990 after ZA439 had spent most of October at RNAS Yeovilton carrying out seventy-six ski-jumps, eight of them at night. These 'leaps' included about every configuration likely with the new aircraft including 1,000lb bombs, tanks, Sidewinders and AMRAAM missiles. The shipboard trials covered every aspect of the aircraft's compatibility with the ship, from deck handling, ski-jumps,

One of the Harrier's portable 'inflatable' intake covers
(© Royal Navy)

Part of No.899 Squadron, a Dark Sea Grey trial scheme without markings
(© Andy Evans Collection)

MADGE transponder. The communications suite consisted of an AD120 VHF radio and an AN/ARC-164 ARC radio with an AN/APX-100 MK12 or the PTR 446 IFF.

Some components, such as the ram air turbine, were removed to save on weight. ZA195, the first pre-series aircraft converted to the FRS.2 configuration (it flew originally in 1983 as FRS.1 DB1), took to the air in September 1988, followed by XZ439 (first flight as an FRS.1 DB2 in March

A Harrier pilots climbs aboard – note the GPS antennae and the single blade aerial
(© Royal Navy)

Two contrasting colour schemes here. The more familiar light grey on the right, and a trial Dark Sea Grey scheme on the left
(© Andy Evans Collection)

An AMRAAM equipped Sea Harrier in the hover
(© Gary Parsons)

Showing its final plumage a No.800 Squadron SHAR
(© Gordon Bartley)

Carrying a centreline CBLS an 899 Squadron bird gets airborne
(© Gordon Bartly)

ZD582 looking factory fresh, and note the Light Grey Winged Fist on the tail
(© Gordon Bartley)

Showing its final plumage a No.800 Squadron SHAR
(© Gordon Bartly)

Carrying the full complement for Combat Air Patrol, Sidewinders, AMRAAMs and wing tanks, ZH803 also displays its white outlined tail emblem
(© Gordon Bartley)

SHARs and MIGs during Exercise Polish Dancer
(© Royal Navy)

An AMRAAM equipped Sea Harrier in the hover
(© Alastair Jones)

ZH798, note the overpainted 899 Squadron tail emblem
(© Gordon Bartley)

A great action shot, but also offering a superb topside view!
(© Alastair Jones)

Quite a 'mongrel' of parts here, but note the roundel on the nose!
(© Andy Evans Collection)

recovery techniques, to handling AMRAAMs. XZ439 now also had the near 'production standard' avionics and radar fit. ZA195 still had its photo reference markings visible and also carried a twin Sidewinder fit, as well as under-fuselage AMRAAM pylons. To bring the aircraft to squadron service an Operational Evaluation Unit was formed at Boscombe Down on 1 June 1993 as an off-shoot of No.899 Squadron and received its first aircraft, ZE695 and ZD616, in August with the aircraft carrying the 'Winged Fist' tail motif with small white 'OEU' lettering on top of the tailfin. No.899 Squadron itself took on charge its first FRS.2, ZA176, later in the same month. Anxious to get the aircraft out to one of the carriers for extended sea trials, four newly designated F/A.2s joined HMS Invincible on an Adriatic cruise, working with the No.800 Squadron's Sea Harrier FRS.1s; these four were ZD612, ZD615, ZE696 and ZE697, all from No.899 Squadron OEU. The Royal Navy's first fully operational F/A.2 Squadron was No.801, which received its first two aircraft, ZA176 and XZ455, on 5 October 1994. The unit replaced No.800 Squadron's FRS.1s aboard HMS Illustrious off the coast of Italy, where it gave support to Operation Sharp Guard, the NATO commitment to the conflict over Bosnia flying a dual role, armed each with a single 10001b bomb on the centreline

Looking to sea, as crews prepare their birds for flight
(© Gordon Bartley)

MiG over SHAR!
(© Royal Navy)

The Sea Harriers have been replaced by the non-radar equipped Harrier GR.9
(© Royal Navy)

Carrying AMRAAM a SHAR gets airbourne
(© Gordon Bartley)

ZH798, note the slightly stylised tail emblem
(© Andy Evans Collection)

Showing its final plumage a No.800 Squadron SHAR
(© Gordon Bartley)

Of note here are the pink walkway and stencil markings – apart from the green wing tank!
(© Gordon Bartley)

FRS.2 development aircraft in Dark Grey
(© Andy Evans Collection)

and two AIM-120Bs on the outboard wing stations together with Aden cannons and the internal F.95 camera. On its return to RNAS Yeovilton, No.800 Squadron retired its FRS.1s and the first F/A.2 joined the unit on 17 March 1995. The first totally 'new build' F/A.2 was delivered in October 1995.

Hughes AIM-120AMRAAM

After protracted development, the AMRAAM entered service in 1992. It is of the same basic layout as the Sparrow III but with increased speed, better guidance, and longer range, less smoke and superior ECM capabilities. Guided by a Nortronics INS and Hughes active radar, it carries a 45lb proximity and impact delay-fused blast/fragmentation warhead rear fuselage has been fitted.

The Sea Harrier Retires

In 2002 the Ministry of Defence announced plans to withdraw the Sea Harrier from service by 2006 to be replaced in the short term by the RAF Harrier GR.7A and latterly the

Note again the lighter radome and the white mailed fist on this aircraft
(© Andy Evans Collection)

GR.9 before they too are to be replaced by the F-35 JSF. Although the Sea Harrier had a good radar and good missiles ultimately the airframe was still the original Harrier I design, and the engine was not suited to hot conditions. So rather than spend on a temporary upgrade, retirement was the MoD's preferred option, and as such during 2006 the Sea Harrier story came to a close.

The Old and the New! A Sea Harrier with a GR.7A, which itself will be supplanted by the GR.9
(© Gordon Bartley)

FRS.2 Development aircraft XZ439 in Light Grey. Note the photographic reference markings
(© Andy Evans Collection)

Sunset on the SHAR!
(© Royal Navy)

F/A.2 AMRAAM Trials

The sea-going Harrier F/A.2 was rather drably adorned for obvious tactical reasons, its all-over coat of Medium Grey broken only by the occasional addition of either black or white squadron markings. However, one of the development aircraft, XZ439, broke the mould when in January 1993 the aircraft was shipped out to the USA to take part in live firing trials of the Hughes AIM-120 AMRAAM missile, which was to be the principle in-service armament. It arrived at Norfolk, Virginia and was unpacked, refuelled and dispatched to Eglin AFB where it expended ten missiles against scale MQM-107 and QF-106 target drones during late March 1993. During this time abroad, the BAe engineers applied the garish, full-colour sharkmouth with staring eyes! In front of the port intake 'mission symbols' were added, visible in the shape of ten AMRAAM missiles, although the significance o f the car is open to conjecture. On both sides of the tail in bright blue was the legend 'British Aerospace Dunsfold'; this was repeated on the

Launching AMRAAM
(© BAe Systems)

intake sides On the tailfin RWR fairing (which contained a transponder linked to the trials equipment) is an excellent Day-Glo variation on No.899 Squadron's badge, now turned to the 'Winged finger'. Also on the RWR, again in Dayglo is a small No.801 Squadron trident, and further down on the rudder were No.809's chequerboards. The crew chiefs' names were also added, but deleted on return to the UK. The Royal Navy wording was in black, with a grey panel at the root and tip of the tailfin, and at several points along the fuselage white photo-reference stripes were added. Full two-colour roundels were carried on the sides of the nose and on the upper and lower wings, as were the normal fire, rescue and access markings. For its trial work the aircraft carried an inert Sidewinder missile tube modified as an instrumentation pod on the starboard outer wing pylon and a converted CBLS pod which served as a centreline camera mount. It is also interesting to note that the aircraft has no pitot tube fitted.

Launching AMRAAM
(© BAe Systems)

The full-blooded sharksmouth! Note the twin yaw vanes on the nose and the ladder attachment
(© Andy Evans Collection)

Looking forward. Of note is the peeling 'Dunsfold' logo, and the stripe down the centre of the cold nozzle
(© Andy Evans Collection)

F/A.2 AMRAAM

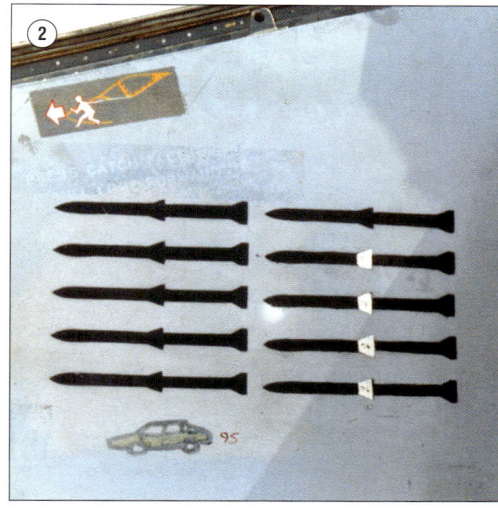

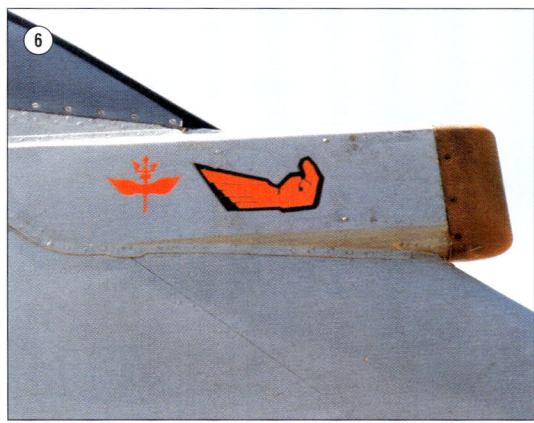

• 1 Close in on the bloodshot eye and the yaw vanes
(© Andy Evans Collection)

• 2 Ten missile launch symbols, and one unidentified 'car' symbol
(© Andy Evans Collection)

• 3 Tail detail, including the small No.801 Squadron chequerboards on the rudder trim tab, the Dark Grey fin top and the No.800 Squadron Day-Glo symbol on the RWR
(© Andy Evans Collection)

• 4 Close in on the sharksmouth, and note the position of the roundel on the nose rather than the intake.
(© Andy Evans Collection)

• 5 On the tip of the tail boom was the rear antenna for the transponder link
(© Andy Evans Collection)

• 6 The 'Winged Finger'!
(© Andy Evans Collection)

• 7 On the tip of the tail boom was the rear antenna for the transponder link
(© Andy Evans Collection)

Harrier T.8N

With the introduction into service of the Sea Harrier F/A.2 and the retirement of the Sea Harrier FRS.1, a new method was urgently required to train the next generation of pilots on the latest version of the naval Harrier. The Navy's existing Harrier T.4A/Ns were therefore upgraded to a new standard, the T.8N, with some ex-RAF Harrier T.4 trainers with acceptable airframe time remaining and held in storage being ear-marked for possible future conversion. Externally, apart from a new paint scheme, they remained unchanged from their former designation; but the internal changes are more significant. It is in the front cockpit where the major upgrades took place, with the FRS.1 style of instrumentation being removed and replaced by the quite different fit of the F/A.2, with the exception of the Blue Vixen radar. Included were a new HUD, UFC and MFD, along with the same data-bus and INS platform. The rear seat retained its FRS.1 ancestry with just a few changes to the technology that allowed the instructor to monitor the student. Sea Harrier Pilots underwent the longest and costliest training programme

ZD990 waits for its next student. Note the Dark Grey wing tanks and the high gloss finish
(© Martin Freer)

ZD990 during a vertical landing. Note the repeated serial number on the tail fin
(© BAe Systems)

in the British services, and around nine pilots a year were so trained. The T.8N was especially good in the air-to-ground mode, and could carry an ACMI pod and additional fuel tanks, thereby making it more economical on the bombing ranges; and some T.8Ns were noted carrying cannon pods. No.899 Squadron operated five Harrier T.8Ns and took delivery of the first conversion, ZB605 (a former T.4N), from BAe Systems on 1 May 1995, the aircraft making its maiden flight on 27 July 1994. In line with the thinking of the late 1990s on high-visibility colour schemes for training aircraft, the T.8Ns received an all-over, high gloss black colour scheme, with white canopy edges, step markings, caution/warning markings and a gloss white intake in front of the Pegasus fan. ZB605 arrived sporting a golden outline of No.899's emblem matched by a white 'Royal Navy' legend beneath it, with its naval ID code of '720' being added later.

ZD805 in the hover. Of note are the white cockpit step markings and the 'trestle' strips under the intakes and rear fuselage
(© BAe Systems)

High visibility was the order of the day for the T.8 Harriers
(© BAe Systems)

ZD990 during a ski-jump training sortie at Yeovilton. Note the placement of the serial number on the bottom of the tailfin
(© Joop Zandbergen)

Caught in the hover as a student learns to stand the Harrier on its thrust
(© Gordon Bartley)

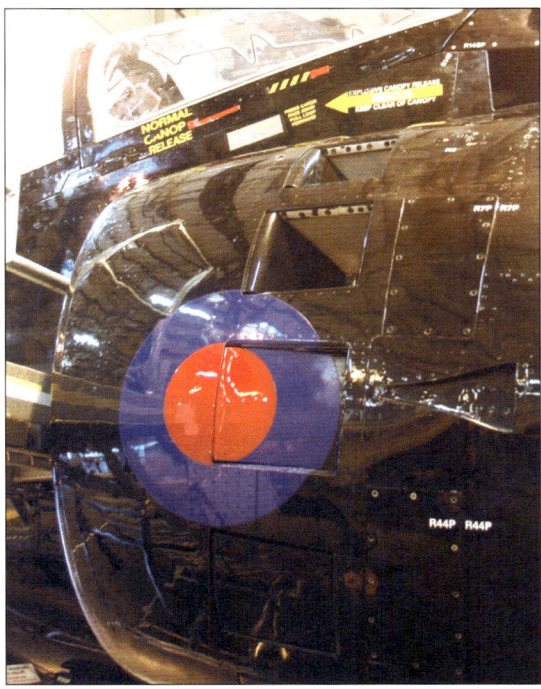

The high gloss finish of the T.8N is evident here
(© via Nick Greenall)

ZB805 high above Yeovilton
(© BAe Systems)

T.8N Walkaround

One of the glass black T.8Ns on the pan at Yeovilton
(© BAe Systems)

T.8N Walkaround

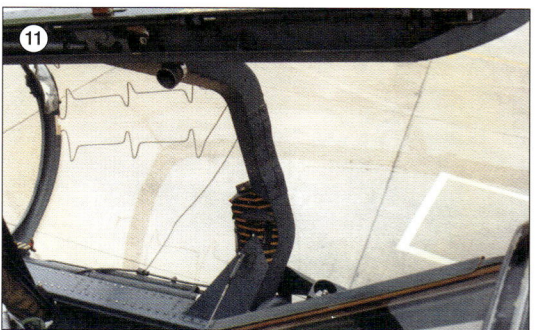

- **7** The rear ejection seat in detail
(© Andy Evans Collection)

- **8** The revised front cockpit of the T.8 made more representative of the Harrier F/A.2
(© Andy Evans Collection)

- **9** Nose detail on the T.8
(© Andy Evans Collection)

- **10** The inner wing pylon showing the attachment points, plus the forward edge of the pylon with its panel removed
(© Andy Evans Collection)

- **11** Canopy interior showing the explosive cord system on the canopy
(© Andy Evans Collection)

- **12** Here we have the rear detail on the airscoops and the grille from the heat exchanger
(© Andy Evans)

A T.8N showing its canopy cover
(© via Nick Greenall)

T.8N Walkaround

• 13 The front cockpit is more representative of the F/A.2
(© Andy Evans Collection)

• 14 The headbox of the ejection seat has angled edges to aid piercing the canopy in the event of an ejection
(© Andy Evans Collection)

• 15 The front cockpit is more representative of the F/A.2
(© Andy Evans Collection)

• 16 The front cockpit is more representative of the F/A.2
(© Andy Evans Collection)

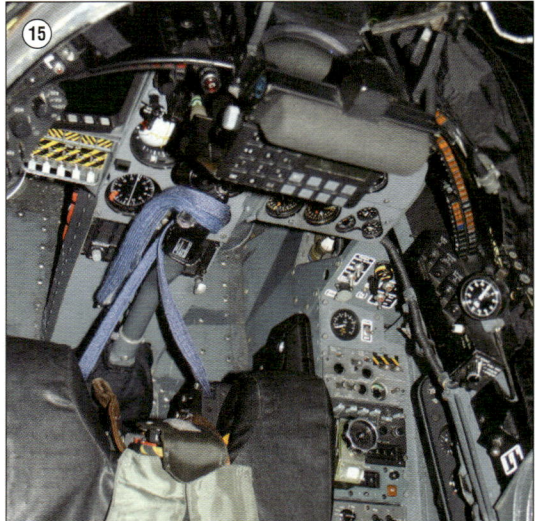

T.8N Walkaround

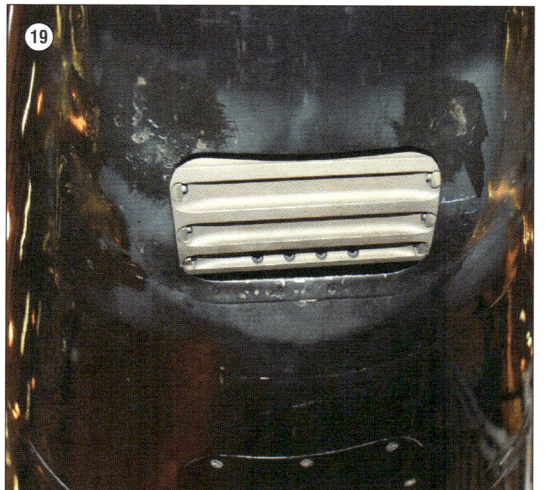

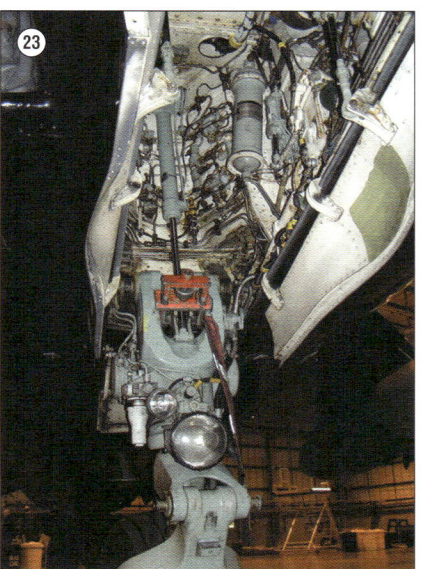

•17 Looking down through the blow-in door at the fan. Note the white insides
(© Andy Evans Collection)

•18 Wing root landing light and fire access port
(© Andy Evans Collection)

•19 Undernose duct
(© Andy Evans Collection)

•20 Looking down on the ejector seat headbox and parachute assembly
(© Andy Evans Collection)

•21 The rear cockpit is in fact a self-contained unit with its own windshield
(© Andy Evans Collection)

•22 The front section on the canopy shown hinged open
(© Andy Evans Collection)

•23 Looking up into the nosewheel bay
(© Andy Evans Collection)

•24 The headbox of the ejection seat has angled edges to aid piercing the canopy in the event of an ejection
(© Andy Evans Collection)

•25 The rear cockpit is in fact a self-contained unit with its own windshield
(© Andy Evans Collection)

No.899 Squadron, Anniversary Scheme

Chapter 9

The Admiral's Barge!

To celebrate No.899 Squadron's 25 year association with the Sea Harrier, and to mark its impending demise, a special colour scheme was commissioned for the occasion. The aircraft chosen was FA.2 ZH809 which received an unusual Roundel Blue and white paint job. It had been proposed that the aircraft should carry the same colours as the Sea Harrier in its original service entry guide, however, there were no stocks of the Dark Sea Gray available, so the most prolific colour left Roundel Blue, was employed. The Squadron's mailed Fist emblem was prominent on the tail matched with a yellow '25 Years' motif above it. The intake roundel was also in full colour with a black ring applied at a different diameter to the roundel. The scheme attracted the name of the Admiral's Barge, and later gained the words 'Fly Navy' on the underside of the wings. The radome was matt Extra Dark Sea Grey with a mixed Medium/Dark Sea Grey band at its rear edge and a DSG/tan mixed radome tip. The

Here we see plain white underwings
(© Royal Navy)

aircraft also had GPS white discs on the upper fuselage and only carried white inner wing pylons for transit fuel tanks.

No.899 Squadron Decommissioning – Additional Notes

As the unit prepared for decommissioning, some anomalies were noted on the last of its aircraft, especially on the Mailed Fist tail markings. In fact, every winged fist was of a different size, especially the amount of black outline. The fists therefore fell broadly into two categories: large and small. Examples of the large fist were found on ZH802/711 ZH796/712, ZE693/714 and ZD579/715/R (the letter R for Ark Royal on the fin tip above the rudder and the number 8 on the starboard outrigger only plus ZE692/718 and ZH800/719/VL - the VL being centred over the rudder hinge line. Small-fisted SHARs were noted as ZE690/713, ZH812/716 and XZ440/717. On the day of Decommissioning, 23rd March 2005, the aircraft on display also had noteworthy details. ZH809 now had the name CDR J Lawler RN in white under both sides of the windscreen and the name of its maintainers in black on its starboard front u/c door. The port door just had the Danger and black nitrogen symbol stencils on it. Following ZH809's example, several other SHARs now had pilot's names in white under their windscreens on both sides of

'Fly Navy' was later applied
(© Royal Navy)

In its glossy blue the aircraft was an impressive sight
(© Royal Navy)

ZH809 makes a hazy getaway
(© Royal Navy)

Applied as decals the 'Fly Navy' legend began to peel
(© Royal Navy)

Splash and Dash!
(© Royal Navy)

899 Squadron's Boss, Commander J 'Chips' Lawler
(© Royal Navy)

Of note here is the thin black outline surrounding the roundel
(© Royal Navy)

the fuselage and a few also had crew names on the front undercarriage doors, such as ZH802/711 – MAJ R J Dresner RN, ZE692/712 – LT CDR P Tremelling RN, ZH800/713 – LT C H Compain RN, but missing the Lt C on the port side. ZD579/715/R – CDR J Lawler RN (again!), and on its port front u/c door in black stencils: AEM 'Baby Dave' Roberts, AEA 'Smudge' SMITH. ZH812/716 – MAJ R J Dresner RM (again!) and on its starboard front undercarriage door in black stencils: AEM Stu Fulcher 'Magnet', AEM Rob Gouldbourne 'Steel' and SAC Hana Lowden 'Bird'; XZ440/717 – LT J Blackmore RN. ZE690/719 – on its starboard side only was: CDR SHAR, CDR T Eastaugh RN, Stiggins. Some other oddities included ZH806/730/N with 899's 730 side codes but with a full set of 801 fin markings, including the ship code for Invincible and ZE693 with a large fist on the fin now carrying 899's 717 side codes in the Haas Helvetica style. The two SHARs flown by 899 for their decommissioning flypast were ZH802/711 and ZD579/715/R.

Getting ready for another display
(© Royal Navy)

The No.899 Squadron Anniversary Scheme
(© Andy Evans Collection)

No.800 Squadron Retirement Scheme

Chapter 10

Satan Special!

This unique eye-catching design started when Commander Paul Stone asked for ideas for a one-off decommissioning for 800 Naval Air Squadron on the 31 March 2004, as Rob Trewinard-Boyle explains: The 'Red Arrow' design started by using the shape of the fin flash that was already applied to the Squadron's Harriers' tails and duplicating this on the upper and lower surfaces. This design was then tweaked to fit over the panel lines to look balanced on the aircraft; harder than it seems with items like vortex generators, pylons etc being in the way. The geometric design, though, was not racy enough for the aircrew on the Squadron who decided that as one of 800 NAS callsigns was 'Satan' they wanted a more devilish design. Adapting the original involved putting a triangular head on the point of the arrow with horns leading onto the cabin-conditioning air intake fairings on either side of the cockpit, as well as taloned claws coming over

The position of the underside marking
(© Royal Navy)

(All images © Royal Navy)

the leading edge of the wing. At one point flames along the forward fuselage, under the canopy, were talked about but discounted due to the risk of them peeling off and getting sucked into the engine. However, the Satan design was not allowed: it was 'too demonic'! So, back to the geometric design, with a few words added to mark the occasion under the canopy. ZD613 (side number 127) was chosen to be painted as it was to be scrapped after the decommissioning. However, the decommissioning aircraft had to have the CO's side number so it was changed to 122. This led to the previous 122 flying with 127 painted on for a while and this showed on some early photos, and hence some models have ZD613 in the decommissioning scheme with the side number 127 on them! The decision to have strakes painted was due to a shortage of gunpods at the time, leading to a less noticeably red fuselage than originally intended.

When final approval came through for the geometric design the aircraft was towed to the paint shop at Yeovilton and, with a few favours pulled in, the design was applied over a long weekend. The white Squadron badge was then applied using an aircraft-specific type of sticky backed plastic called Spandex. Also, when the masking tape on the wings had been removed, a noticeable ridge of paint could be seen. This had to be smoothed and edge-sealed to prevent the paint chipping/flaking in the airflow. The final design definitely made an impact and became one of the most photographed Sea Harriers ever, a fitting reminder of the aircraft and 800 NAS.

Additional Notes
800 Squadron's Disbandment

After 24 years of SHAR operation, 800 Squadron disbanded at RNAS Yeovilton on the 31st March 2004. The six aircraft that took part in the flypast were: ZD613/122/R, ZE698/123/R, ZE696/124/R, ZH801/125/R, ZD610/126/R and ZH806/127/R, with ZD579/128/R as the reserve. ZD613 was in 800's decommissioning scheme, and carried strakes and 190 gallon tanks, with both outer pylons being empty. All the other SHARs in the flypast carried gun pods, 190s and some carried centre-line pylons and were all in 800's standard finish, with the red pennant on the fin containing the Squadron's white crossed swords and trident. ZE698, ZE696, ZH801 and ZD579 all carried the respective last digit of their side codes high up on both outriggers: 3, 4, 7 and 8. The positioning of the letter R on the fin varied slightly between each aircraft, ZE696's starboard side R was uniquely centred over the rudder hinge line, whilst ZH806's starboard R was just back of the hinge line. All the aircraft carried pilot's names under the windscreens. Anomalies worth noting included ZE696/124/R - two patches on the port side of the fin appear to be dark green or, more likely, Dark Sea Grey and on her starboard outrigger only the diagonal of the numeral 4 remained. Also noted on ZD579/128/R was that the front section of the port 190 tank was Dark Sea Grey with a heavily weathered chromate yellow tip.

No.801 Squadron – Last of the Sea Harriers Chapter 11

Aboard HMS Illustrious
(© Gordon Bartley)

The last unit to continue to fly the Sea Harrier, No.801 Squadron, had a memorable last few months of operations, and remained a potent fighting force to the end. To mark the passing of the unit and the Sea Harrier a black 'Omega' symbol was added to their usual tail emblems.

The 'Last Cruise' HMS Illustrious November 2005

The last ocean shout for the SHARs took place aboard HMS Illustrious in the November of 2005. The Aircraft involved were: ZH796/001/L CDR A J Rae RN; XZ440/002/L LT CDR I C Tidball RN; ZE690/003/L LT C H Compain RN; ZH803/004/L MAJ B H Ritterby plus crew names in black on the port front undercarriage door: AEM Martin, AEM Ibbotson; ZH813/006/L LT K N Steen RN (port side only) The last SHAR to leave was ZH796/001/L flown by Lt Cdr I C Tidball on 29 November 2005; taking off at 09:17 GMT. This occasion also saw one of the first SHARs, XZ440 (first flight as an FRS.1 on 6 June 1979) flying alongside the last SHAR F/A.2 built, ZH813 (which took its first flight in November 1998).

801 Squadron's Last Gunfight: RAF Lakenheath, 12th February 2006

899's penultimate outing was against the F-15Cs of the 493rd Fighter Squadron of the USAFE at Lakenheath. The aircraft on the squadron at this time were: ZH797/000/L CDR A J Rae RN; ZH796/001/L CDR A J Raern: ZH811/002/L LT CDR I C Tidball RN; ZE690/003/L LT C H Compain RN; ZH803/004/L MAJ B H Ritterby; ZH811/005/L LT P H Lee RN; ZH813/006/L LT K N Steen RN, plus crew names AEM Price and AEM Gray in black on the port front u/c door; and ZH804/007/L. The pilot's names were still in black. H803/004/L was by now missing large parts of her rudder markings on both sides. The SHARs' last shout came on a dull, wet 9th March 2006 when the unit flew the SHARs' last ever tactical mission as 'Blue Force' protecting ground targets near Sennybridge in South Wales from the enemy 'Red' Force of four Tornado GR.4s from No IX(B) Squadron and a pair of Jaguar GR.3As from No 41(F) Squadron, with their air cover being provided by eight F-15Cs from the 493rd FS USAFE. It was appropriate that this, last trip was from Yeovilton. The SHARs and pilots for this the final 'Venom Flight' were: Venom 1 - Cdr Tony Rae (Stinger) in ZH812/005/L; Venom 2 - Lt Chris Roy (Casper) in ZE690/007/L; Venom 3 - Lt Kieron Steen (Zippy) in ZH804/003/L; Venom 4 - Lt Cdr Ian Tidball (Tidders) in ZH811/002/L and Venom 5 - Major Brett Ritterby (Critter) in ZH803/004/L.

RAF Lakenheath
(© Gary Parsons)

The Last Gunfight
(© Gary Parsons)

The Sea Harrier's last cruise aboard HMS Illustrious
(© Gordon Bartley)

Aboard HMS Illustrious
(© Gordon Bartley)

Aboard HMS Illustrious
(© Gordon Bartley)

Aboard HMS Illustrious
(© Gordon Bartley)

ZH813 with some non-standard final markings!

The final line-up
(© Mathew Clements)

James Bond no less!

Tails to the sun with the Omega added
(© Gary Parsons)

801 Squadron's Disbandment - Yeovilton, 28 March 2006

801 had all their SHARs prepared for their disbandment flypast well ahead of time and the aircraft that comprised 801's ceremonial 5-ship flypast were: ZH796/001/L CDR A J Rae RN (AEM Price, AEM Barry, crew names port door), starboard 'panel 12' was of the older F/A.2 style with a bulge, pushing the 001 side code back. ZH811/002/L LT CDR I C Tidball RN (AEM Teas, E Alderson, ZH804/003/L LT K N Steen RN, ZH803/004/L MAJ B H Ritterby USMC AEM Martin, AEM Ibbotoson, ZH812/005/L LT CA Roy RN (AEM STU Fulcher with 'Magnet' on the starboard front undercarriage door, together with AEM Rob Goldbourne 'Steel' and Hana Lowden 'Bird'. All SHARs were similarly equipped with fuselage strakes, 190 gallon tanks and AMRAAM drill rounds on their outer pylons. Typically the black and white chequers on the fins were differently aligned on each aircraft as detailed: ZH811/002/L aligned to leading edge, but with quite a gap at the leading edge, ZH803/004/L mixed alignment to leading edge around the strake, ZH812/005/L aligned to trailing edge, ZE690/007/L aligned to leading edge, ZH796/001/L aligned to leading edge, ZH804/003/L aligned to the leading edge.

Flying Into Oblivion

Having had their AMRAAM drill rounds removed, the five SHARs that comprised 801's flypast were flown to RAF Shawbury on 29 March and put into storage. The spare aircraft for the disbandment was ZE690/007/L on which had been some considerable touching up to areas on its nose, and it only had the letter L on the port side of the fin. It carried the pilot's name: LT C H Compain RN in black under the windscreen on both sides of the fuselage and had no numbers on its outriggers. This aircraft was also the last service SHAR to leave Yeovilton on 29 March 2006, being flown by the last holder of the title Commander SHAR, Cdr Henry Mitchell RN, to RNAS Culdrose where it was put to use with the SFDO: School of Flight Deck Operations.

Farewell Sea Harrier
(© Royal Navy)

Colour Side-views • 1 • FRS.1

XZ450 the first Sea Harrier to fly, piloted by John Farley on 20th August 1978, BAE Dunsfold. The first to operate from a ski-jump and be demonstrated to the public at the SBAC Farnborough Show on 2nd September 1978 by John Farley; the first equipped to carry and fire Sea Eagle missiles. The first loss in the Falklands War, Lt Nick Taylor KIA, 4th May 1982 during an attack on Goose Green.

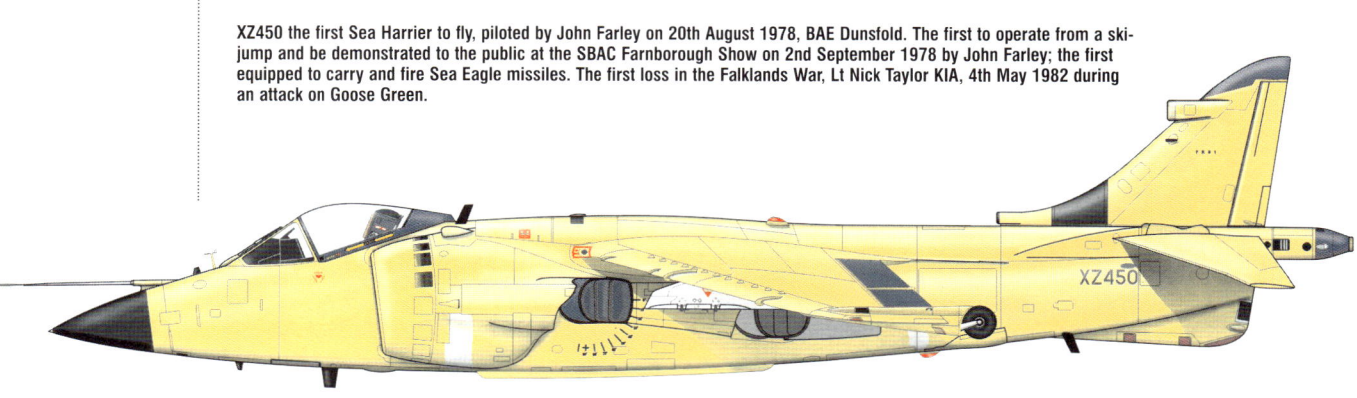

XZ455/102 of 700A Flight, the Sea Harrier Intensive Flying Trials Unit (IFTU), during working-up trials on HMS Hermes in 1979. It is believed Lt Cdr David Braithwaite is the only SHAR pilot to have flown with all five Royal Navy SHAR squadrons.

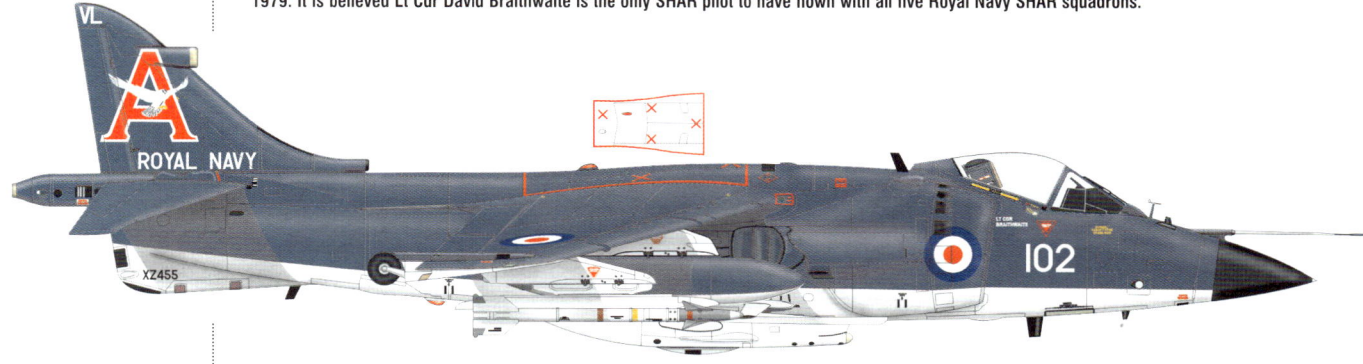

XZ492/123/H, 5th April 1982 when she departed with 800NAS on HMS Hermes for the South Atlantic. On 21st May 1982, Lt Cdr Neill Thomas destroyed an A-4C Skyhawk, either C-309 or C325, of Grupo 4 with an AIM-9L. Later converted to an FA.2, XZ492 is now a privately owned wreck at Faygate, West Sussex.

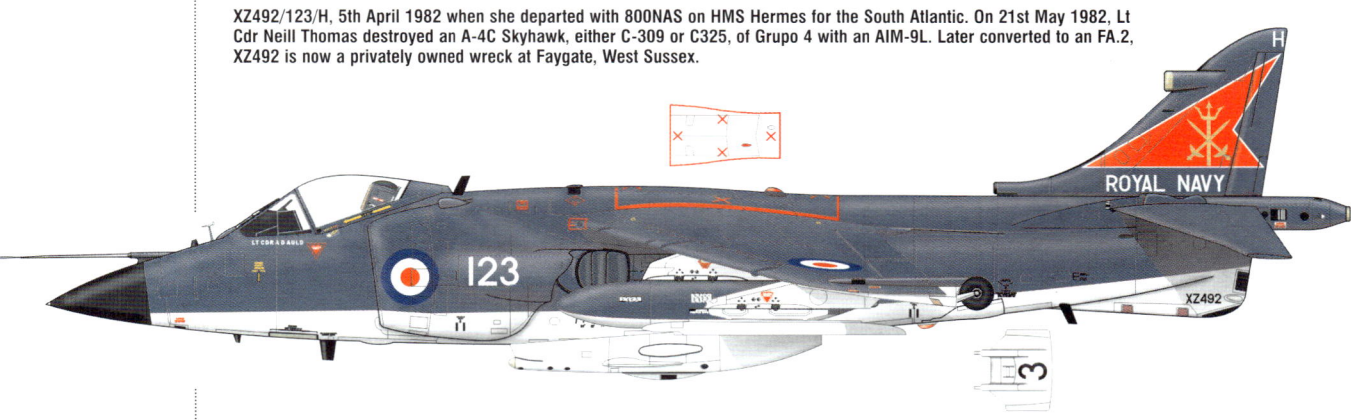

ZA175/004/N, 5th April 1982 when she departed with 801NAS on HMS Invincible for the South Atlantic. On 01 May 82, Lt Cdr Mike Broadwater fired two AIM-9L Sidewinders at a Canberra of Grupo 2, neither finding its mark. On 21-May-82, Lt Cdr 'Sharkey' Ward shot down Dagger C407 of Grupo 6 with an AIM-9L. Later converted to an FA.2 in 1994, it has been acquired by the IWM Duxford and is preserved at the Norfolk & Suffolk Aviation Museum, Flixton, Suffolk.

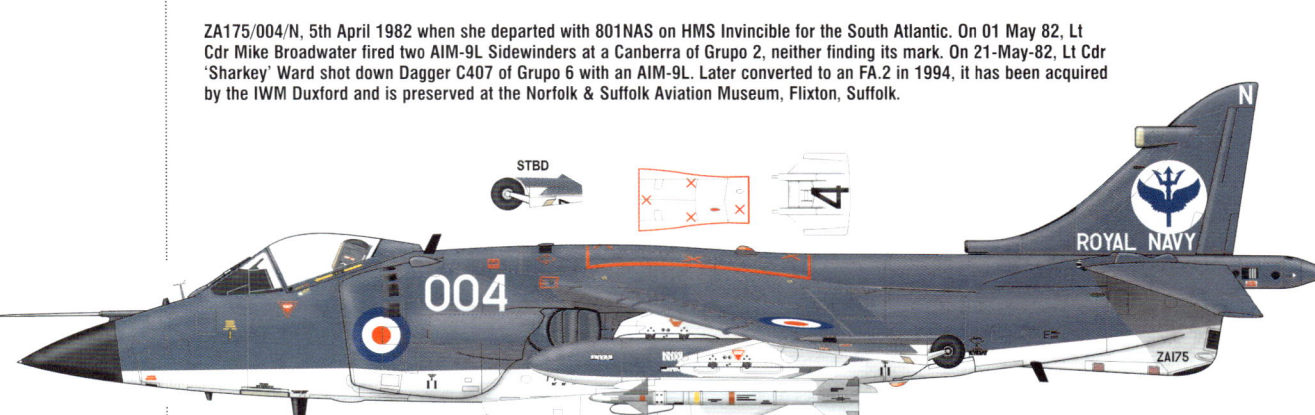

Colour Art © David Howley

XZ453/105, July 1981. Flt Penfold was one of the first two pilots pilots to qualify on the SHAR being on 899's first course - OFT1, with Lt Cdr Ogilvy. As 009 of 801NAS, lost on 6th May 1982 killing its pilot Lt Alan Curtis, either colliding with Lt Cdr John Eyton-Jones in XZ452/007 or striking the sea in bad weather. Lt Curtis received a posthumous Mention in Despatches.

XZ496/27 ex-127/H with 800NAS of the 800/899NAS HMS Hermes Air Group, 21st May 1982. On this date Lt Cdr Mike Blissett destroyed an A-4C Skyhawk, either C-309 or C-325 of Grupo 4 with an AIM-9L fired from the starboard rail. Note how the (brush) overpainted white undersides and fin markings just visible through the overpaint which became a common feature. On its return to the UK it had medium sea grey replacement rudder and port foward nozzle and a white Skyhawk stencil under the cockpit on the starboard side. Lost on 16th March 1984 when it ditched in the North Sea off Norway alongside HMS Illustrious after engine failure.

XZ457/14 ex-714/VL with 899NAS of the 800/899NAS, the top scoring SHAR with the HMS Hermes Air Group, May/June 1982. On 21st May 1982 Lt Clive Morrell destroyed A-4Q Skyhawk 0660/3-A-307 of 3 Escuadrilla with an AIM-9L and damaged A-4Q Skyhawk 0665/3-A-312 of 3 Escuadrilla with cannon fire, this A-4 being lost while attempting an emergency landing. On 24th May 1982 Lt Cdr Andy Auld destroyed 2 Daggers - C419 and, probably, C-430 of Grupo 6 with 2 AIM-9Ls. Later converted to FA.2 standard in 1993. On 20th October 1995 as 714 of 899 NAS caught fire while preparing for take off at Yeovilton. Now in the Boscombe Down Aviation Museum.

ZA177/77 one of the 809NAS SHARs that joined the Hermes Air Group. On 8th June 1982 Flt Lt David Morgan destroyed two A-4B Skyhawks, C226 and C-228 of Grupo 5, with AIM-9Ls during a 'Duskers' sortie. On 21st January 1983 as 711 of 899NAS crashed in a spin; Lt Fox ejected but suffered spinal injuries.

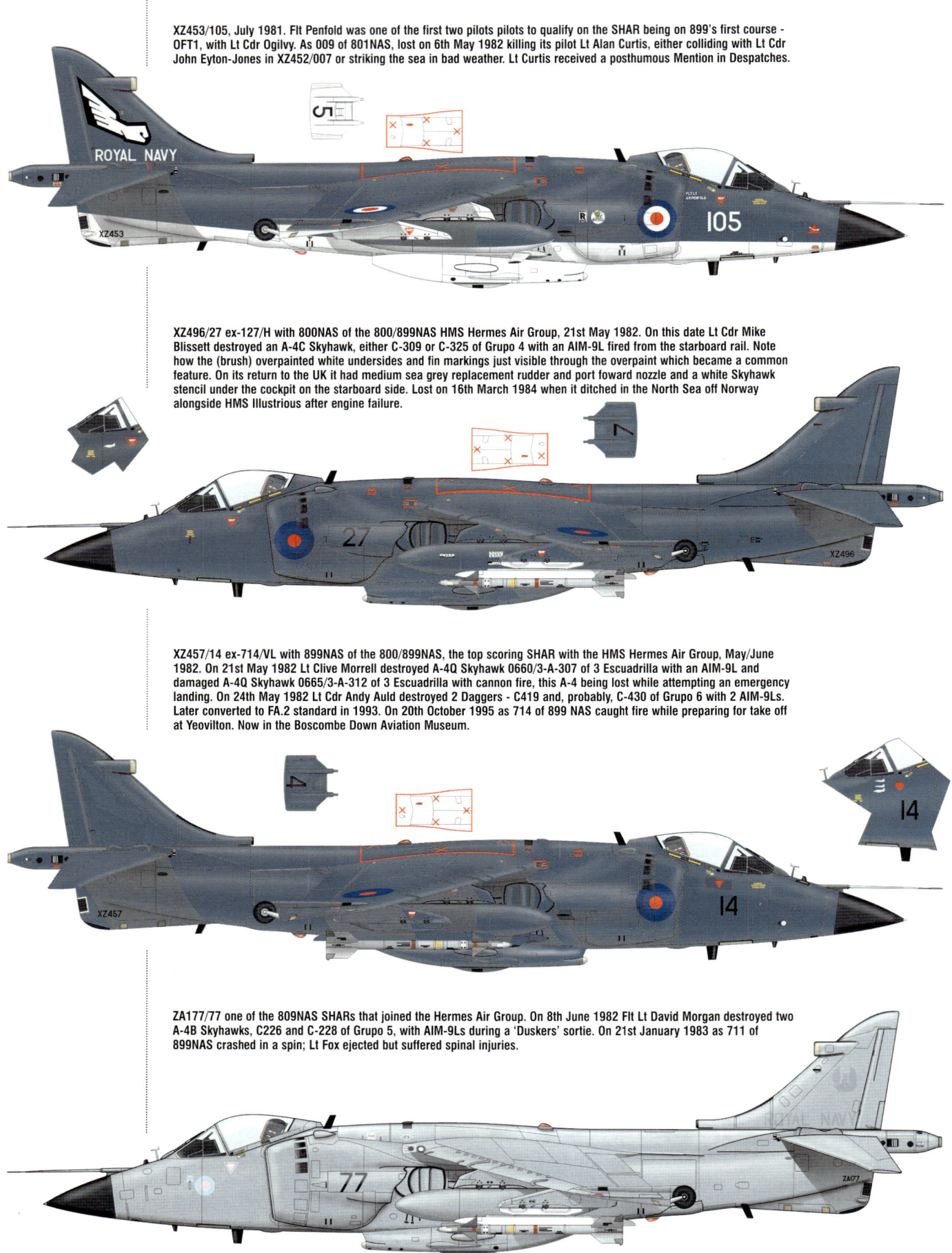

Colour Art © David Howley

Colour Side-views • 3 • FRS.1

XZ499 of 809NAS on departure from RNAS Yeovilton, 1st May 1982. On 8th June 1982 Lt Dave Smith destroyed A-4B Skyhawk C204 of Grupo 5 with an AIM-9L. Later converted to Sea Harrier FA.2 and now in the Fleet Air Arm Museum Reserve Collection at RNAS Yeovilton.

XZ451/006 became the top scoring SHAR with 801NAS on HMS Invincible during the Falklands War. Note how the spray painted EDSG undersides appear slightly lighter. On 1st May 1982 Lt Alan Curtis destroyed Canberra B-110 of Grupo 2 with one of two AIM-9Ls fired. On 21st May 1982 Lt Cdr 'Sharkey' Ward destroyed Grupo 3 Pucara A-511 flown by Mayor Carlos Tomba with cannon fire and on 1st June 1982 he destroyed Hercules TC-63 of Grupo 1 with one of two AIM-9Ls fired and cannon fire. On 30th November 1989 as 005 of 801NAS, crashed near Sardinia; Lt Auckland ejected safely.

ZA190/099 of 801NAS on 21st May 1982 when Lt Steve Thomas destroyed two Daggers, C-404 and C403 of Grupo 6, with two AIM-9Ls. On 15th October 1987 as 006 of 801 NAS operating from HMS Ark Royal it crashed in the Irish Sea after a bird strike.

XZ496/257 'Mrs Robinson' of 809NAS on HMS Illustrious in early December 1982, just prior to its return to the UK at the end of Illustrious' deployment to the Falkland Islands. This was the only deployment 809 NAS undertook as an independent SHAR unit.

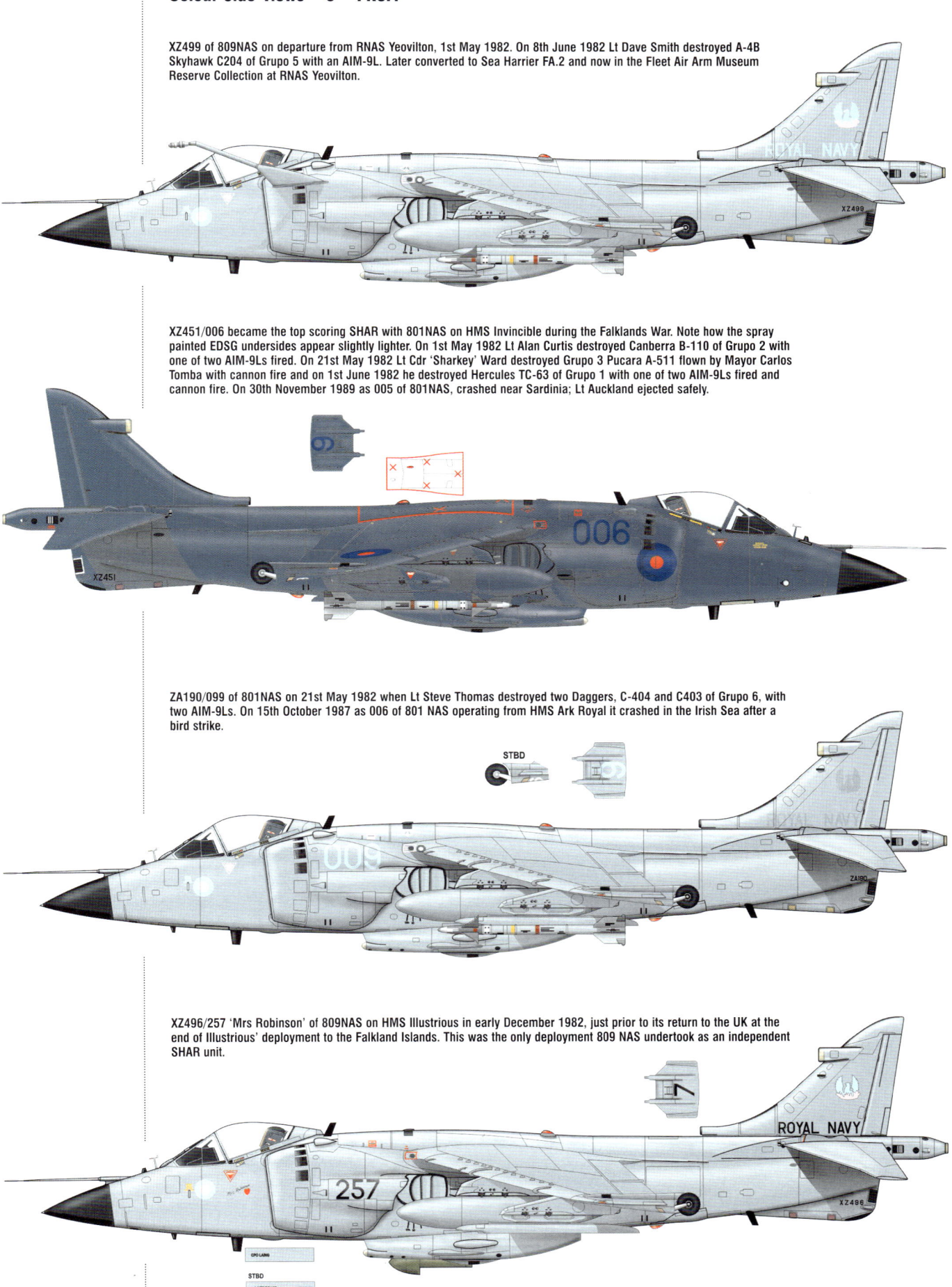

Colour Art © David Howley

ZD698/127 of 800NAS flew the last Combat Air Support operational sortie of an FRS.1 over Bosnia, as part of Op Deny Flight on 18th February 1995. As an FA.2 wearing the codes 123/R on 31st March 2004 she was one of the SHARs flying when 800 NAS Decommissioned at RNAS Yeovilton.

ZD609/000/R the nominal mount of Lt Cdr M W 'Soapy' Watson the CO of 801NAS during its deployment on HMS Ark Royal during mid-1990.

XZ494/716 of 899NAS during the late 1980s. An ex-899NAS Falklands veteran, as black-16 armed with 3x 1,000lb delayed action bombs she was flown by Lt Cdr Andy Auld the CO of 800NAS on the 1st May 1982 when he led the attack on Stanley Airfield, immortalised by Brian Hanrahan of the BBC when he reported: ""I counted them all out and I counted them all back.

ZA175/717 in the stunning scheme to mark 899's 50th Anniversary in December 1992. and was still being worn in 1994. 717 was nominally the aircraft of CO Lt Cdr Simon Hargreaves.

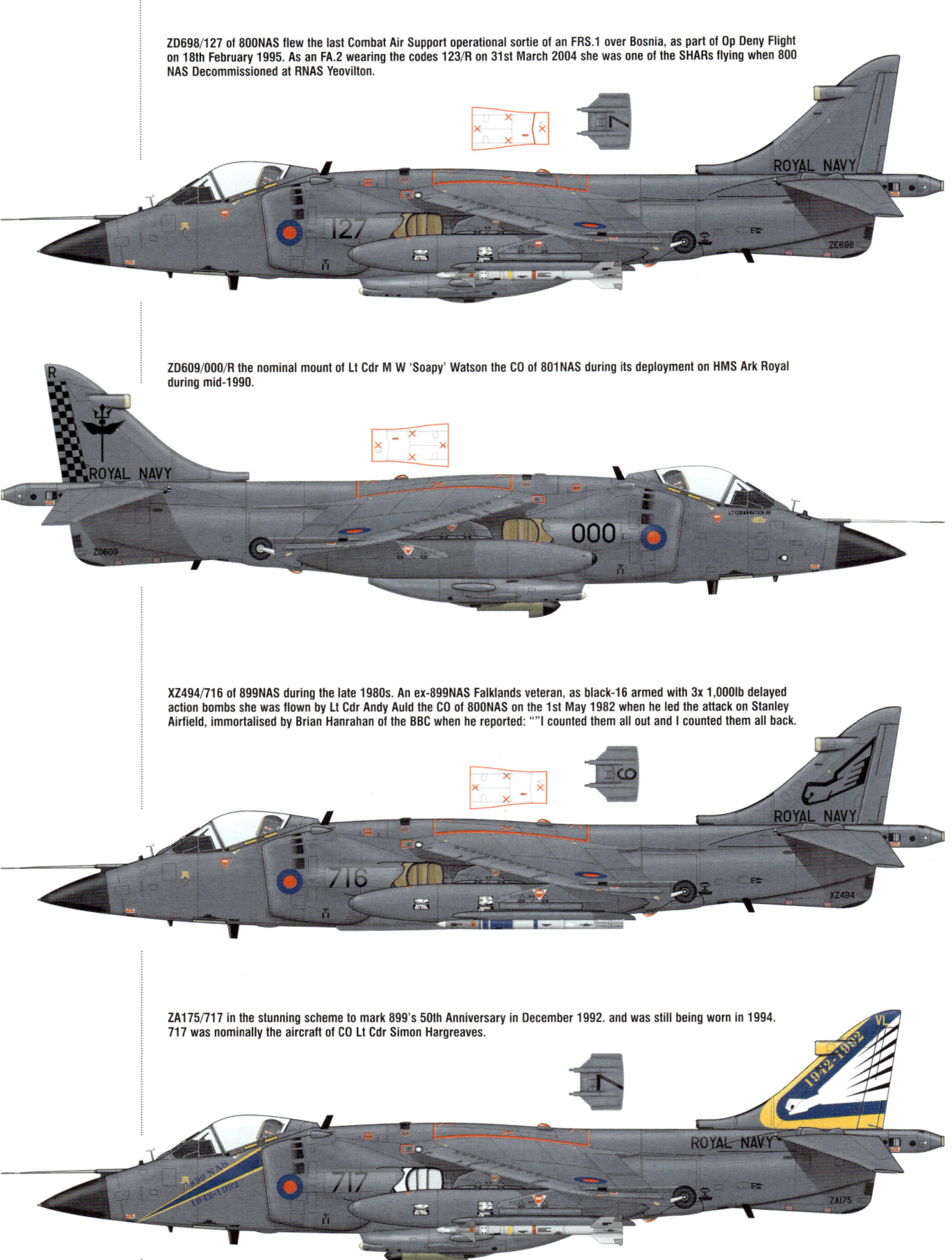

Colour Art © David Howley

XZ455/12 seen in Extra Dark Sea Grey, Falklands camouflage scheme.

ZE690/713 was the usual mount of 899's last CO, Cdr Jon 'Chips' Lawler in late 2004 - early 2005. Cdr Lawler had re-introduced the 713 side code to the Squadron which had not used it for some years after two 713s had been lost in quick succession.

Colour Art © David Howley

Colour Side-views • 6 • FRS.2 and F/A.2

ZA195 FRS.2 Prototype. This aircraft was first flown in FRS.2 configuration from BAE Dunsfold by Heinz Frick on 19th September 1988 in overall DSG with black Sea Harrier FRS.2 logos on her nose sides. While able to carry a full warload from an early stage, ZA195 was not fitted with a radar so could accommodate a nose mounted pitot. As depicted here in November 1990, she conducted carrier trials on HMS Ark Royal.

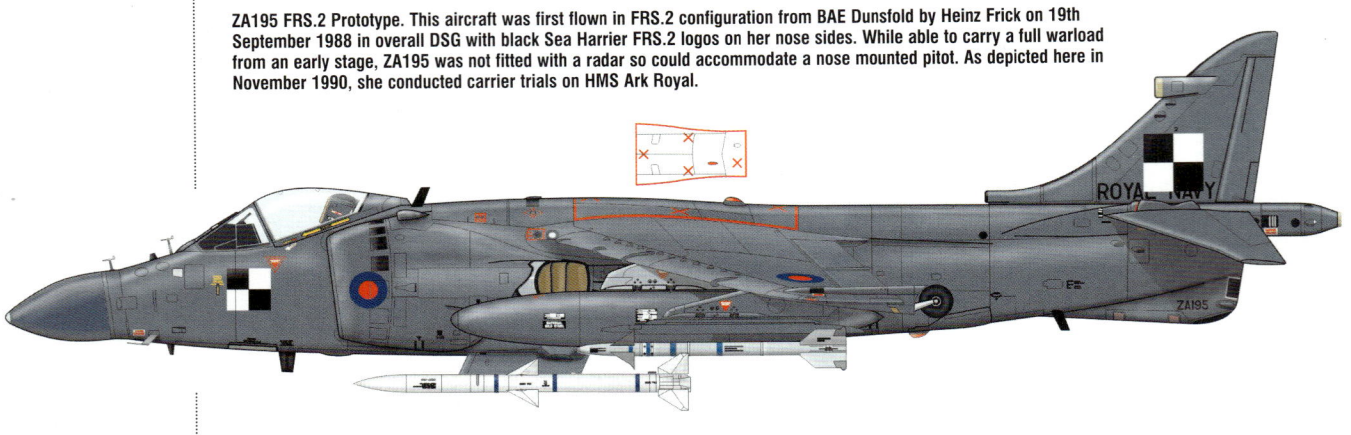

ZD615/712 was the first FA.2 delivered to the OEU on 21st June 1993. In September 1994 the OEU embarked on HMS Invincible alongside 800NAS's FRS.1s and were active over Bosnia later that year armed with Sidewinders.

ZD608/128 of 800NAS aboard HMS Invincible during NATO's operation 'Deliberate Force' over Bosnia from July 1995. The markings denote six 1,000lb bombs dropped.

ZD579/128/R at the time of 800NAS, Decommissioning, 31st March 2004, RNAS Yeovilton. Lt Cdr Mould was the SPLOT, Senior Pilot, of 800NAS.

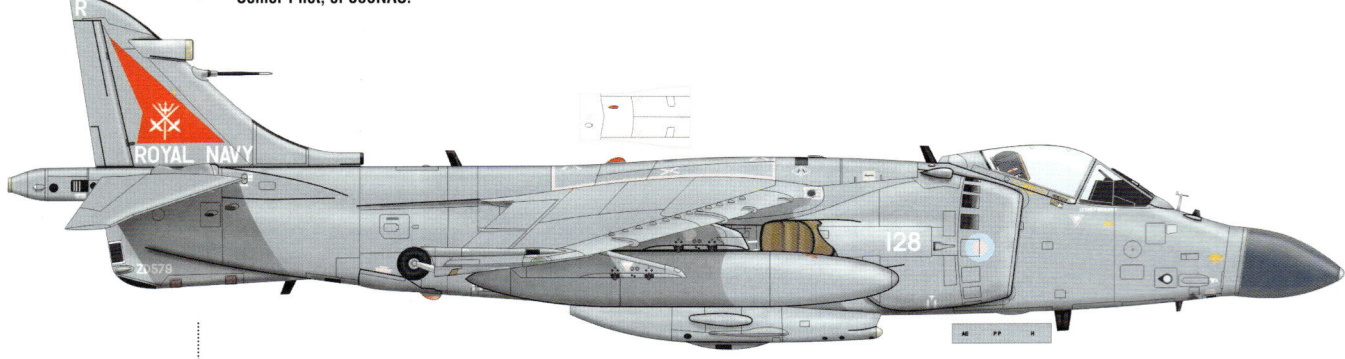

Colour Art © David Howley

Colour Side-views • 7 • F/A.2 and Trainers

ZD613/122 of No.800 Sqn. Seen here in its SATAN 1 decomissioning scheme as designed by Rob Trewinnard-Boyle.

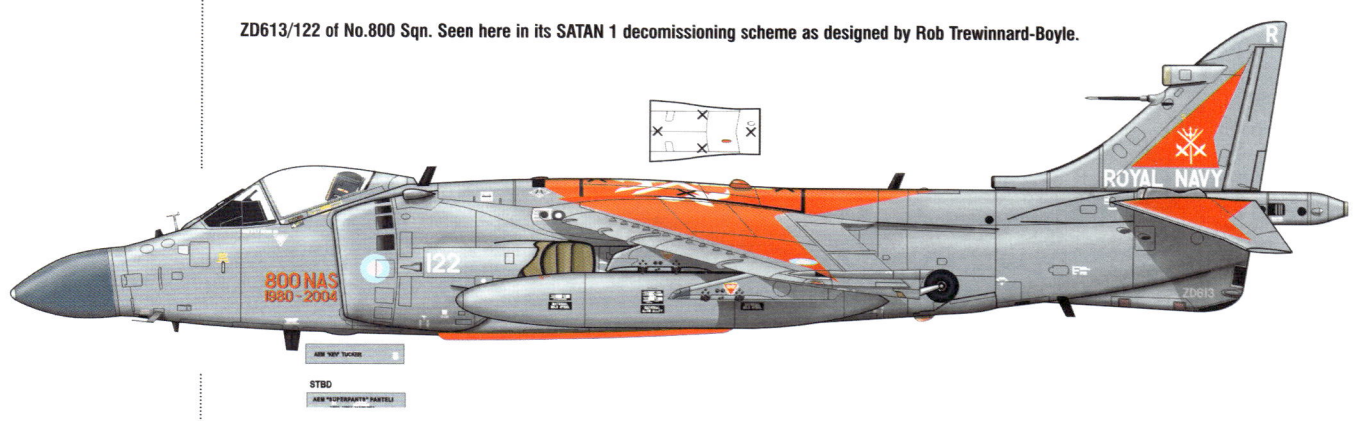

ZH809/(710) in No.899 Sqns 'Admiral's Barge' scheme first unveiled in 2004 to celebrate the 25th Year of the SHAR entering service with the Fleet Air Arm of the Royal Navy. Due in part to a lack of EDSG paint being available the original SHAR scheme was replicated with gloss roundel blue upper surfaces. To differentiate the roundels a black ring was applied at the correct distanc from the whote/red centres. The fuselage roundels were relocated to a higher rearward position on the intake sides. During its life various stencils disppeared, while at the end the name of 899's CO, Cdr J Lawler RN, was in white lettering under the windscreens. In late 2004 it carried the words FLY NAVY under the wings: FLY under the starboard wing.

XW266/719 T.4N of No.899 Sqn. Early T-4, seen here in Dark Sea Grey colour scheme, the T.4 was replicated the FRS.1 in the training regime.

ZD990/721 T.8N of No.899 Sqn. The all-black T.8's were so painted for high conspicuity and replicated the FA.2 in cockpit in the front seat. This aircraft is depicted at the time of No.899 Squadrons decomissioning.

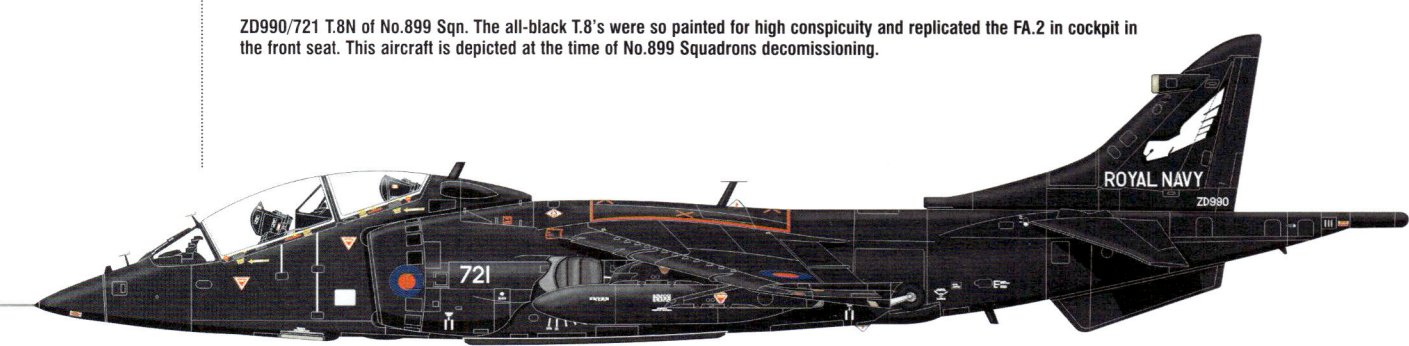

Colour Art © David Howley

Colour Side-views • 8 • FRS.51 Indian Navy

IN606/606/W Sea Harrier FRS.51 from No. 300 Sqn of INAS 551B 'Braves' of the Sea Harrier Operational Flying Training Unit 2005, depicted here in its Extra Dark Sea Grey and White colours.

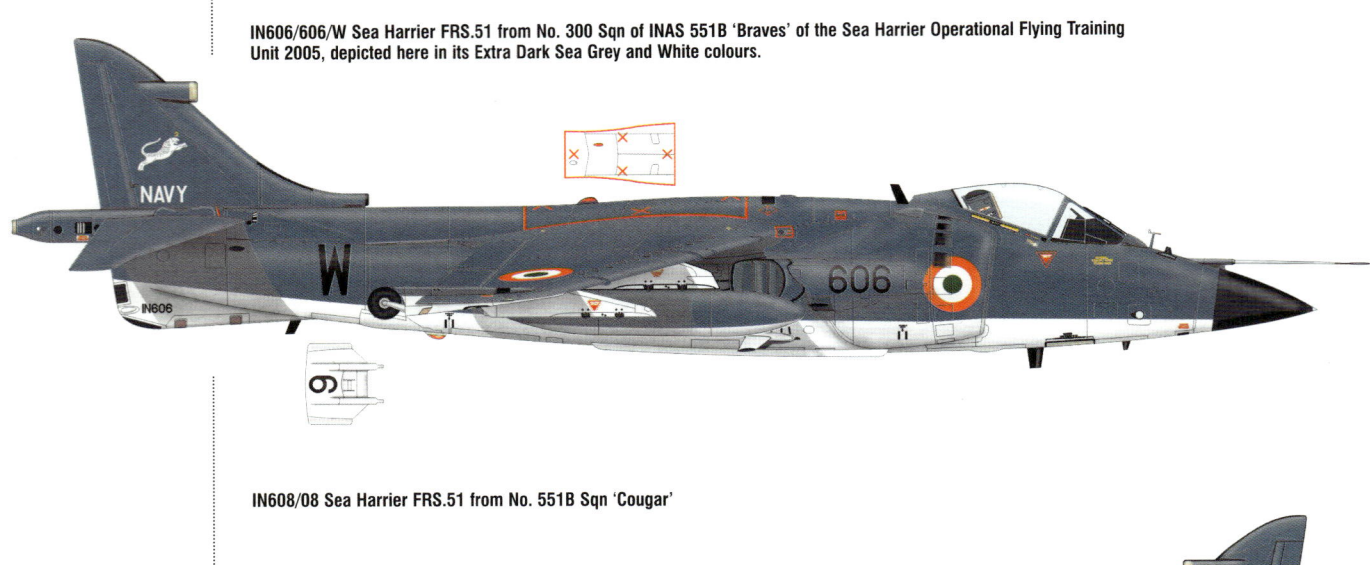

IN608/08 Sea Harrier FRS.51 from No. 551B Sqn 'Cougar'

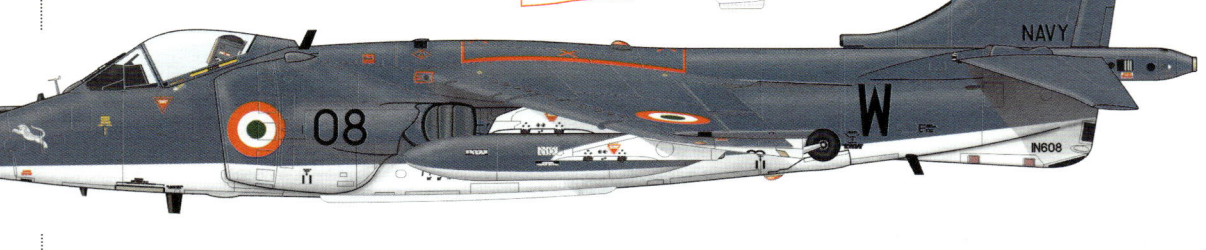

IN603/603 Sea Harrier FRS.51 from No. 300 Sqn aboard INAS Viraat in 2004, show in its Medium Sea Grey finish.

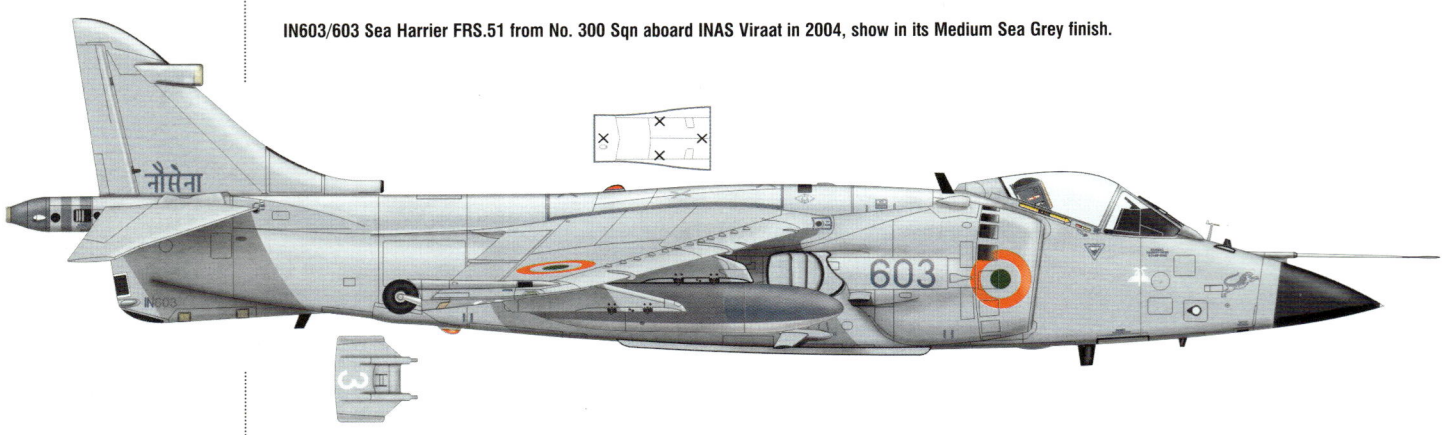

IN651/651 T.60/T.4(I) Sea Harrier Operational Flying Training Unit (SHOFTU)

Colour Art © David Howley

Sea Harrier Squadrons

Chapter 12

800 Squadron

Formed on 3 April 1933, together with 801, with which it had a strong bond and friendly rivalry. Its motto, 'Nunquam Non Paratus', means 'Never Unprepared', and it was the first jet unit within the Fleet Air Arm. First aircraft in 1933 were Hawker Nimrods, the navalised version of the Fury, and during the Second World War the squadron operated from HMS Ark Royal, flying Blackburn Skuas against such targets as the battleship Scharnhorst. Sea Hurricanes replaced the Skuas later in the war to support the North African landings, and towards the end of the war Hellcats from the unit helped 617 Squadron in the destruction of the Tirpitz. Seafires followed post-war, then the first jets in the shape of the Sea Hawk FGA.6 during the Suez Crisis, flying from HMS Albion, progressing through the Scimitar and Buccaneer until disbandment in 1972. Reformed on 31 March 1980 with the Sea Harrier FRS.1, the squadron saw action in the South Atlantic two years later with HMS Hermes, its pilots being awarded many decorations for their heroic efforts against the Argentine forces.

801 Squadron

Formed in 1933 as a Fleet Fighter Squadron, 801 saw extensive service during the Second World War protecting the Malta convoys, battling in North Africa and against the German battleship Tirpitz. Types flown throughout the conflict included the Skua, Sea Hurricane and Seafire. It later saw action in Korea, with the Sea Hornet and Sea Fury, and in 1982 was heavily involved in the Falklands conflict where eight Argentine aircraft were shot down by the Squadron's recently acquired Sea Harrier FRS.1s. More recently it has seen action in Yugoslavia and Bosnia, losing a Sea Harrier in the latter while trying to defend a town against Serb tanks.

899 Squadron

The squadron originally formed at Hatston in December 1942 as a fighter squadron with twelve Seafire IICs, and in March 1943 embarked on HMS Indomitable for the Mediterranean to take part in the landings on Sicily. When the ship was damaged by a torpedo the squadron disembarked at North Front, Gibraltar. In August the squadron embarked on HMS Hunter to provide cover in the landings in Salerno the following month, one detachment being shore based at Paestrum. In April 1944 the squadron embarked on HMS Khedive with twenty Seafire L.IIIs and took part in the landings in the south of France in August 1944. In September 1944 the squadron took part in attacks off Crete and Rhodes,

subsequently spending most of winter at Long Kesh. In February 1945 the squadron embarked on HMS Chaser with 24 Seafire L.IIIs, and subsequently disembarked at Schofield, Australia in April 1945 to became the Operational Training squadron with the task of training experienced former RAAF pilots for naval duties to form the nucleus of the Australian Fleet Air Arm of the Royal Australian Navy. The Squadron was training on HMS Arbiter on VJ-Day. Post-war, by 1956 the Squadron, by then flying Seahawks, took part in the Suez Campaign, and ten years later, equipped with the Sea Vixen, enforced the Beira Blockade during the Rhodesian UDI Crisis. A Sea Vixen of 899 NAS was the last aircraft to leave Aden after the British withdrawal in 1967 and carried the Union Flag back to HMS EAGLE. The Squadron disbanded in 1972. It reformed in 1980 with the Sea Harrier FRS.1 and became the Royal Navy's fixed wing training squadron. Despite periods embarked in HMS Hermes during the Falklands Campaign and a detachment to HMS Invincible for operation in the Adriatic and Bosnia-Herzegovina, the Squadron has continued in the training role, upgrading to the F/A.2 in 1993.

809 Squadron

809 squadron was reformed on the 15th of January 1963, at Lossiemouth in the strike role, operating the Blackburn Buccaneer S.1 aircraft. It operated as the Operational Flying Training Squadron for all Buccaneer crew training, but lost its identity in March 1965 when it was downgraded to second-line status and redesignated as 736 Squadron. 809 next reformed at Lossiemouth again in January 1966 with the Buccaneer S.2, and embarked on HMS Hermes in January 1967. In November 1978 its aircraft were disembarked to RAF St. Athan for disposal to the RAF. The squadron was hastily reformed during the Falklands War and disestablished soon after.

800 Squadron

801 Squadron

809 Squadron

899 Squadron

Broken or Preserved

One of the major concerns for many aviation enthusiasts is that once an aircraft type is retired from service, very few examples are saved for posterity, and in many cases in the past no examples of a particular aircraft were ever preserved for future generations to examine. Thankfully, thus far retired Sea Harrier airframes seem to have been well received by many institutions, Naval Bases or museums, which have seen that the unique contribution the aircraft has made to UK history and is worth saving. Sadly, at the time of writing a great number of Sea Harriers will have been scrapped, but many will have found their way to dealers like Everett Aero who have sold them on to collectors or interested parties. Here we have a brief look at some aircraft that have remained intact, and other that sadly have not!

ZA192 not looking too bad!
(© Simon Gregory)

ZH801 at Greenwich

ZD691's stripped out cockpit

ZE961 fares not much better!

A sad end to T-Bird too!

ZD578 is the gate guard ay Yeovilton

ZD 582 at Predannack

ZD614 in pieces

A sad sight as this SHAR awaits its fate in a scrap yard in Birmingham

Sea Harrier F/A.2 Walkround

An F/A.2 caught just at the moment of full throttle for take-off. Of note is the nose-wheel landing light, and the huge 'elephant ear' intakes, a trademark of the Harrier
(© Royal Navy)

The wing tanks on the Sea Harrier take a severe weathering in the harsh ocean environment, as can be seen here
(© Gordon Bartley)

A sight now consigned to history, as a Sea Harrier F/A.2 'ski-jumps' from the bow of HMS Illustrious
(© Royal Navy)

Taken with a wide-angle lens, this shot accentuates the rather compact radar nose of the F/A.2 containing the Blue Vixen radar
(© Royal Navy)

Nose

• 1 The Sea Harrier carries the same 'bolt-on' in-flight refuelling pod as the earlier Harrier GR.3
(© Paul Wakely)

• 2 Head-on, the bulbous nose contours become clear. Note also the windscreen wiper and its associated fairing
(© Andy Evans Collection)

• 3 The unpainted radome of the F/A.2 housing the Blue Vixen radar set
(© Andy Evans Collection)

• 4 A view of the port side of the nose showing panel lines and details such as pitot tubes and air scoops
(© Andy Evans Collection)

• 5 Windscreen wiper and 'bulge' detail
(© Andy Evans Collection)

• 6 The position of the access ladder
(© Andy Evans Collection)

• 7 Looking down on the nose and wiper
(© Andy Evans Collection)

The shape of the in-flight refuelling probe can be seen in this view
(© Geoff Hibbert)

ZF130, a HS-125 converted for trials of the Blue Vixen radar system
(© Joop de Groot)

A good view of the top surfaces of the Sea Harrier, showing the two GPS antennae, shown as white discs behind the cockpit and in front of the tail
(© P Tonna)

Looking across the upper starboard side forward fuselage
(© Andy Evans Collection)

On the GPS fitted aircraft the Doppler panel was removed
(© Andy Evans Collection)

Looking upward under the nose at the yellow antennae of the Doppler set
(© Andy Evans Collection)

Tail

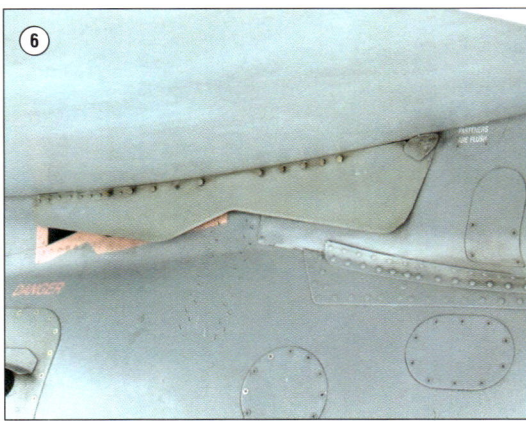

- 1 No.801 Squadron's F/A.2 tail markings
(© Andy Evans Collection)

- 2 Tail detail. Note the exhaust vents below the tailplane differ from those on the FRS.1
(© Andy Evans Collection)

- 3 ZH800 in the lighter tail markings of No.899 Squadron also shows the fuselage 'plug' just behind the wing training edge added to increase the length of the F/A.2 to balance the larger radome
(© Ian Howat)

- 4 Looking up under the tail section
(© Andy Evans Collection)

- 5 ZH811 caught at take-off. Note the slightly shaded trident on the tail
(© Glenn Beasley)

- 6 Tailplane plate
(© Andy Evans Collection)

- 7 An excellent view of the Sea Harrier F/A.2 showing the tail markings of No.801 Squadron before the Omega symbol was applied
(© Chris Lofting)

Wheels

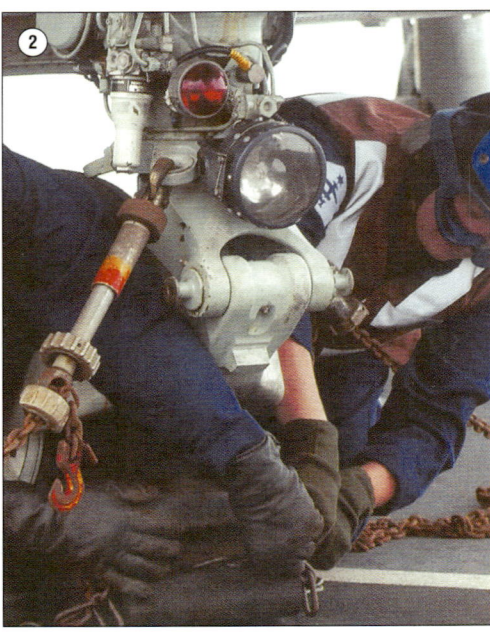

• 1 Front mainwheel details
(© Royal Navy)

• 2 Front mainwheel details
(© Royal Navy)

• 3 Mainwheel Detail
(© Andy Evans Collection)

• 4 Front mainwheel details
(© Royal Navy)

• 5 Outrigger wheel detail,
note the tie-down lugs added
to the Sea Harrier
(© Andy Evans Collection)

• 6 Front mainwheel details
(© Andy Evans Collection)

• 7 Heavy staining on the rear
'hot' exhaust nozzle and
baffle plate
(© Andy Evans Collection)

Vents and nozzles

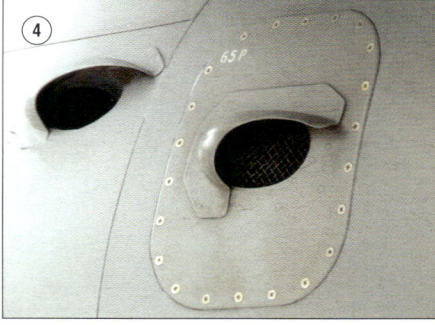

•1 Exhaust vents at the rear of the F/A.2 which differ from those on the FRS.1
(© Andy Evans Collection)

•2 Close in on the exhaust vents at the rear of the F/A.2 which differ from those on the FRS.1
(© Andy Evans Collection)

•3 & 4 Rear vents
(© Andy Evans Collection)

•5 Exhaust vent on the port rear fuselage
(© Andy Evans Collection)

•6 The port side cold nozzle and attendant detail. Note increment markings around the nozzle. Also note the vane below, often mistaken for an aerial it is in fact the vent for the engine
(© Andy Evans Collection)

•7 Heavy staining on the rear 'hot' exhaust nozzle and baffle plate
(© Andy Evans Collection)

•8 Rear 'hot' nozzle in a downward pose
(© Andy Evans Collection)

Details

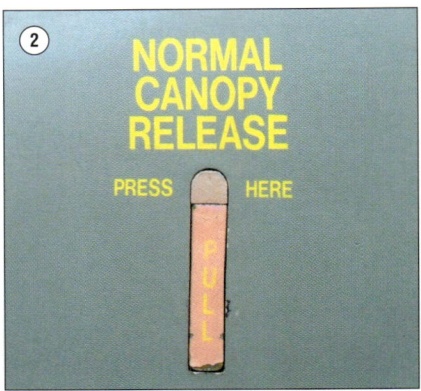

NORMAL CANOPY RELEASE

PRESS HERE

PULL

HAZARD
SONAR LOCATION BEACON
& LITHIUM
SO2 BATTERY

- 1 Fire access panel and landing light at the wing root
(© Andy Evans Collection)

- 2 Canopy release handle
(© Andy Evans Collection)

- 3 Undernose antennae
(© Andy Evans Collection)

- 4 Close in on one of the Hazard Warning Panels
(© Andy Evans Collection)

- 5 Air data sensor
(© Andy Evans Collection)

- 6 Wingtop vortex generators
(© Andy Evans Collection)

- 7 Looking down on the front GPS antennae
(© Andy Evans Collection)

- 8 Markings on the refuelling panel
(© Andy Evans Collection)

- 9 Upper fuselage anti-collision light
(© Andy Evans Collection)

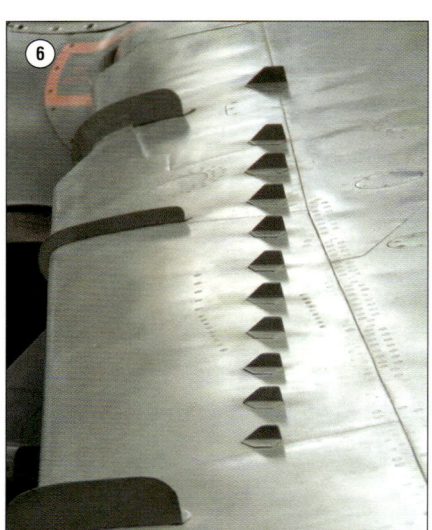

Details

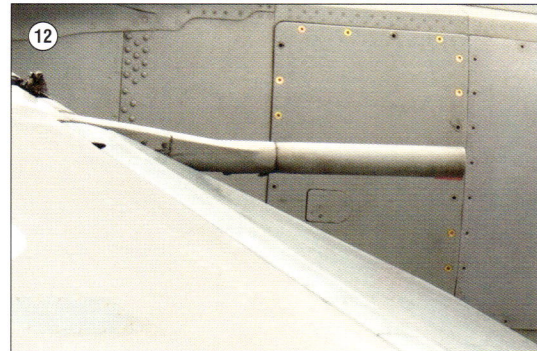

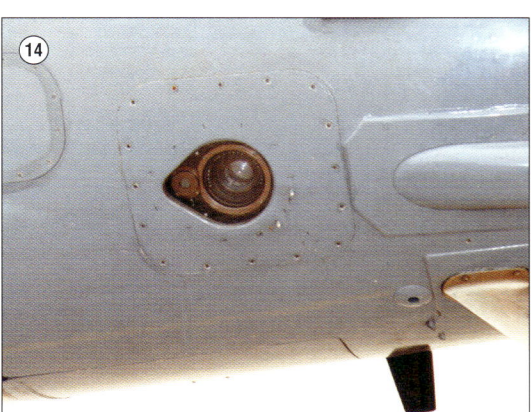

ZE698 taxis back into Yeovilton after a training sortie. Of note here is the heavy staining around the gun-pods and the weathering on the top of the radome
(© Gordon Bartley)

Intakes

• 1 Looking up across the intake to the bubble canopy. Note the characteristic droop of the spring-mounted blow-in doors on the upper side, often a problem for kit manufacturers!
(© Andy Evans Collection)

• 2 Note how the blow-in doors open when the engine requires extra air
(© Andy Evans Collection)

• 3 The blow-in doors mechanism up close
(© Andy Evans Collection)

Air Brake

• 1 Inside the airbrake
(© Andy Evans Collection)

• 2 Looking up into the airbrake assembly
(© Andy Evans Collection)

Armament and stores

• 1 Looking up at the outrigger wheel, but primarily focussing on the ACMI pod on the wing pylon
(© Gary Parsons)

• 2 The F/A.2's principle armament was the AIM-120 AMRAAM, seen on the under fuselage and wing pylons
(© Andy Evans Collection)

• 3 For short range engagements te F/A.2 carried the AIM-9 Sidewinder missile
(© Royal Navy)

• 4 The F/A.2's principle armament was the AIM-120 AMRAAM, seen on the under fuselage and wing pylons
(© Andy Evans Collection)

• 5 The principal anti-ship missile was the sea-skimming BAe Systems Sea Eagle, still in service with the Indian Navy
(© BAe Systems)

• 6 One of the results of the Falklands War was the 'twin-Sidewinder' fit that became standard for all SHARS
(© via Nick Greenall)

• 7 A good view of the outer wing pylon with its Sidewinder missile rail and adapter
(© via Nick Greenall)

• 8 One of the stores carried by the Sea Harrier was the centreline 'baggage pod'
(© Robert Pittuck)

ZD608 showing a white No.899 Squadron mailed fist on the tail, plus an intriguing 'AMRAAAM' marking under the canopy
(© Gordon Bartley)

ZH802 seen here outbound carrying CBLS (Carrier Bomb Light Store) practice bomb under its wings
(© Anthony Osbourne)

XZ440 carrying a Sidewinder acquisition round used for training purposes
(© Chris Lofting)

The F/A.2's principle armament was the AIM-120 AMRAAM, seen on the under fuselage and wing pylons
(© Andy Evans Collection)

Carrying a pair of Sidewinder acquisition rounds a Sea Harrier edges over the deck for a vertical landing
(© Gordon Bartley)

Armed with both Sidewinder and AMRAAM missiles, the Sea Harrier was a potent force!
(© Gordon Bartley)

Armament and stores

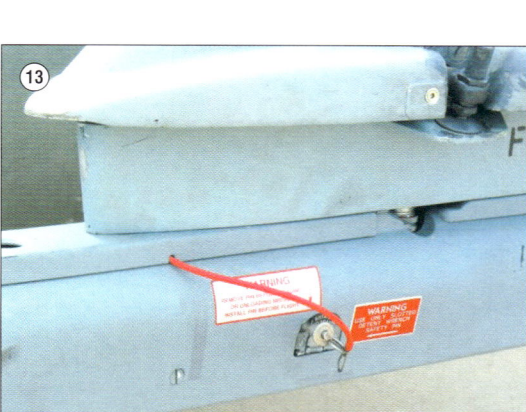

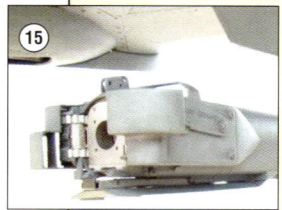

- **9** The trusty 30mm ADEN cannon pods on the undersides
(© Andy Evans Collection)

- **10** The ADEN gun pod
(© Andy Evans Collection)

- **11** The Swedish made BOL chaff launcher rail
(© Andy Evans Collection)

- **12** One of the practice bombs fitted into the CBLS carriers
(© Royal Navy)

- **13** Close in on the wing mounted AMRAAM adaptor rail
(© Andy Evans Collection)

- **14** Looking up at the centreline pylon
(© Andy Evans Collection)

- **15** The rear of the Swedish made BOL launcher rail
(© Andy Evans Collection)

- **16** The trusty 30mm ADEN cannon pods on the undersides
(© Andy Evans Collection)

- **17** Sidewinder launch rail details
(© Andy Evans Collection)

Technical Diagrams and Details

Chapter 15

Cutaway

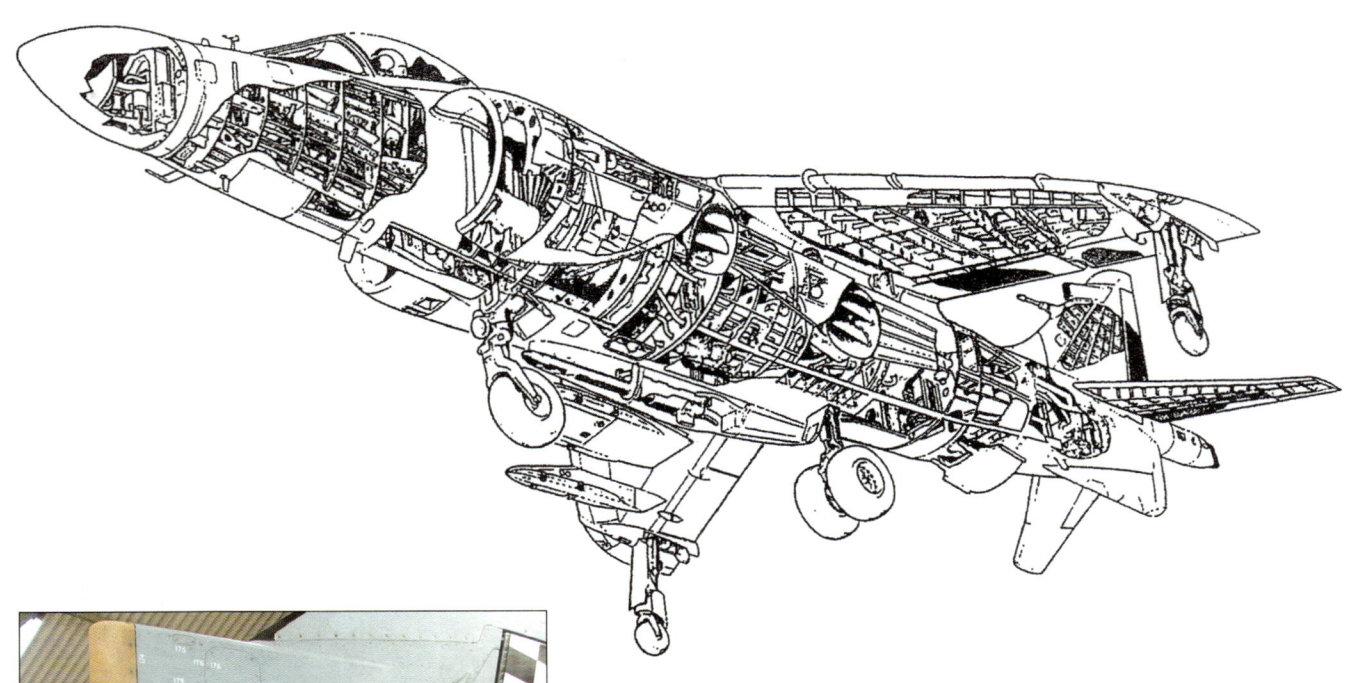

A mongrel's tail, showing traces of 800, 899 as well as 801 squadron markings

Underfuselage pylon attachment point

Painting

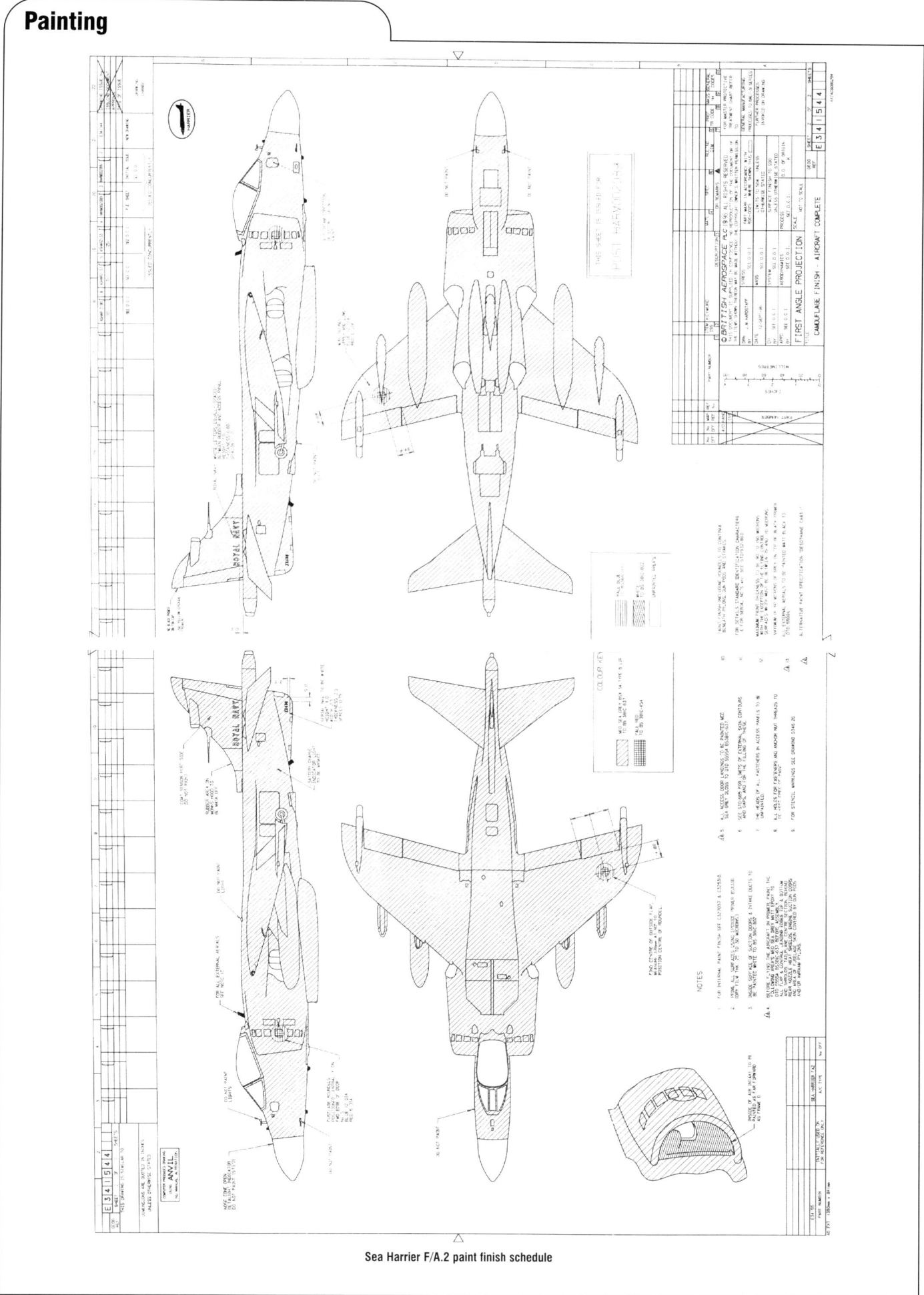

Sea Harrier F/A.2 paint finish schedule

Panel Chart

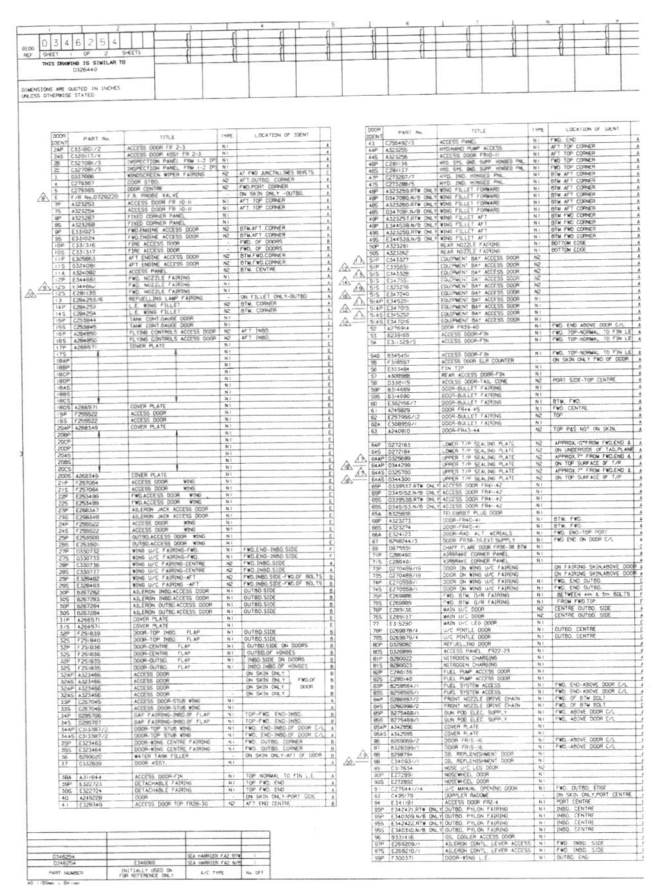

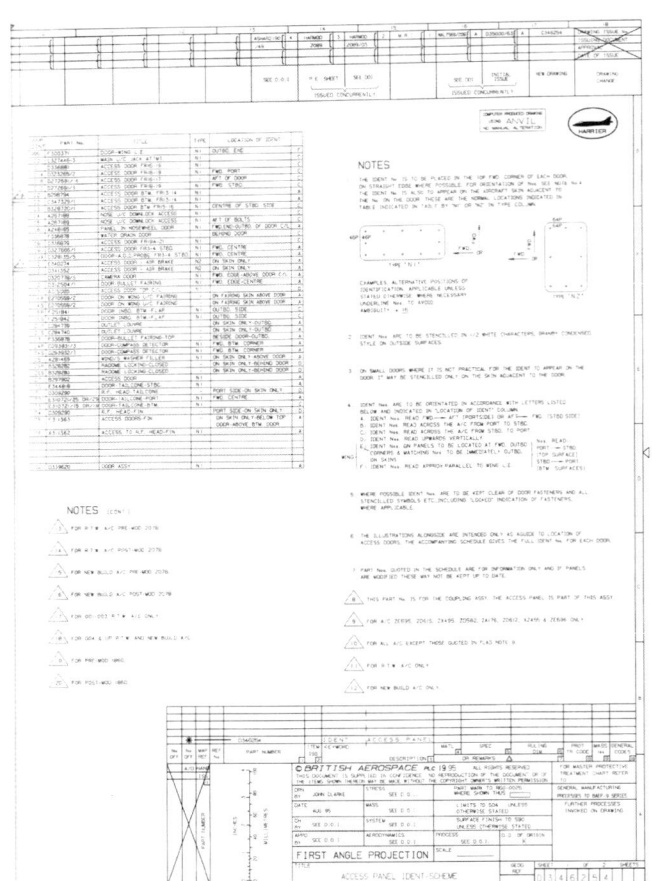

Sea Harrier F/A.2 panel reference chart

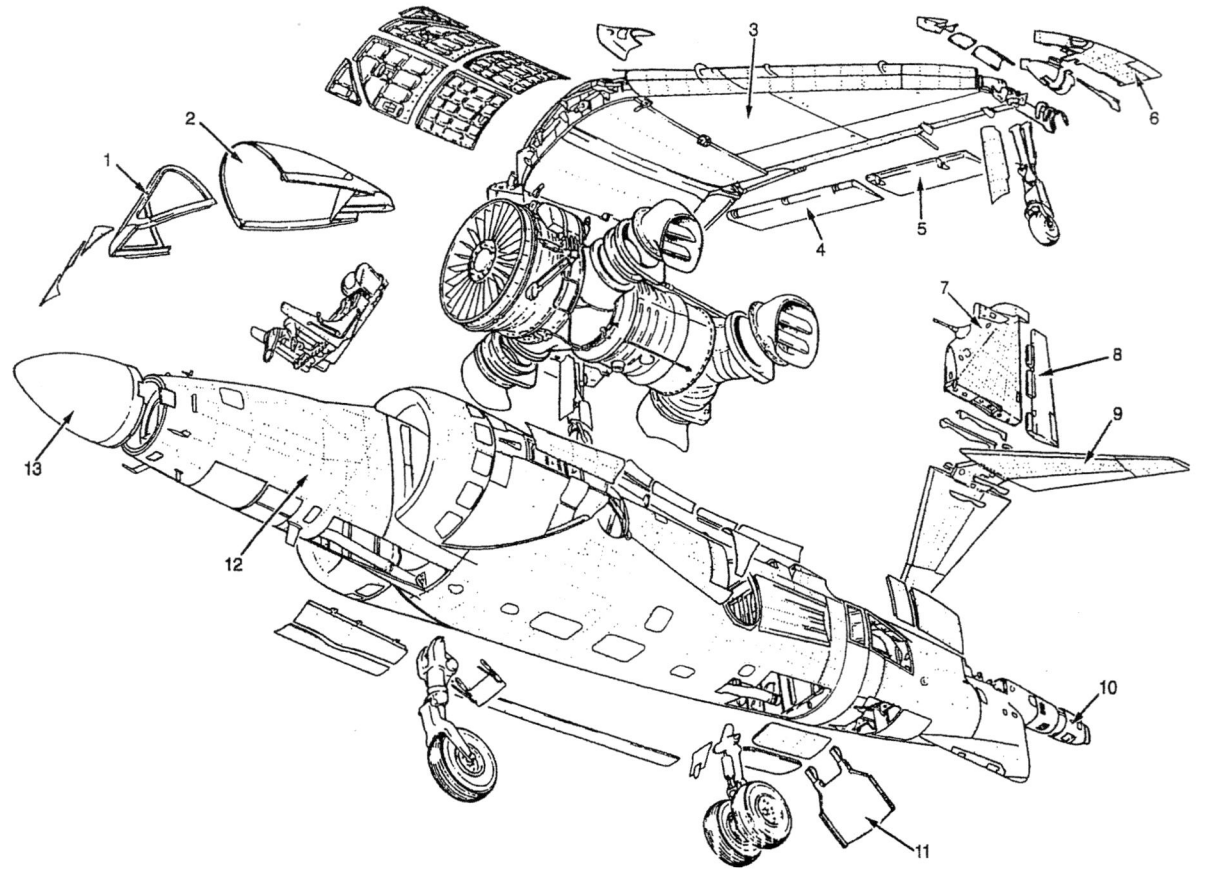

Stencils and Panels

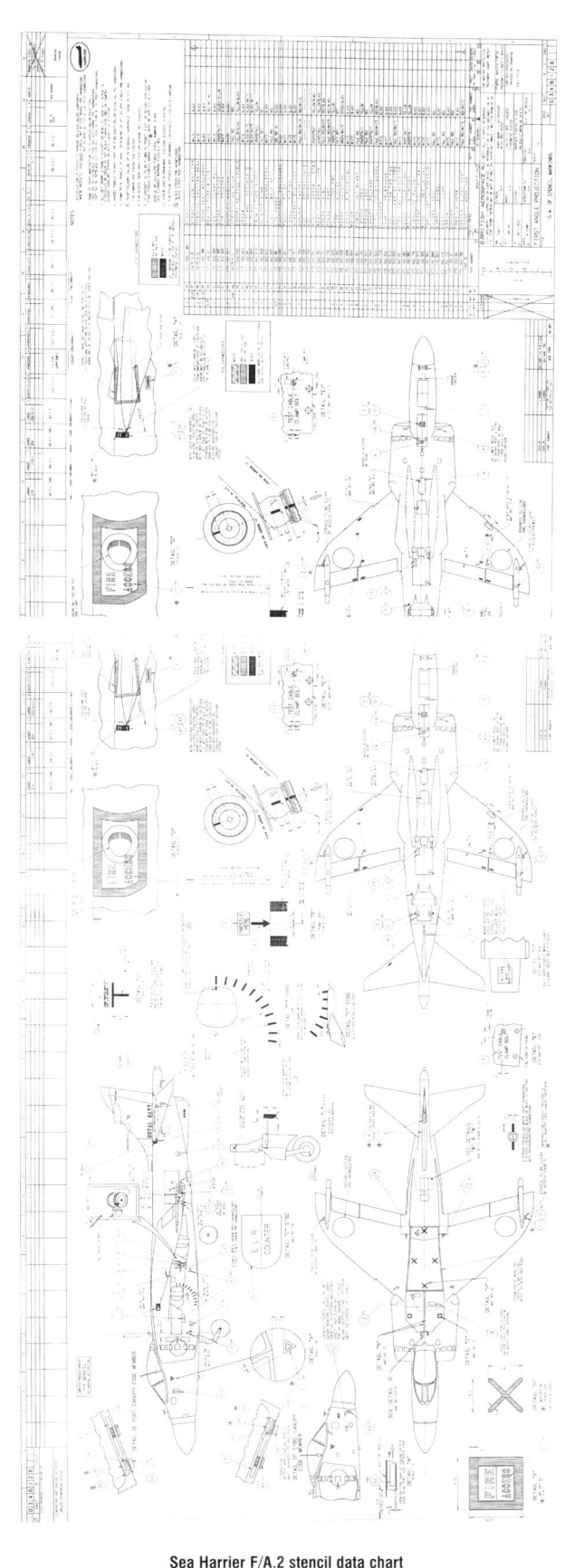

Sea Harrier F/A.2 stencil data chart

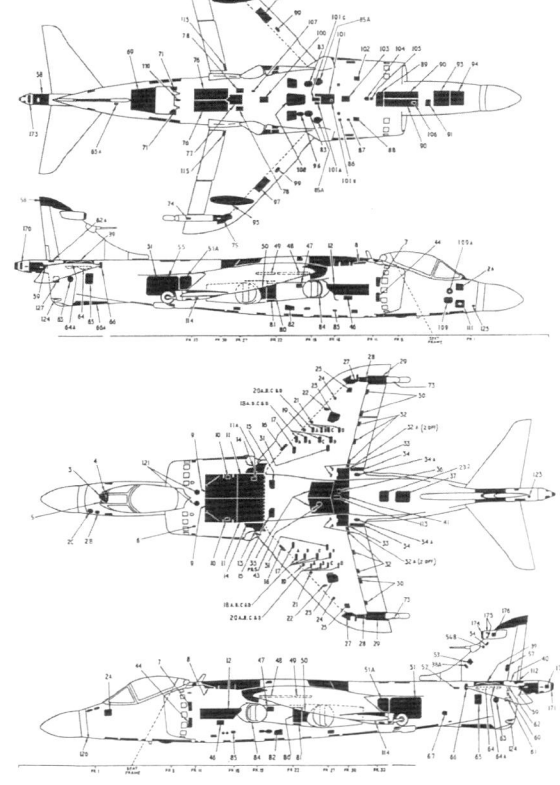

Sea Harrier F/A.2 panel data chart

Sea Harrier F/A.2 panel data chart

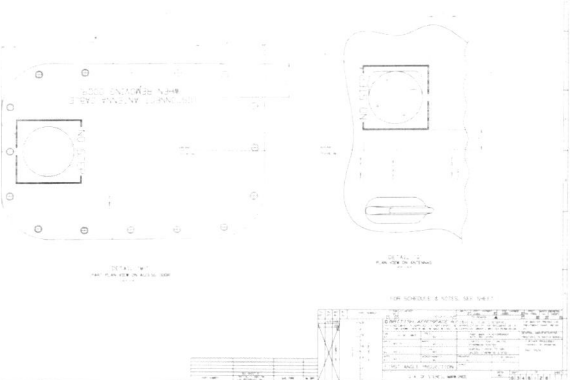

Details of the GPS fit on the upper fuselage

Nose, Fuselage, Stores

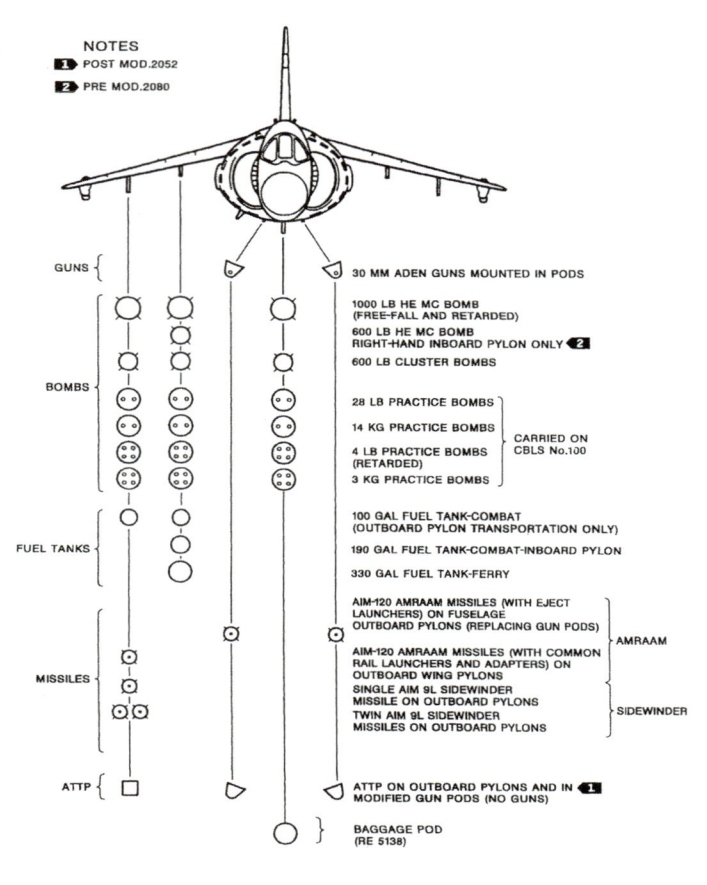

NOTES

1 POST MOD.2052

2 PRE MOD.2080

GUNS — 30 MM ADEN GUNS MOUNTED IN PODS

BOMBS
- 1000 LB HE MC BOMB (FREE-FALL AND RETARDED)
- 600 LB HE MC BOMB RIGHT-HAND INBOARD PYLON ONLY **2**
- 600 LB CLUSTER BOMBS
- 28 LB PRACTICE BOMBS
- 14 KG PRACTICE BOMBS
- 4 LB PRACTICE BOMBS (RETARDED)
- 3 KG PRACTICE BOMBS

CARRIED ON CBLS No.100

FUEL TANKS
- 100 GAL FUEL TANK-COMBAT (OUTBOARD PYLON TRANSPORTATION ONLY)
- 190 GAL FUEL TANK-COMBAT-INBOARD PYLON
- 330 GAL FUEL TANK-FERRY

MISSILES
- AIM-120 AMRAAM MISSILES (WITH EJECT LAUNCHERS) ON FUSELAGE OUTBOARD PYLONS (REPLACING GUN PODS)
- AIM-120 AMRAAM MISSILES (WITH COMMON RAIL LAUNCHERS AND ADAPTERS) ON OUTBOARD WING PYLONS

AMRAAM

- SINGLE AIM 9L SIDEWINDER MISSILE ON OUTBOARD PYLONS
- TWIN AIM 9L SIDEWINDER MISSILES ON OUTBOARD PYLONS

SIDEWINDER

ATTP — ATTP ON OUTBOARD PYLONS AND IN **1** MODIFIED GUN PODS (NO GUNS)

BAGGAGE POD (RE 5138)

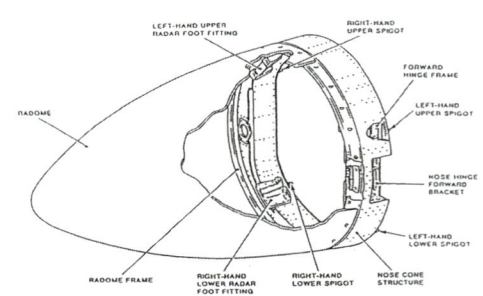

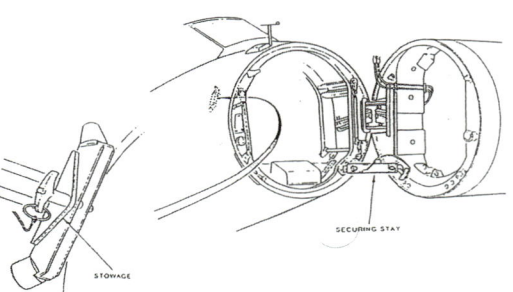

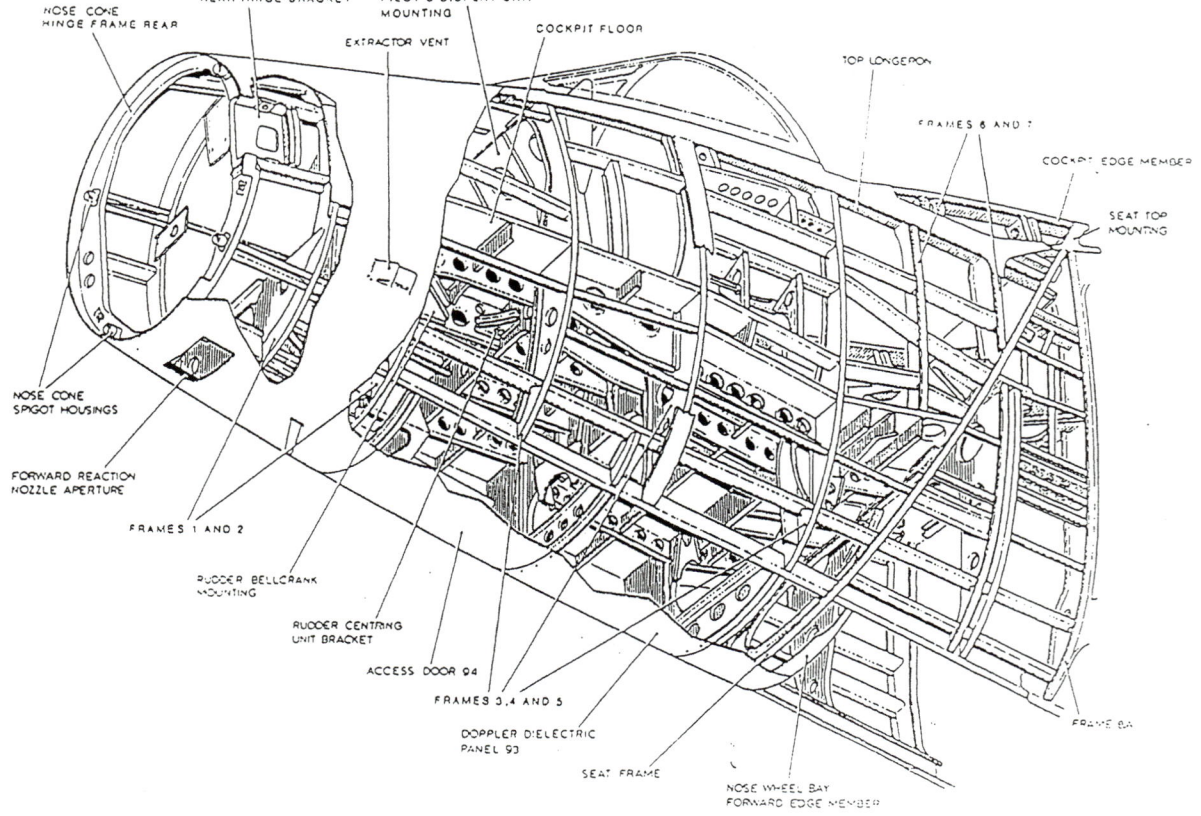

Stencil detail on the port side of the nose

Engine Bay

Inside the engine bay with the Pegasus powerplant removed

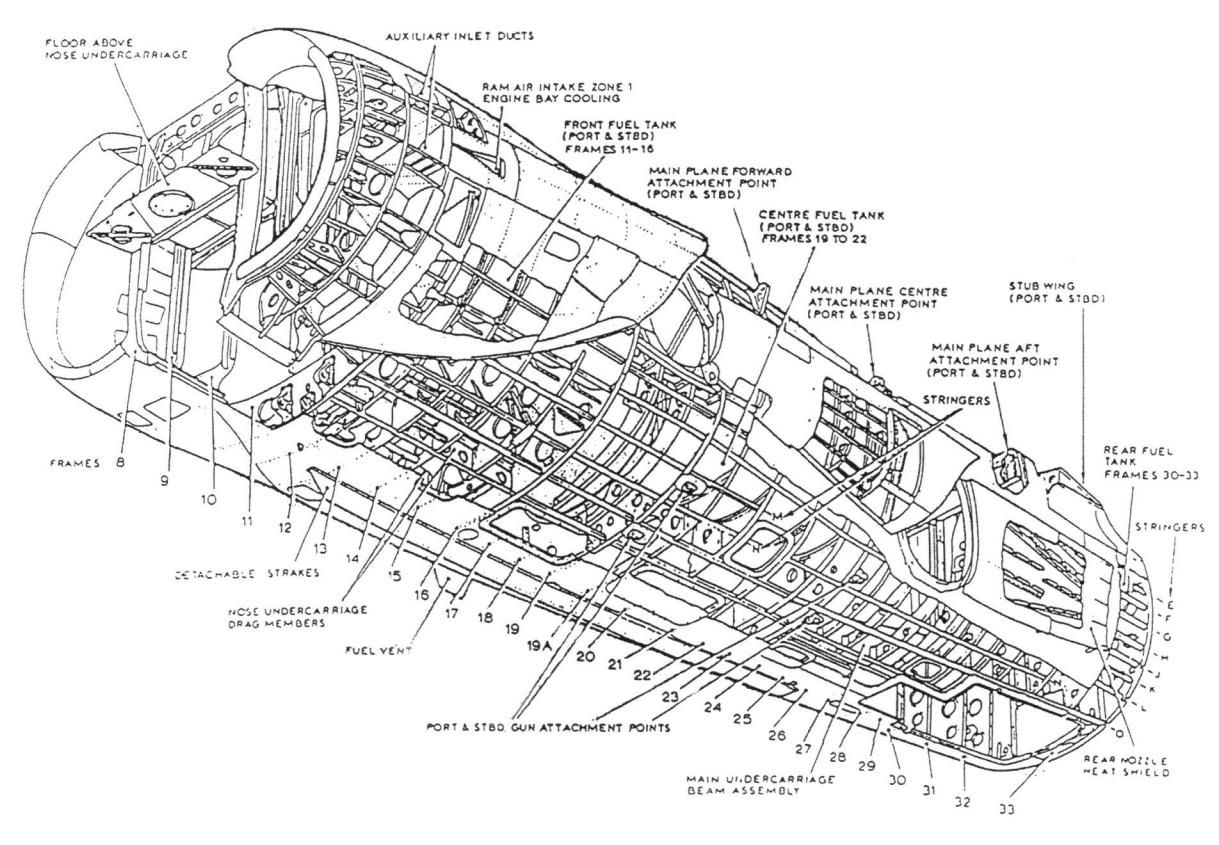

Gas deflector, fuselage

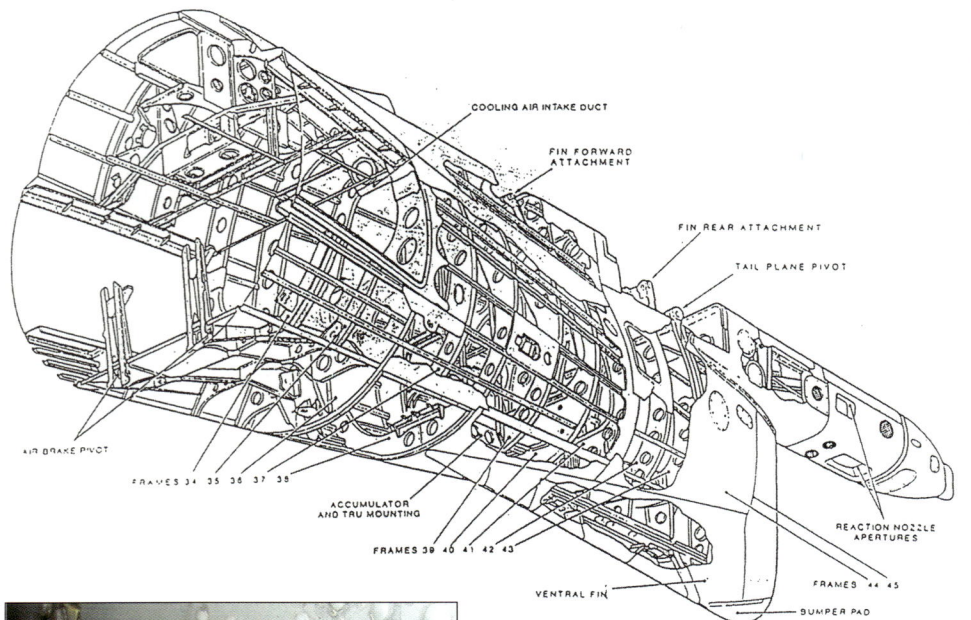

COOLING AIR INTAKE DUCT
FIN FORWARD ATTACHMENT
FIN REAR ATTACHMENT
TAIL PLANE PIVOT
AIR BRAKE PIVOT
FRAMES 34 35 36 37 38
ACCUMULATOR AND TRU MOUNTING
FRAMES 39 40 41 42 43
VENTRAL FIN
REACTION NOZZLE APERTURES
FRAMES 44 45
BUMPER PAD

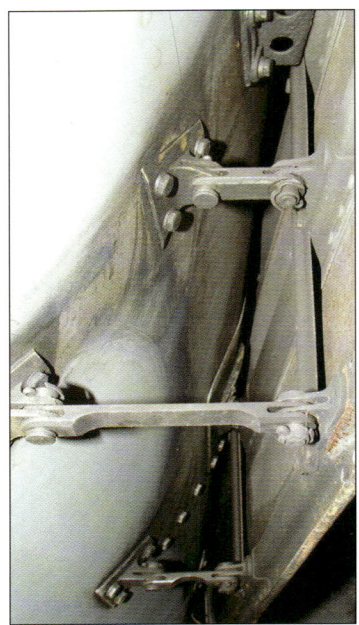

The fixings that keep the hot gas deflector plate away from the main fuselage, not readily detailed on any kits

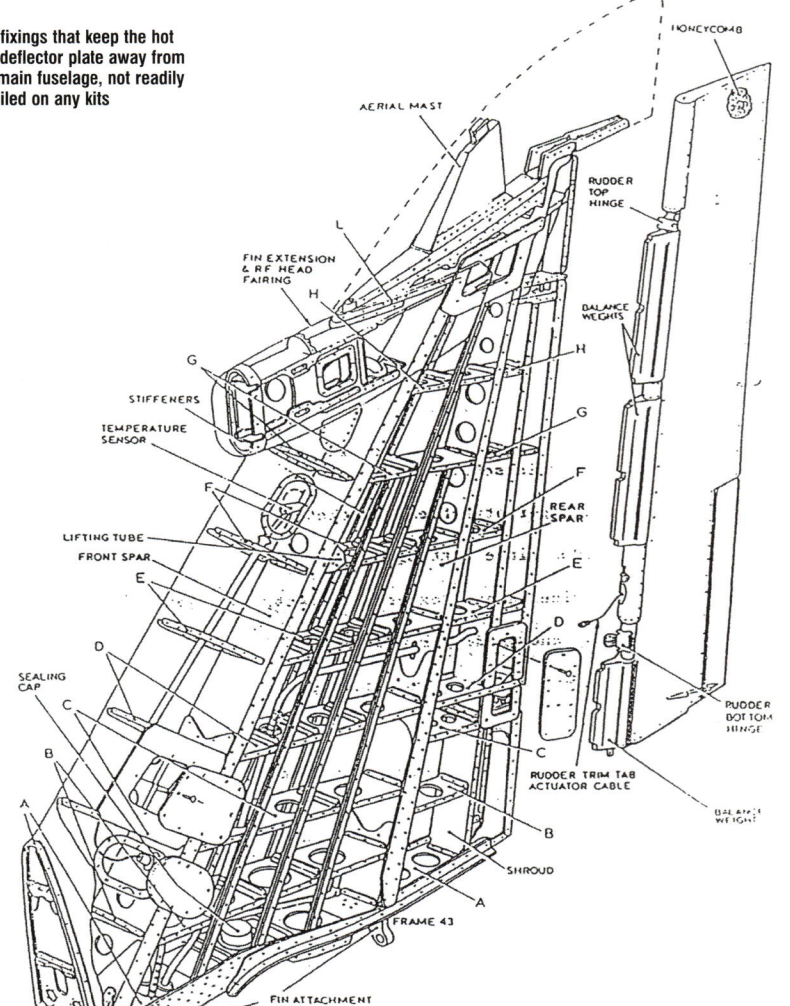

HONEYCOMB
AERIAL MAST
RUDDER TOP HINGE
FIN EXTENSION & RF HEAD FAIRING
BALANCE WEIGHTS
STIFFENERS
TEMPERATURE SENSOR
REAR SPAR
LIFTING TUBE
FRONT SPAR
SEALING CAP
RUDDER BOTTOM HINGE
RUDDER TRIM TAB ACTUATOR CABLE
BALANCE WEIGHT
SHROUD
FRAME 43
FIN ATTACHMENT BRACKETS
FRAME 40

Electrics, Stencils

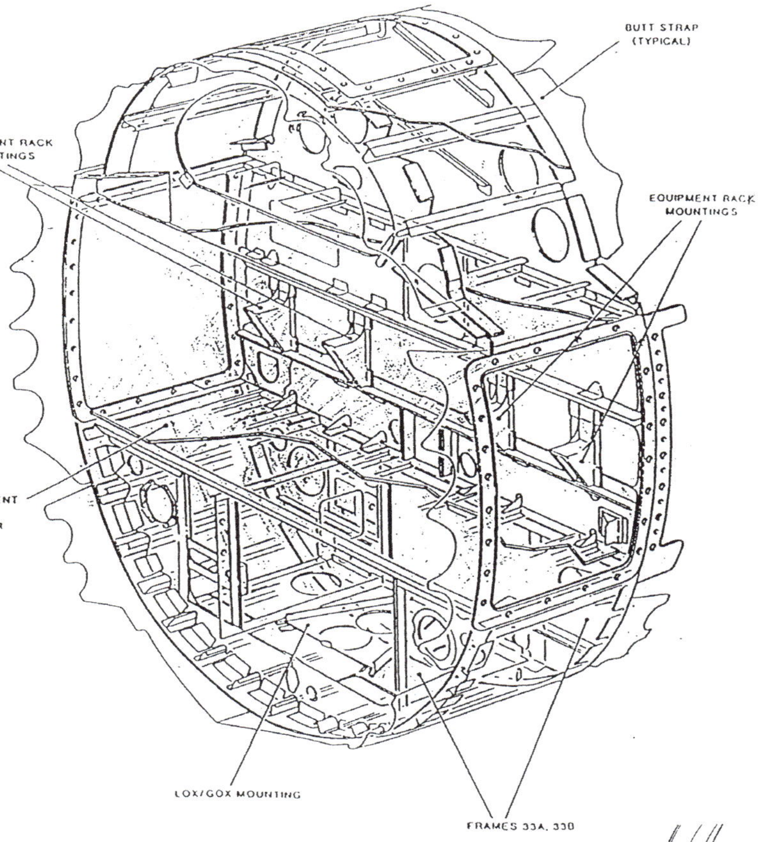

BUTT STRAP
(TYPICAL)

EQUIPMENT RACK
MOUNTINGS

EQUIPMENT RACK
MOUNTINGS

EQUIPMENT
BAY
FLOOR

LOX/GOX MOUNTING

FRAMES 33A, 33B

AIR BRAKE
GROUND LOCK

FREE

Stencil detail for the air brake lock

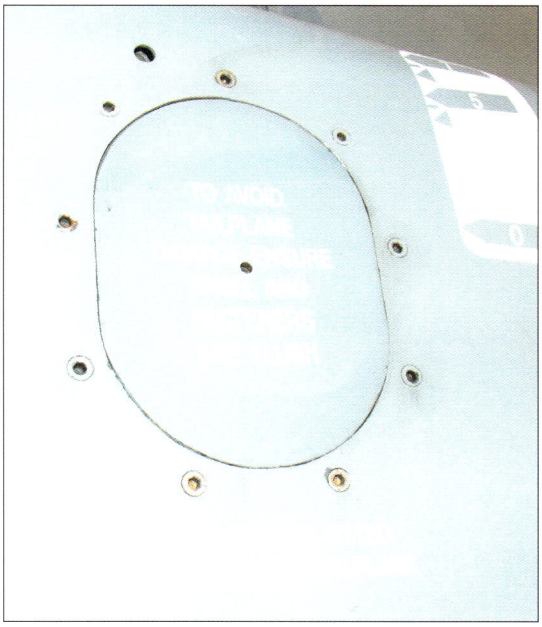

MIC-TEL SOCKET
IN LEFT-HAND
MAIN PLANE
FAIRING

MIC-TEL SOCKET
(TELELINK)

TELELINK

No1 A/C   No.2 BATT   No.1 BATT   AC

No.2 A/C   DC

EXT SUPPLY/APU
SWITCH OFF BEFORE
DISCONNECTING

GROUND SERVICING

TEST SOCKET PANEL

E

SERVICING
GROUND SUPPLY

200 VOLTS
400 CYCLES

N   C

E   B

F   A

EXTERNAL POWER SUPPLY CONNECTION

Panel and stencil detail just in front of the moving tailplanes

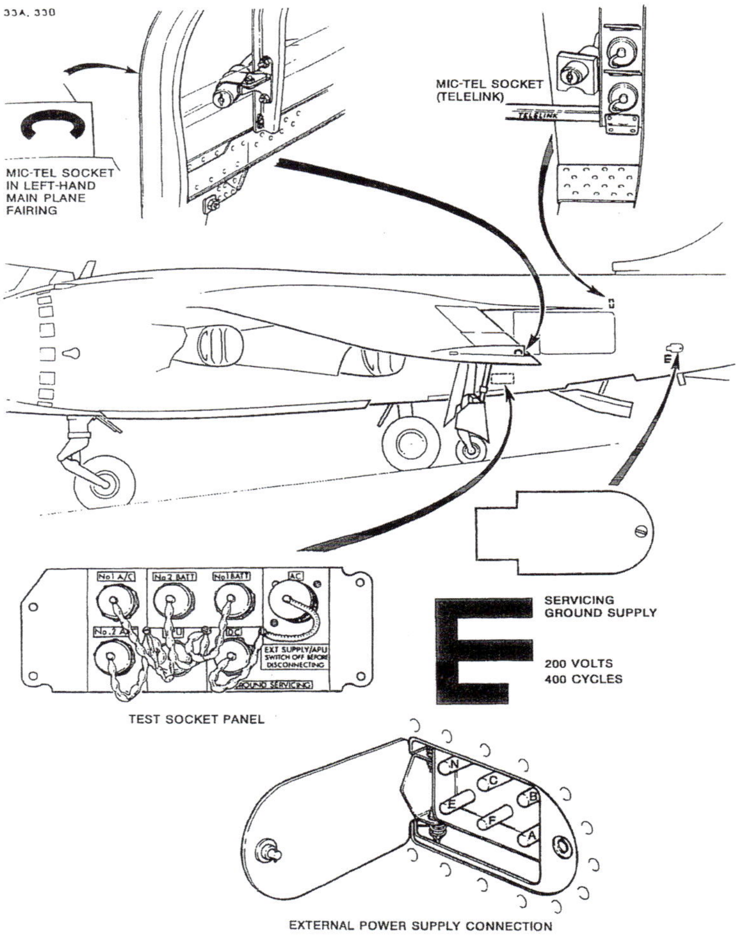

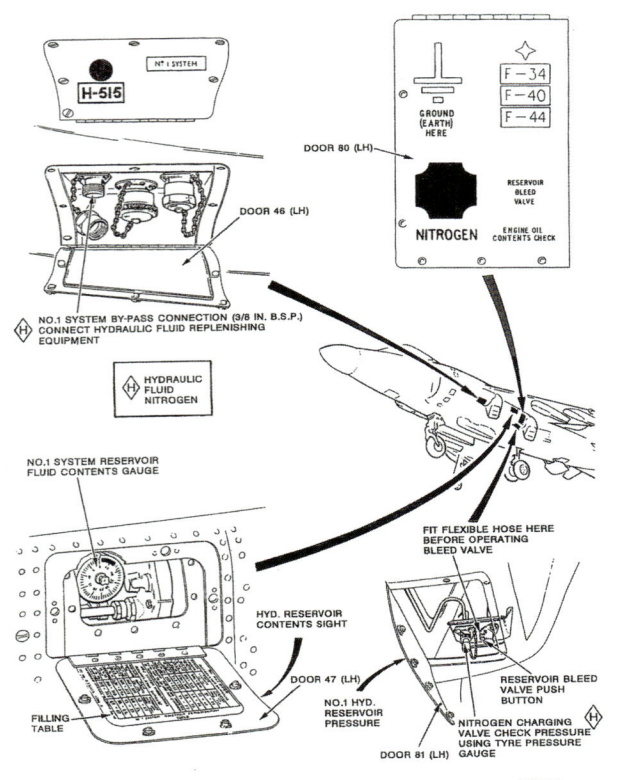
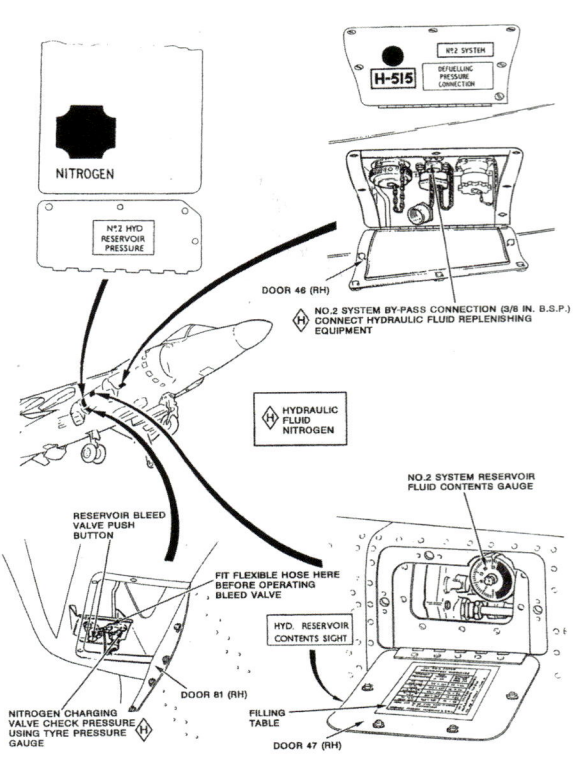

S.10304/1

Fire Access panel detail

The ELR Counter window

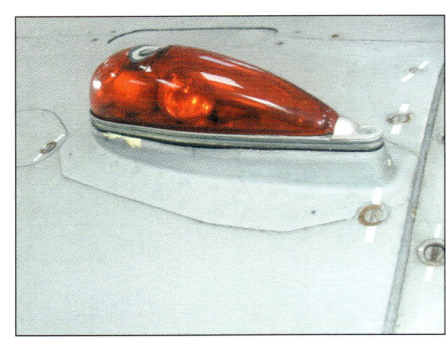

Upper anti-collision light

Stencil detail on the main undercarriage doors

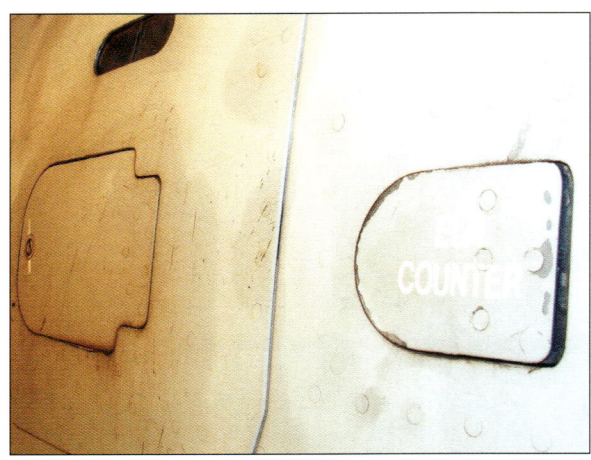

Located on the rear port side is the ELR Counter and its associated window

GPS, Oil, Wheelwell

Detail of the forward GPS antennae located behind the cockpit

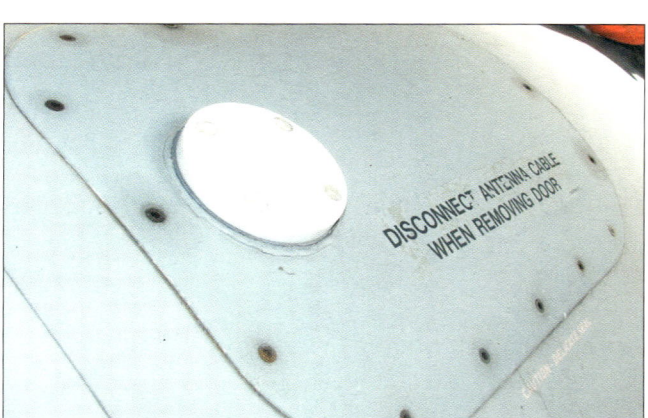

Detail of the rear GPS antennae. Note the stencil marking on the access panel

DISCONNECT ANTENNA CABLE WHEN REMOVING DOOR

Looking up into the nosewheel bay

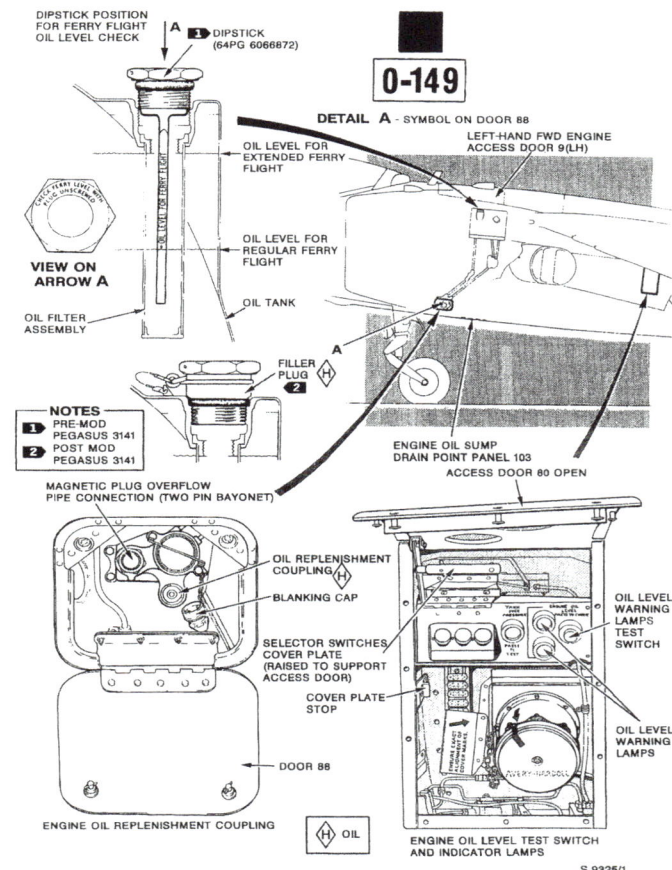

DIPSTICK POSITION FOR FERRY FLIGHT OIL LEVEL CHECK

DIPSTICK (64PG 6066872)

0-149

DETAIL A - SYMBOL ON DOOR 88

OIL LEVEL FOR EXTENDED FERRY FLIGHT

LEFT-HAND FWD ENGINE ACCESS DOOR 9(LH)

VIEW ON ARROW A

OIL LEVEL FOR REGULAR FERRY FLIGHT

OIL FILTER ASSEMBLY

OIL TANK

FILLER PLUG 2

NOTES
1 PRE-MOD PEGASUS 3141
2 POST MOD PEGASUS 3141

ENGINE OIL SUMP DRAIN POINT PANEL 103

ACCESS DOOR 80 OPEN

MAGNETIC PLUG OVERFLOW PIPE CONNECTION (TWO PIN BAYONET)

OIL REPLENISHMENT COUPLING

BLANKING CAP

SELECTOR SWITCHES COVER PLATE (RAISED TO SUPPORT ACCESS DOOR)

COVER PLATE STOP

DOOR 88

ENGINE OIL REPLENISHMENT COUPLING

OIL

OIL LEVEL WARNING LAMPS TEST SWITCH

OIL LEVEL WARNING LAMPS

ENGINE OIL LEVEL TEST SWITCH AND INDICATOR LAMPS

S.9325/1

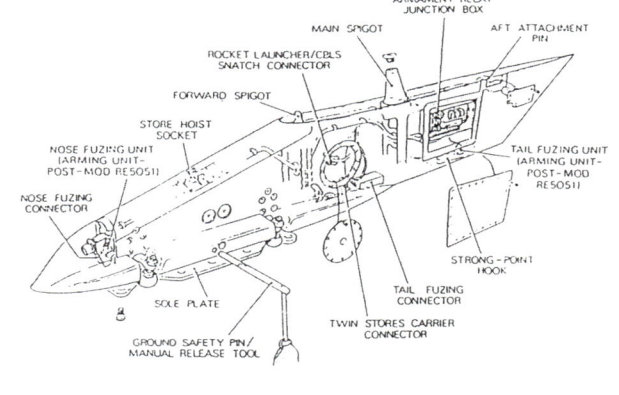

ARMAMENT RELAY JUNCTION BOX

MAIN SPIGOT

AFT ATTACHMENT PIN

ROCKET LAUNCHER/CBLS SNATCH CONNECTOR

FORWARD SPIGOT

STORE HOIST SOCKET

NOSE FUZING UNIT (ARMING UNIT- POST-MOD RESOS1)

TAIL FUZING UNIT (ARMING UNIT- POST-MOD RESOS1)

NOSE FUZING CONNECTOR

TAIL FUZING CONNECTOR

STRONG-POINT HOOK

SOLE PLATE

GROUND SAFETY PIN/ MANUAL RELEASE TOOL

TWIN STORES CARRIER CONNECTOR

Wheels

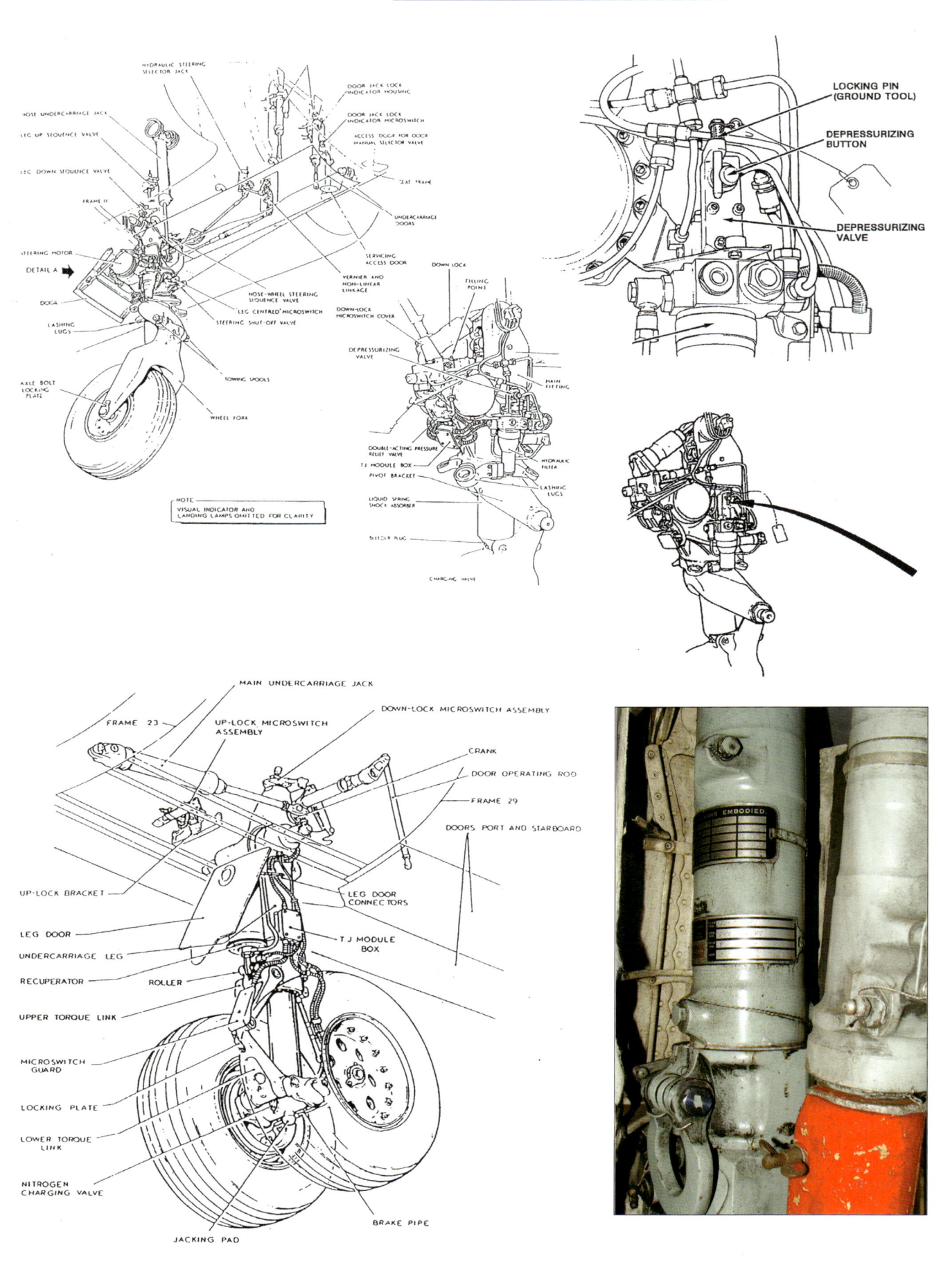

HYDRAULIC STEERING SELECTOR JACK

DOOR JACK LOCK INDICATOR HOUSING

DOOR JACK LOCK INDICATOR MICROSWITCH

ACCESS DOOR FOR DOOR MANUAL SELECTOR VALVE

NOSE UNDERCARRIAGE JACK

LEG UP SEQUENCE VALVE

LEG DOWN SEQUENCE VALVE

FRAME 11

STEERING MOTOR

DETAIL A

DOGS

LASHING LUGS

AXLE BOLT LOCKING PLATE

SEAT FRAME

UNDERCARRIAGE DOORS

SERVICING ACCESS DOOR

VERNIER AND NON-LINEAR LINKAGE

NOSE-WHEEL STEERING SEQUENCE VALVE

'LEG CENTRED' MICROSWITCH

STEERING SHUT-OFF VALVE

TOWING SPOOLS

WHEEL FORK

NOTE
VISUAL INDICATOR AND LANDING LAMPS OMITTED FOR CLARITY

DOWN LOCK

FILLING POINT

DOWN-LOCK MICROSWITCH COVER

DEPRESSURIZING VALVE

MAIN FITTING

DOUBLE-ACTING PRESSURE RELIEF VALVE

TJ MODULE BOX

PIVOT BRACKET

HYDRAULIC FILTER

LASHING LUGS

LIQUID SPRING SHOCK ABSORBER

BLEED PLUG

CHARGING VALVE

LOCKING PIN (GROUND TOOL)

DEPRESSURIZING BUTTON

DEPRESSURIZING VALVE

MAIN UNDERCARRIAGE JACK

DOWN-LOCK MICROSWITCH ASSEMBLY

FRAME 23

UP-LOCK MICROSWITCH ASSEMBLY

CRANK

DOOR OPERATING ROD

FRAME 29

DOORS PORT AND STARBOARD

UP-LOCK BRACKET

LEG DOOR CONNECTORS

LEG DOOR

UNDERCARRIAGE LEG

RECUPERATOR

ROLLER

TJ MODULE BOX

UPPER TORQUE LINK

MICROSWITCH GUARD

LOCKING PLATE

LOWER TORQUE LINK

NITROGEN CHARGING VALVE

JACKING PAD

BRAKE PIPE

Panels, Stencils, Ducts

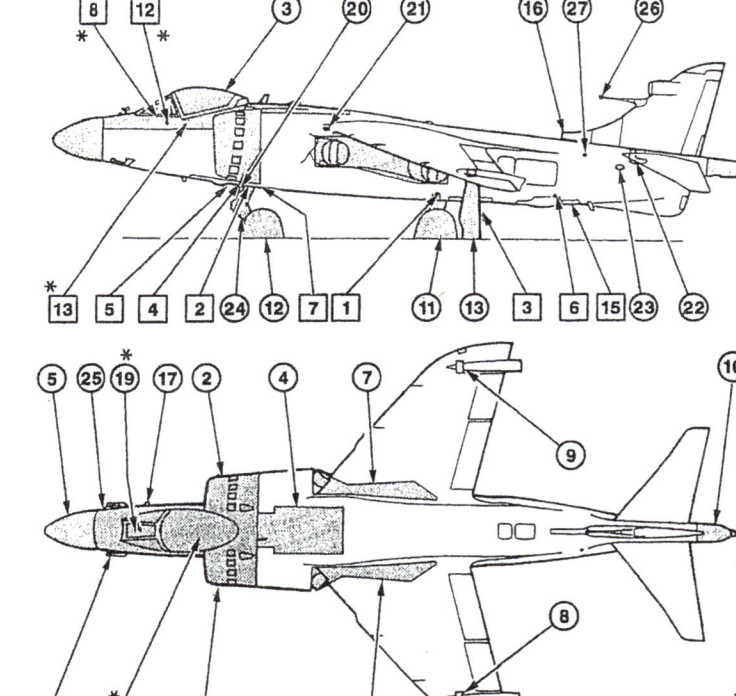
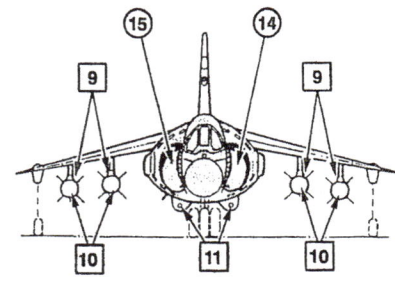
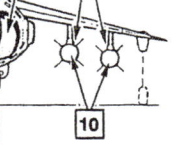

Fig. 6 Safety devices and protective covers

S.1058B/1

KEY

COVERS AND BUNGS ○

1 AIR INTAKE COVER LH
2 AIR INTAKE RH
3 COCKPIT COVER
4 SPINE COVER
5 NOSE CONE COVER
6 ENGINE NOZZLE COVER LH
7 ENGINE NOZZLE COVER RH
8 WINGTIP REACTION NOZZLE COVER LH
9 WINGTIP REACTION NOZZLE COVER RH
10 TAIL REACTION NOZZLE COVER
11 MAIN WHEEL COVER
12 NOSE WHEEL COVER
13 MAIN PLANE UNDERCARRIAGE WHEEL COVER (LH AND RH)
14 MAIN AIR INTAKE BLANK LH
15 MAIN AIR INTAKE BLANK RH
16 BUNG REAR FUSELAGE COOLING
17 GUARD ADD PROBE
18 PITOT HEAD COVER (LH AND RH)
✱19 PILOT'S DISPLAY UNIT COVER
20 LANDING LAMP COVER
21 AIR DUCT BUNG (LH AND RH)
22 TAILPLANE APERTURE COVER
23 COOLING DUCT BUNG
24 NOSE LEG COVER
25 RAM AIR INLET BUNG
26 FIN MOUNTED STATIC PROBE COVER
27 REAR BAY AUXILIARY AIR SYSTEM INLET

SAFETY LOCKS □

1 MAIN UNDERCARRIAGE GROUND LOCK
2 NOSE UNDERCARRIAGE GROUND LOCK
3 MAIN PLANE UNDERCARRIAGE GROUND LOCK
4 NOSE UNDERCARRIAGE DOORS MANUAL SELECTOR GROUND LOCK
5 NOSE UNDERCARRIAGE DOOR JACKS GROUND LOCK (2 OFF)
6 AIR BRAKE SAFETY KEY
7 LOCKING PIN NOSEWHEEL STEERING DE-PRESSURISATION
✱8 MASTER ARMAMENT SAFETY SWITCH
9 PYLON SAFETY PINS
10 WEAPON SAFETY PINS
11 GUN ELECTRICAL CONNECTIONS
✱12 RUDDER PEDAL LOCK
✱13 PARKING BRAKE
✱14 SEAT AND MDC SAFETY PINS
15 CHAFF/FLARE DOOR ASSY SAFETY PIN

✱ LOCATED IN COCKPIT

Close-up details of the 'puffer ducts' located above and below the wings

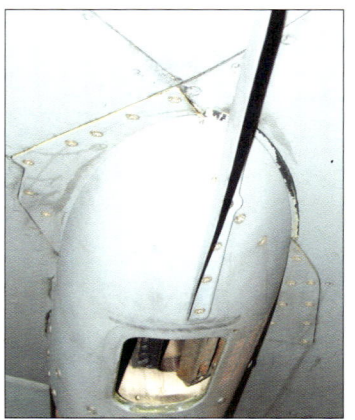
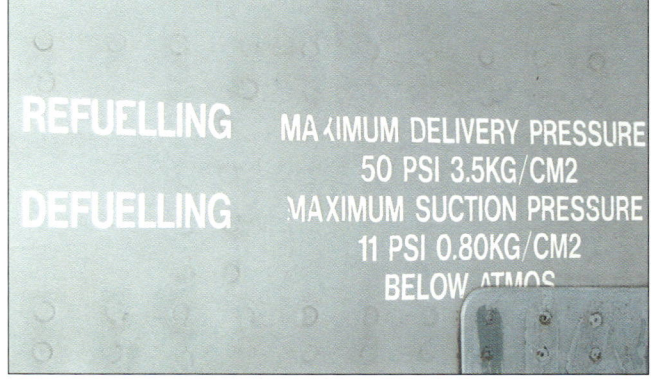

Stencil detail above the refuelling panel

Sea Harrier F/A.2 Cockpit Walkround

The cockpit of the Sea Harrier F/A.2 retains its first generation harrier heritage, despite being modernised from the FRS.1. What makes the Sea Harrier unique is the throttle lever with its associated engine nozzle controls that allow the aircraft to hover and take off and land vertically, not to mention its ability to fly backwards, always a crowd pleaser at airshows! The layout remained a mix of conventional dials interspersed with modern heads down radar and RWR displays. A Smiths Industries head up display (HUD) dominated the pilots forward view, and although the cockpit was relatively small by comparison to later Harriers, pilots nevertheless found it a good working environment and straightforward to manage.

Cockpit

- 1 Looking forward at the stick and HUD controls

- 2 Down toward the rudder pedals

- 3 The right-hand panel section

- 4 A close-up on the radio panels

Cockpit – Front

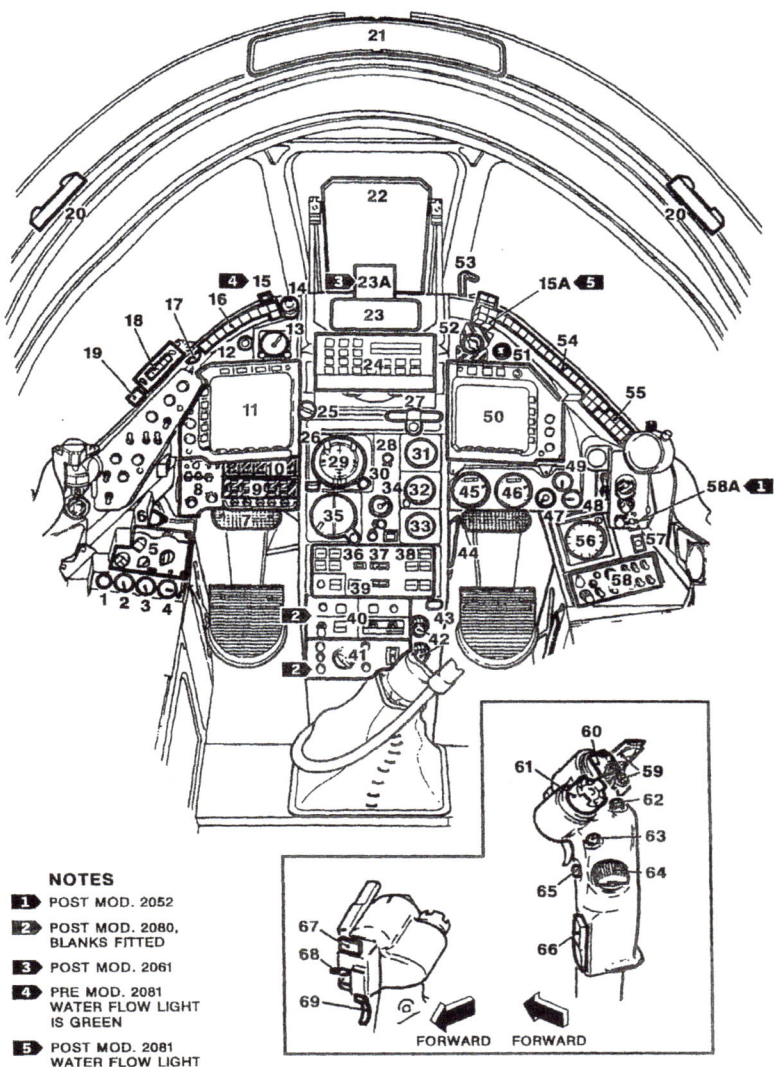

NOTES

1 POST MOD. 2052

2 POST MOD. 2080, BLANKS FITTED

3 POST MOD. 2061

4 PRE MOD. 2081 WATER FLOW LIGHT IS GREEN

5 POST MOD. 2081 WATER FLOW LIGHT IS BLUE AND RELOCATED

FORWARD   FORWARD

S.9371/5
AA000049

The area to the rear of the canopy

1   NOSE WHEEL CENTRED MAGNETIC INDICATOR - Black when nose wheel centred.
    White when nose wheel not centred or if no electrical supply
2   AILERON TRIM INDICATOR
3   RUDDER TRIM AND YAW AUTOSTAB TEST INDICATOR
4   TAIL PLANE SETTING INDICATOR
5   V/UHF CONTROL UNIT
6   LANDING GEAR EMERGENCY LOWERING CONTROL, engraved U/C. Press centre
    button and pull control to lower landing gear
7   WHEEL BRAKES. Depress toe pedals to apply wheel brakes
8   WEAPON CONTROL PANEL (WCP)
9   'CLEAR AIRCRAFT' STORES JETTISON BAR
10 PYLON STORES JETTISON PUSH SWITCHES (five)
11 MULTI-FUNCTION DISPLAY (MFD)
12 WINDSCREEN WASHER BUTTON, labelled WASH. Press momentarily to initiate
    six-second flow of washing fluid to windscreen
13 RADAR HEIGHT INDICATOR
14 COMBINED ATTENTION GETTER-CANCEL-MUTE SWITCH, engraved C
15 WATER INJECTION FLOW LIGHT, engraved H_2O (pre Mod.2081)
15A WATER INJECTION FLOW LIGHT, engraved H_2O (post Mod.2081)
16 CENTRALIZED WARNING SYSTEM (CWS) PRIMARY (RED) WARNING ARRAY
17 WANDER LAMP CLIP
18 REMOTE FREQUENCY AND CHANNEL INDICATOR
19 REFUELLING INDICATOR LIGHTS
20 CANOPY HANDLES (TWO) - LH and RH
21 REAR VIEW MIRROR
22 PILOT'S DISPLAY UNIT (PDU) COMBINER
23 CRASH PAD - (Location for video recorder camera)
24 UP-FRONT CONTROL PANEL
25 WINDSCREEN WIPER CONTROL engraved PARK-RUN. Rotate clockwise towards
    RUN to start and increase wiper speed, turn fully counterclockwise to
    PARK to stop wiper
26 MADGE RANGE INDICATOR
27 CANOPY RELEASE HANDLE, engraved HOOD. Pull to release canopy locks
28 ATTITUDE INDICATOR BATT-NORM S/W, engraved Att Ind, Norm-Batt. Set
    down to introduce emergency DC supply to attitude indicator
29 ATTITUDE DIRECTION INDICATOR
30 ATTITUDE INDICATOR FAST ERECTION BUTTON
31 VERTICAL SPEED INDICATOR (VSI)
32 BAROMETRIC ALTIMETER
33 AIR SPEED INDICATOR (ASI)
34 ANGLE OF ATTACK INDICATOR
35 COMPASS GYRO INDICATOR (CGI)
36 COMPASS-DG SWITCH, engraved Comp-DG. Set down for DG
37 COMPASS-BATT NORM SWITCH, engraved Comp-Batt. Normally set to Comp
    (left). Set to Batt (right) to introduce emergency DC supply to
    CGI (35)
38 MACH INDICATOR. Digital display
39 MISSILE CONTROL PANEL (MCP)
40 BOMB RELEASE SAFETY LOCK (BRSL)
41 FUZE CONTROL UNIT (FCU)
42 COCKPIT LIGHTING DIMMER CONTROLS. Two pairs of concentric knobs;
    rotate clockwise to increase lighting brilliance
43 RUDDER PEDALS ADJUSTMENT KNOB, labelled Rudder Pedal Adjust. Pull knob
    to free pedals for leg reach adjustment; release knob and move pedals
    to engage lock
44 RUDDER LOCK HANDLE - With rudder bar central, pull handle and turn 45
    deg to the right to lock rudder and bar. To unlock, pull handle, turn
    to the left and release into stowage
45 ENGINE REV/MIN INDICATOR (PER CENT) - Normally displays LP rev/min.
    Press and hold button on instrument face for display of HP rev/min
46 JET PIPE TEMPERATURE (JPT) GAUGE
47 WATER CONTENTS GAUGE
48 ENGINE NOZZLES POSITION INDICATOR
49 INLET GUIDE VANE (IGV) POSITION INDICATOR
50 RADAR DISPLAY UNIT (RDU) - A cover plate is fitted in lieu of RDU, when
    radar not fitted
51 OXYGEN FLOW MAGNETIC INDICATOR, labelled OXY. Main oxygen supply
    indicator. Black when no oxygen flow - white bar when oxygen flowing
52 MASTER ARMAMENT SAFETY SWITCH (MASS), engraved SAFE-STBY-LIVE, from
    SAFE - no power to armament systems, turn switch clockwise to STBY -
    armament test supplies only. From STBY pull switch and turn clockwise
    to LIVE - armament power supplies available
53 MASS INDICATOR FLAG - Green flag erect when armament circuits safe,
    partially erect for stby, not visible for live
54 CWS SECONDARY (AMBER) WARNING ARRAY
55 CWS SYSTEMS STATUS (BLUE) INDICATOR LIGHTS, comprising:-
        ATT   - Attitude
        HGT   - Height
        A/P   - Autopilot engaged
        APU   - APU generator on line
        Cam   - Camera running
        Dopp - Doppler
        A/B   - Air brake position indication
        Cmbt - Combat selected
        Land - Water injection, Landing selected
        T/O   - Water injection, Take-Off or Manual Water on selected
        Skid - Anti-skid system off
56 PASSIVE WARNING RECEIVER (PWR) DISPLAY
57 BUS CONTROL INTERFACE UNIT RESET SWITCH, labelled BCIU Reset. Push
    button (guarded)
58 PWR CONTROL UNIT
58A ATTP RESET SWITCH, labelled ATTP Reset. Toggle switch

CONTROL COLUMN HANDLE (Inset)

59 WEAPON RELEASE BUTTON AND SAFETY GUARD
60 AILERON/TAIL PLANE TRIM SWITCHES
61 WEAPON SELECTOR SWITCH - 4-way selector spring-loaded to centre.
    Sidewinder left; AMRAAM right, guns forward; Reject rearward
62 WEAPON AIMING ACCEPT SWITCH
63 TARGET DESIGNATE BUTTON - Push button switch for manual designation of
    radar targets
64 WEAPON MODE SELECT SWITCH - 5-way selector spring-loaded to centre.
    Function depends on missile control system (MDC) state
65 NAVIGATION FIX BUTTON - Dual function pushbutton: MCS in air-to-air
    mode, button selects/deselects an AMRAAM mode. MCS not in air-to-air
    mode, button initiates FIX
66 NOSE WHEEL STEER/AUTOPILOT - ENGAGE-DISENGAGE/CAMERA SWITCH - Two-
    position paddle switch spring-loaded to Off. Three functions: When
    weight-on-wheel and anti-skid on press and hold paddle switch for nose
    wheel steering. With landing gear up: camera master switch off; AFCS
    and autopilot master switches on, paddle switch operation engages/
    disengages autopilot. When landing gear up and camera master switch
    on, press and hold paddle switch to run camera. Release paddle switch
    to stop camera.
67 GUN SAFETY CATCH POSITION INDICATOR
68 GUN SAFETY CATCH
69 GUN FIRING TRIGGER

Key to Figure 13

1   MINIATURE DETONATING CORD (MDC) FIRING HANDLE. With safety pin removed, pull to shatter canopy transparency
2   AIR DATA COMPUTER TEST PUSHBUTTON SWITCH, labelled ADC Test 1. Press for readout on PDU
3   AIR DATA COMPUTER TEST PUSHBUTTON SWITCH, labelled ADC Test 2. Press for readout on PDU
4   STANDBY COMPASS LIGHT UNIT
5   STANDBY COMPASS
6   PILOT'S CONTROL PANEL (PCP). Controls pilot's display unit (PDU) head-up display (HUD)
7   WHEEL BRAKES EMERGENCY BUTTON, engraved B. Press to apply and lock wheel brakes in emergency
8   ALE-40 INDICATOR LAMPS - Front to rear: Flar Emty - flare empty (red), Flar - flare selected (white), Chff Emty - chaff empty (red), Chff - chaff selected (white)
9   COCKPIT AIR CONDITIONING VENT (Post Mod.2194). Drilled end plate consisting of 19 holes. No adjustment possible.
10 CANOPY LOCK INDICATOR (LH), engraved Locked. Indicates correct engagement of canopy lock (LH)
11 BORE SIGHT SELECT SWITCH, labelled AAM Bore Sight. Up for Sidewinder missile system bore sight mode
12 WATER INJECTION SWITCH, labelled Take-Off - Off - Landing. Up for Take-off, mid for Off, down for landing
13 COMBAT SELECT SWITCH, labelled Combat-Off. Up for combat, down for Off
14 MANUAL WATER SWITCH labelled Manual Water, On-Off. Up for On, down for Off
15 NAVIGATION LIGHTS SWITCH, labelled Nav. Flash-Off-Nav. Steady. Up for Nav. Flash, centre Off, down for Nav. Steady
16 ANTI-SKID TEST BUTTON. Press for brake-release test of anti-skid
17 WHEEL BRAKES ANTI-SKID SWITCH, labelled Anti Skid, On-Off. Up for On, down for Off (and, with landing gear down, to engage continuous nose wheel steering)
18 NOSE WHEEL STEERING ACCUMULATOR PRESSURE GAUGE, engraved Steer Acc
19 WHEEL BRAKES ACCUMULATOR PRESSURE GAUGE, engraved Brake Acc
20 WHEEL BRAKES APPLIED PRESSURE GAUGE, engraved Brake press
21 No.2 HYDRAULIC SYSTEM PRESSURE GAUGE, engraved Hyd 2
22 No.1 HYDRAULIC SYSTEM PRESSURE GAUGE, engraved Hyd 1
23 WANDER LAMP - switch on by pulling lamp-head. Stowed lead allows lamp to be hand-held or clipped under LH glareshield
24 PERSONAL EQUIPMENT CONNECTOR (PEC) DUST COVER STOWAGE
25 VISUAL IDENTIFICATION LAMP SWITCH, labelled Landing Lamps, Aux-Off. forward for Aux (On) rearward Off
26 LANDING LAMP SWITCH, labelled Landing Lamps, Approach-Off. forward for Approach, centre position unmarked (hover), rearward Off
27 FLIGHT REFUELLING TANK DEPRESS SWITCH, labelled Flight Refuelling-Tank Depress. Lift and set forward for Tank Depress to shut off tank transfer air and energize refuelling valves for flight refuelling
28 FLIGHT REFUELLING PROBE LIGHT SWITCH, labelled Flight Refuelling-Probe Light. Forward for probe light on. Light fitted in wing root when flight refuelling probe fitted
29 ALTERNATIVE PRESS-TO-TRANSMIT BUTTON, labelled PTT. Use as alternative to throttle switch (76) after selection at station box (Fig.14)
30 SIDEWINDER JETTISON BUTTON, labelled S/W Jettison. Press to jettison missiles by forward firing (unguided, unarmed)

31 CHAFF SELECT SWITCH, labelled Chaff Manual-Chaff Auto-Off. forward for Chaff Auto, rearward for Off
32 FLARE SELECT SWITCH, labelled Flare, On-Off. Lift toggle and push forward for On
33 FLARE JETTISON PUSHBUTTON SWITCH, labelled Flare Jettison. Press to jettison ALE-40 flares
34 WATER JETTISON SWITCH, labelled Water Jettison, On-Off. forward for On, rearward for Off
35 ADD AUDIO ON-OFF VOLUME CONTROL, labelled A.D.D Vol-Off. Rotate clockwise from Off to increase volume
36 COCKPIT CONDITIONING AIR LOUVRE (LH) non-adjustable; fitted on both LH and RH ducting
37 LP FUEL COCK LEVER, engraved LP. Quadrant labelled LP Cock-On-Off
38 SWITCH GANGBAR. Push forward against spring to switch on switches 38 to 43
39 AUTOSTABILIZER ROLL AND YAW CHANNELS SELECTOR SWITCH, labelled Roll Yaw-Off-Roll On. Set forward to engage Roll Yaw, centre for Off and set rearward to engage Roll On
40 AUTOSTABILIZER PITCH CHANNEL SELECTOR SWITCH, labelled Pitch. Set fwd to engage pitch channel
41 AUTOMATIC FLIGHT CONTROL SYSTEM (AFCS) MASTER SWITCH, labelled AFCS. Controls AC supplies to autostabilizer and autopilot. Set forward for on. Lift and set rearward for Off
42 AIR DATA COMPUTER (ADC) SWITCH, labelled ADC. Set forward for on
43 AIRSTREAM DIRECTION DETECTOR (ADD) PROBE HEATER SWITCH, labelled ADD. Set forward for on
44 PITOT/STATIC PROBE HEATER SWITCH, labelled Pitot. Set forward for On
45 COCKPIT MAIN LIGHTING SWITCH, labelled Main Ltg, Norm-Bright-Off. Set forward for Norm, centre for Bright, rearward for Off
46 NAVIGATION LIGHTS SWITCH, labelled Nav-Ltg-Bright-Dim. Set forward for Bright, rearward for Dim
47 ANTI-COLLISION LIGHTS SWITCH, labelled Anti-Coll, On-Off. Set forward for On, rearward for Off
48 COCKPIT EMERGENCY LIGHTING SWITCH, labelled Emerg Ltg-Off. Set forward for on, rearward for Off
49 AFCS TEST BUTTON, labelled AFCS-Test. Press to test AFCS
50 q-FEEL SWITCH, labelled Q Feel, On-Off. Forward for on, rearward for Off
51 RUDDER PEDAL SHAKER (RPS) SWITCH, labelled RPS, On-Off. Forward for On, rearward for Off
52 RPS/YAW AUTOSTAB TEST BUTTON, labelled RPS, Yaw-Test. Press for associated system test
52A VIDEO SOURCE SWITCH (post Mod.2061), labelled DVC/MFD-DVC/RAD- RAD/MFD. Set forward for direct view camera (DVC - view of head-up display and outside world) and MFD video sources, centre for DVC and radar, rearward for radar and MFD.
52B MODE SELECT SWITCH (post Mod.2061), labelled VRS, Rec-Stby-Off. Set forward for record mode, centre for standby mode, rearward for off.
53 TAIL PLANE STANDBY TRIM SWITCHES AND COVER, labelled Lift for Standby Tail plane Trim. Lift cover fully to isolate main trim (control column) and to gain access to two standby switches
53A INERTIAL NAVIGATION/GLOBAL POSITIONING SYSTEM (IN/GPS) MODE SELECT SWITCH (IMSS) (Post Mod.2094) labelled IMSS-OFF, STBY, LAND-AIR, SEA, TA1 and TA2.

54 RUDDER TRIM SWITCH, labelled Rudder Trim and arrowed to left and right. Spring-loaded to centre off. Hold left for 'left' trim and vice versa
55 AUTOPILOT MASTER SWITCH, labelled Auto-Pilot, On-Off. Forward for on, rearward for Off
56 AUTOPILOT MODE SELECTOR SWITCH, labelled Auto-Pilot, Attitude-Height. Forward for attitude, rearward for height
56A VRS EVENT SWITCH (post Mod.2061), labelled VRS Event. Momentarily setting to outboard against spring pressure will provide event mark on video recording. Spring return to inboard 'off' setting.
57 ENGINE NOZZLES CONTROL LEVER DAMPER NUT - Preset by maintenance personnel to give correct lever damping
58 THROTTLE LEVER FRICTION DAMPER, labelled Throttle Damper. Rotate clockwise to increase friction
59 ADJUSTABLE FULL THROTTLE STOP CONTROL, 97-95-OUT (Labelled Out)
60 NOZZLE BRAKING STOP
61 HOVERING STOP
62 ENGINE NOZZLES CONTROL LEVER, labelled Do not operate without air supply on Air Motor. Fully forward for nozzles fully rearward. Move rearwards to increase nozzle deflection. Lift lever to clear STO stop (64) CAUTION Nozzles and lever must be moved together if no air available at AMSU

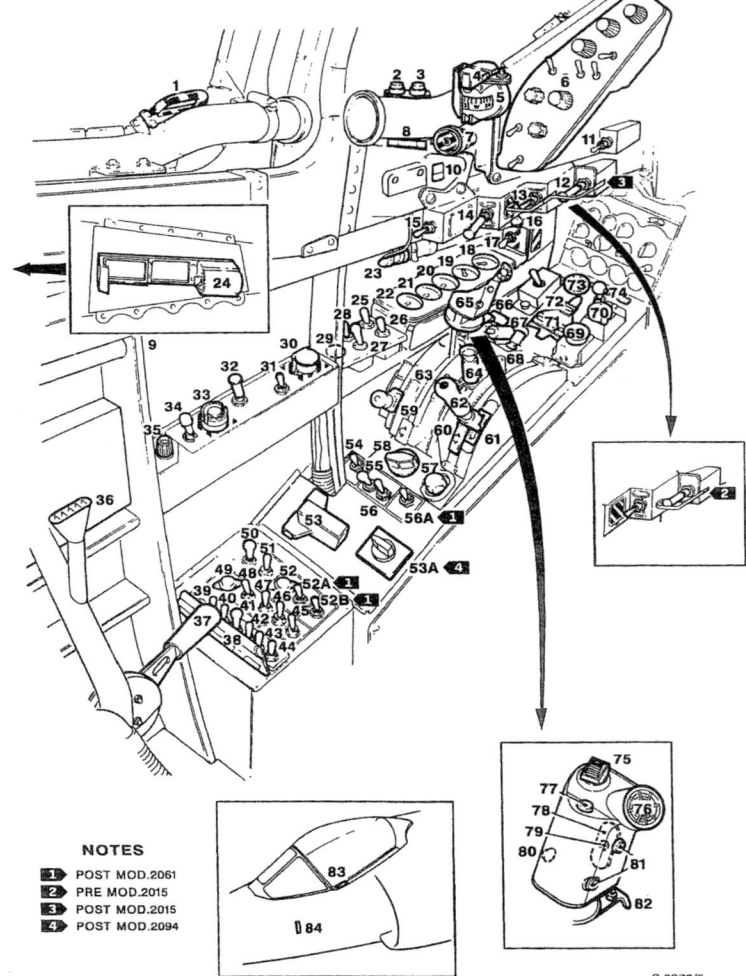

NOTES

▶1 POST MOD.2061
▶2 PRE MOD.2015
▶3 POST MOD.2015
▶4 POST MOD.2094

S.9372/5

62 ENGINE NOZZLES CONTROL LEVER, labelled Do not operate without air supply on Air Motor. Fully forward for nozzles fully rearward. Move rearwards to increase nozzle deflection. Lift lever to clear STO stop (64) CAUTION Nozzles and lever must be moved together if no air available at AMSU
63 CHAFF/FLARE RELEASE INITIATE BUTTON - Press to release chaff/flares
64 ENGINE NOZZLES STO STOP CONTROL. Presets stop on nozzle lever quadrant. Lift knob, move to desired nozzle angle setting on nozzle index plate, labelled 35 to 75, and release knob to engage stop
65 THROTTLE LEVER (Ref. inset). Controls engine fuel supply via engine fuel control unit (FCU)
66 WHEEL BRAKES PARKING LEVER AND RELEASE TRIGGER, labelled Brake Lock. With throttle closed and brake pedals depressed, pull lever fully rearward to apply parking brake. To release parking brake, press trigger and allow lever to spring forward
67 SPRING-LOADED FULL THROTTLE STOP - Limits throttle full-forward travel
68 ENGINE LIMITERS ON-OFF SWITCH, labelled Limiters, Off-On. Controls jet pipe temperature limiter (JPTL) and pressure ratio limiter (PRL). Set forward for Off, either manually or by fully opening throttle so that striker operates the switch. Must be set On (rearward) manually
69 LANDING GEAR DOWN SELECTOR BUTTON, engraved DOWN. Push fully in for landing gear down
70 LANDING GEAR UP SELECTOR BUTTON AND GROUND LOCK OVERRIDE, engraved UP. Push in for landing gear up. To override ground lock for emergency retraction rotate button 60 deg clockwise and press fully in
71 LANDING GEAR POSITION INDICATOR - Four windows displaying coloured indicators. Green - locked down; red - unlocked or no electrical supply; white on black background - locked up. Labelled Nose-P-S-Main
72 MANUAL FUEL SYSTEM SELECTOR SWITCH, labelled MANL FUEL. Lift MANL FUEL guard and set switch forward to select manual fuel control system (MFCS) on
73 FLAP POSITION INDICATOR
74 FLAP SELECTOR SWITCH DOWN-MID-UP. Labelled Flaps Up-Down. Forward for flaps up, mid for flaps mid, rearward for flaps down
75 AIRBRAKE/SPEED-TRIM SELECTOR SWITCH - With landing gear up, set rearward for air brake Out; forward for air brake In. With landing gear down, set rearward for nozzles trim down; forward for nozzles trim up
76 RADAR SLEW CONTROL - Operate 'eyeball' control to position target marker displayed on RDU and post Mod.2193 in combat area search mode (CAS) controls selection of CAS mode ranges
77 RADIO PRESS-TO-TRANSMIT BUTTON
78 RADAR ELEVATION CONTROL - Rock switch to control elevation of radar scanner. Press upper portion of switch to increase, and lower portion to decrease scanner elevation
79 RADAR TRANSMIT/STANDBY BUTTON - Operate to switch radar transmitter between transmit and standby
80 ENGINE RELIGHT BUTTON - Press to energize engine ignition
81 RADAR RANGE BUTTONS - Operate upper button to increase and lower button to decrease, radar range scale displayed on RDU and post Mod.2193 in air-to-air track while scan mode, controls selection of RDU expanded display
82 ENGINE IDLING STOP TRIGGER - Lift trigger to clear stop to move throttle lever fully rearward for engine shut-down

Canopy External Controls (inset)

83 MINIATURE DETONATING CORD (MDC) EXTERNAL FIRING HANDLE ACCESS (LH) - Fitted on both LH and RH sides of canopy frame
84 CANOPY EXTERNAL RELEASE HANDLE - Press thumb plate and pull down extended handle to release canopy locks

Cockpit – Right

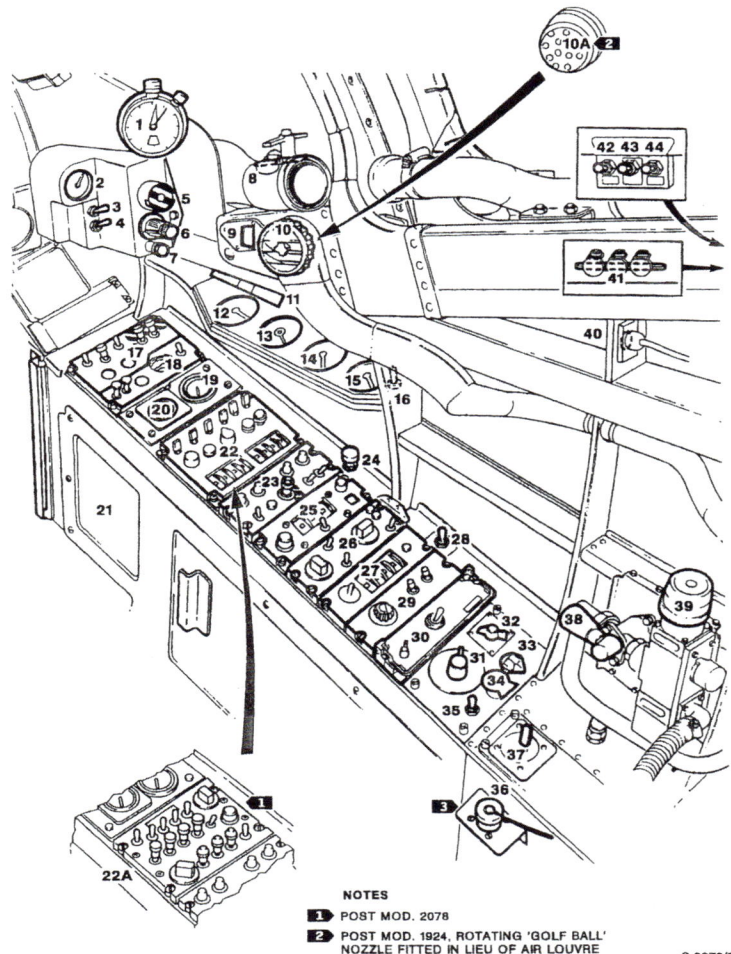

The right-hand panel section

NOTES

1 POST MOD. 2078

2 POST MOD. 1924, ROTATING 'GOLF BALL' NOZZLE FITTED IN LIEU OF AIR LOUVRE

3 PRE MOD. 2057

S.9373/5
AA000050

1 ELAPSED-TIME CLOCK - Outer buttons - press to zero hands. Centre button - re-wind; press to start/stop
2 DUCT PRESSURE INDICATOR
3 CAMERA SPEED SWITCH, labelled Camera, Fast Speed-Slow. Up for fast; down for slow
4 CAMERA MASTER SWITCH, labelled Camera, On Master-Off. Up for on
5 ENGINE FIRE WARNING LIGHT, engraved F.
6 DIMMER CONTROLS.
    Outer (large) knob controls:
      CWS primary warning lights
      CWS attention light
      Engine fire warning light
      Refuelling lights
    Inner (small) knob controls:
      CWS secondary warning lights
      Systems status lights
      Water injection flow light
      Radar height indicator warning light
7 TEST BUTTON, labelled CWP Test - Press to test:
      CWS primary and secondary warning lights
      Systems status lights
      CWS attention light and audio warning
      Engine fire detection circuits and warning light
      Refuelling lights
      Water injection flow light
      Digital Mach indicator
      Tacan control unit TEST light
      MCP and BRSL indicator lights
      ADI range display
8 SAFETY PINS STOWAGE - Stowage for seat firing handle and MDC firing handle safety pins
9 CANOPY LOCK INDICATOR (RH), labelled Locked. Indicates correct engagement of canopy lock (RH)
10 COCKPIT AIR CONDITIONING LOUVRE (RH) - (pre Mod.1924) adjust as required for ventilation air flow
10A COCKPIT AIR CONDITIONING 'GOLF BALL' NOZZLE (RH) - (post Mod.1924) depress gently against system pressure and rotate to direct ventilation air flow
11 FREQUENCY CARD HOLDER - Operate latch and lower the holder for access to fold-over cards
12 COCKPIT PRESSURE ALTIMETER
13 OXYGEN PRESSURE GAUGE
14 OXYGEN CONTENTS GAUGE
15 CORRECTED OUTSIDE AIR TEMPERATURE (COAT) GAUGE
16 COAT GAUGE CHANGEOVER SWITCH, engraved COAT-OAT. Normally at COAT. Set inboard to OAT for COAT gauge display of maximum permissible LP rev/min (engine performance assessment)
17 FUEL SWITCH PANEL.
    Inboard to outboard (front):
      LH booster pump switch, engraved Port Pump and On, set forward for On
      Fuel flow proportioner switch, engraved Flow Prop and On, lift and set forward for On
      RH booster pump switch, engraved Stbd Pump and On, set forward for On
      Fuel jettison switches (LH & RH), engraved Fuel Jettison, Port and Stbd - lift and set forward for fuel jettison
17 FUEL SWITCH PANEL.
    Inboard to outboard (rear):
      Fuel contents check button, engraved Contents Check - press and hold to check total internal fuel on gauge pointers during refuelling or when no transfer air pressure. Pointers revert to normal indication when button released.
      Fuel gauge check button, engraved Gauge Check - press and hold to check gauge and CWS fuel low level warnings; gauge pointers move counterclockwise to zero and warnings flash. Indications revert to normal when button released.
      To check total fuel (all tanks) press and hold contents check and gauge check simultaneously
18 ELECTRICAL SWITCH PANEL
    Inboard to outboard:
      No.1 battery master switch, engraved Battery Master No.1 On-Off-Ext
      No.2 battery master switch, engraved Battery Master No.2 On-Off-Standby
      AC reset button engraved AC Reset (press to bring main AC generator on line after transient fault)
      Voltmeter, marker BATTERY VOLTS
      Voltmeter changeover switch, engraved Ext-Pwr Off/Test Battery hold rearward to TEST for emergency busbar voltage on voltmeter
19 FUEL CONTENTS GAUGE
20 FUEL FLOW METER
21 DOCUMENT CASE STOWAGE
22 IFF/SSR CONTROL UNIT (pre Mod.2078)
22A IFF CONTROL UNIT (post Mod.2078)
23 COMMUNICATIONS CONTROL SYSTEM (CCS) STATION BOX
24 UNDERVOLT/OVERLOAD AND CHANGEOVER TEST SWITCH, labelled U/Volt - O/Load Elect Test - push to Test (engine running), lamp in pushbutton illuminates, O/L caption on RH glareshield flashes
25 TACAN CONTROL UNIT
26 I BAND TRANSPONDER CONTROL UNIT
27 MADGE CONTROLLER
28 SEAT HEIGHT ADJUSTMENT SWITCH, labelled Seat Lower-Seat Raise. Spring-loaded centre off; hold forward for seat lower, rearward for seat raise
29 NAVIGATION SWITCH PANEL
30 SOUND RECORDER
31 COCKPIT TEMPERATURE CONTROL - Rotary switch with Auto and Manual temperature control sectors
32 COCKPIT PRESSURIZATION/CONDITIONING AIR ROTARY CONTROL SWITCH, labelled Off-Normal-Demist-Flood
33 GTS/APU MODE SELECTOR, labelled OFF-APU-ECU START - Rotary switch (clockwise only). Set as required and press starter button (34) to initiate GTS ground run or engine start sequence
34 STARTER BUTTON AND GUARD FLAP, labelled Starter. Lift flap and press button to initiate GTS/engine start cycle as selected at 33
35 EQUIPMENT BAY CONDITIONING CONTROL SWITCH, labelled Eqpt. Bay Cool. Set On-Norm-Off. Spring-loaded to centre; set momentarily forward or rearward for system on or off respectively
36 BUS CONTROL INTERFACE UNIT GROUND TEST SOCKET, labelled BCIU GROUND TEST SOCKET (not used) (pre Mod.2057)

MAIN OXYGEN CONTROL, labelled OXYGEN ON-OFF. Set outboard to turn on main oxygen supply
ANTI-g SYSTEM SELECTOR LEVER, engraved ON-OFF. Down for ON
ANTI-g GRADIENT SELECTOR AND TEST BUTTON, engraved H-L. Set rotary selector to H (high) or L (low) for, high/low pressure gradient and cut-off; press button for suit inflation test
GROUNDCREW INTERCOM SOCKET
SAFETY PIN STOWAGE. Stowage for three ejection seat servicing/maintenance safety pins
ENGINE IGNITION SWITCH, labelled Isolate Ignition. Lift and set down to isolate engine ignition
JET PIPE TEMPERATURE LIMITER (JPTL) CHECK SWITCH, labelled Max Thrust-Response. Spring-loaded centre off. Lift and set up to Response for post engine start JPTL confidence check. Lift and set down to MAX THRUST during ground servicing testing
COMBAT/MAX THRUST RPM CHECK SWITCH, labelled NL Speed Check. Set down for test position

Cockpit

•1 The rear bulkhead seen after removal of the ejector seat

•2 To the left of the ejector seat is the Armament Power Supply breaker box

•3 The section on the left side once the ejector seat is removed

•4 and •5 Looking to the left at the throttle and nozzle controls

•6 Looking forward to the left side at the HUD and radar display

Ejector Seat

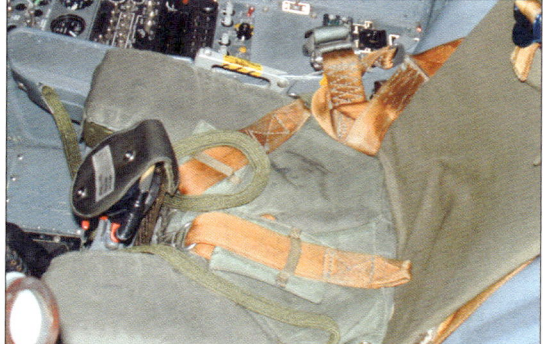

The Sea Harrier FRS.1 and F/A.2 both used the Martin Baker Mk 10 zero-zero ejector seat

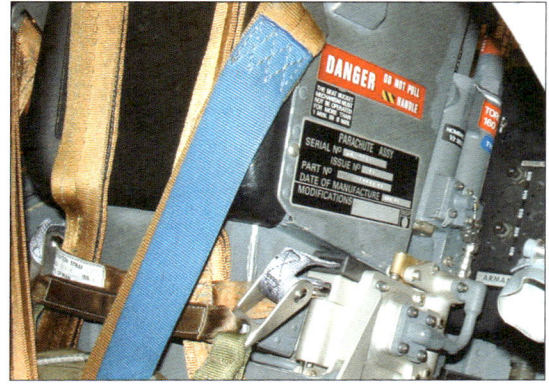

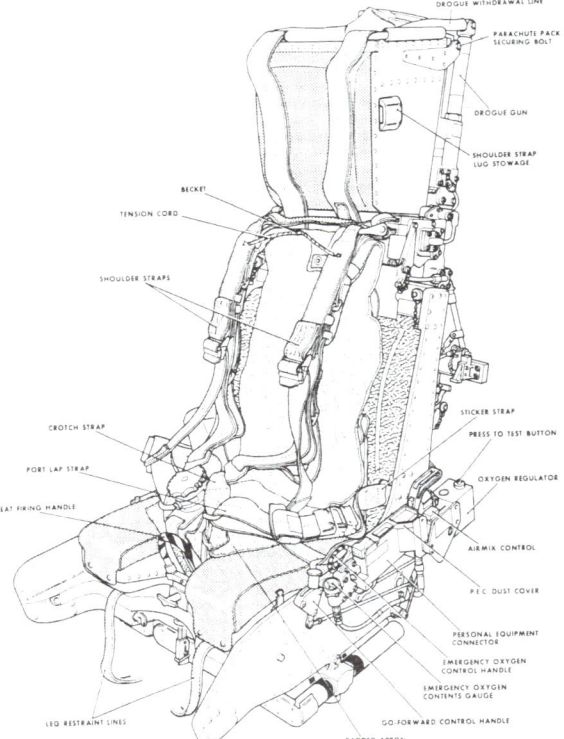

DROGUE WITHDRAWAL LINE

PARACHUTE PACK SECURING BOLT

DROGUE GUN

SHOULDER STRAP LUG STOWAGE

BECKET

TENSION CORD

SHOULDER STRAPS

STICKER STRAP

PRESS TO TEST BUTTON

CROTCH STRAP

OXYGEN REGULATOR

PORT LAP STRAP

SEAT FIRING HANDLE

AIRMIX CONTROL

PEC DUST COVER

PERSONAL EQUIPMENT CONNECTOR

EMERGENCY OXYGEN CONTROL HANDLE

EMERGENCY OXYGEN CONTENTS GAUGE

LEG RESTRAINT LINES

GO-FORWARD CONTROL HANDLE

PADDED APRON

Super-detailing the Airfix 1:24 FRS.1

Chapter 18

XZ455/12, 899/800 NAS, HMS Hermes

Operation Corporate, Falklands Islands, May – June 1982

Modelled by Nick Greenall

Here we have a 'super-detailer's' guide to producing a 1:24th Sea Harrier FRS.1. Nick Greenall guides you through how to model an excellent large scale SHAR using the Airfix kit applying 'traditional' construction methods without resorting to aftermarket add-ons, thereby giving you the opportunity to try new modelling techniques and improve your skills. Nick's model was originally built in the mid-1980s but he stripped it down and restored and upgraded it using a variety of methods to achieve a stunning result.

The Airfix 1:24th SHAR

For those used to the standards of current large-scale kits it must be remembered that the kit on which the FRS.1 is based is 33 years old! Ground-breaking in 1974, its age is now showing.

Here is a brief summary of the kit:

High points

- Excellent overall dimensions and outline accuracy
- The model captures superbly the sit and feel of the real aircraft
- Reasonably good fit of the major components, with care, except for the forward engine cover
- The decal sheet

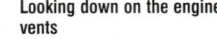

Looking down on the engine vents

Low points

- Too many gimmicks such as moving control surfaces and undercarriage, the Pegasus engine has rotating nozzles and poor rubber tyres
- The overall 'rough-cast' finish of the plastic with over-deep rivet detail
- Inaccuracies in the panel lines and fastenings, the airbrake bay, wing pylons, and cockpit intake cut-outs
- Poor definition especially around the nozzle openings and the nose cone profile
- Poor detail in the cockpit, wheel wells, intakes and compressor blades

If you want an accurate large scale Sea Harrier then this project is not so much 'shake and bake' but more a labour of love, and if you are prepared to do some concerted modelling and put in the time a stunning replica will be the result.

Surface detail – rivets and panels

Photos and drawings show that in addition to the over-deep rivet detail on the kit, several panel lines and inspection plates are incorrectly located. They need attention by adding better definition, especially around the rear engine bay covers. The re-scribing of the airframe is a big job and is best done after the various remedial steps for each major section are completed. 5 thou strip is used for the many slightly raised panels across the airframe and templates for the small inspection panels are made from clear acetate for easy, accurate location on the model. Access panel fastenings should be engraved using a hand-held 1mm round reamer bit with different depths and widths of scribing being used for different panels.

Tailfin

- The RWR pod and fairing need some work as it is 1.5mm too low and needs raising up. Use 10 thou, strip and filler for the fairing flanges, sanding these down to about 5 thou, also correcting the various panel lines in that area
- The rudder control inspection panel needs adding to the port side
- Hinge cut-outs need to be added to the fin trailing edge
- Fin leading edge HF notch antenna needs to be built up on top of the fin with microstrip and faired in
- Pressure vane on port side needs to be fashioned from scrap
- Rudder trailing edges need to be sharpened
- Strakes need to be created from microstrip
- Rudder control and trim-tab actuator need adding from

Looking down on the engine access panels

strip and rod
- Rudder base 'bevel and step' should be cut in

Tailplane

- Leading and trailing edges need to be sharpened, and tips re-profiled as the kit items are too round
- Gaps for the sealing plates need to be filled with card and new correctly shaped plates made from 10 thou card, with 5 thou fastening bracket details using rod at pivot point for fitting tailplanes to fuselage

Fuselage – aft of wings

- Plastic tubing needs to be used to make new tailplane/fuselage attachments

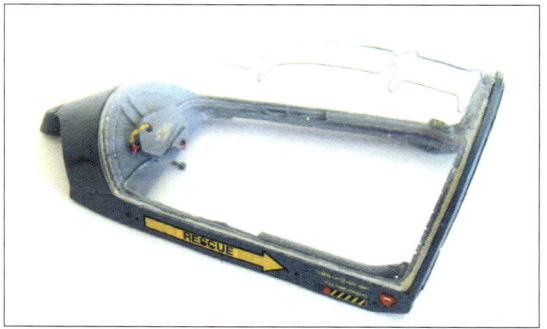

Looking down on the engine access panels

Cockpit

Canopy details showing the redefined MDC

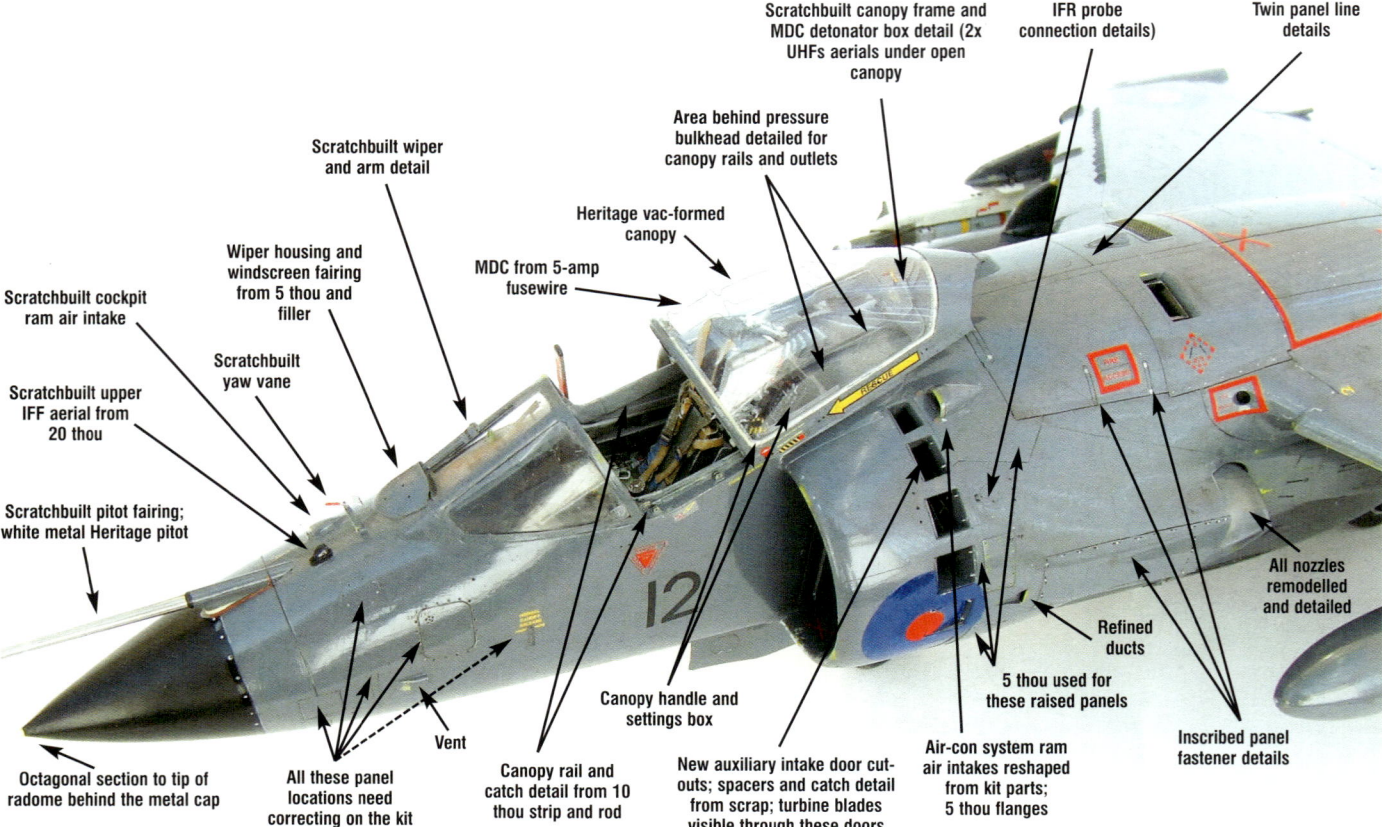

Scratchbuilt canopy frame and
MDC detonator box detail (2x
UHFs aerials under open
canopy

IFR probe
connection details)

Twin panel line
details

Area behind pressure
bulkhead detailed for
canopy rails and outlets

Scratchbuilt wiper
and arm detail

Heritage vac-formed
canopy

Wiper housing and
windscreen fairing
from 5 thou and
filler

MDC from 5-amp
fusewire

Scratchbuilt cockpit
ram air intake

Scratchbuilt
yaw vane

Scratchbuilt upper
IFF aerial from
20 thou

Scratchbuilt pitot fairing;
white metal Heritage pitot

All nozzles
remodelled
and detailed

Refined
ducts

5 thou used for
these raised panels

Canopy handle and
settings box

Octagonal section to tip of
radome behind the metal cap

Inscribed panel
fastener details

All these panel
locations need
correcting on the kit

Vent

Canopy rail and
catch detail from 10
thou strip and rod

New auxiliary intake door cut-
outs; spacers and catch detail
from scrap; turbine blades
visible through these doors

Air-con system ram
air intakes reshaped
from kit parts;
5 thou flanges

**Port side landing light as
described in the text**

- The all-moving tailplane slots need to be cut out, new tailplane joining plate and actuation mechanism detail need to be added directly into the fuselage
- Bulges need to be added on top of the fuselage each side of fin above the cut-outs
- Reaction Control Valves need detailing using four pieces of microstrip glued to 10 thou, cut to size, bent to shape and fitted into the openings; in the case of the side ones these need to be opened out and backed with card, with the underside one having a box made from 10 thou for the mechanism to fit into
- 5 thou card should be used for the raised inspection panels under the tailplanes
- Rear position lights from clear sprue need adding to the tailboom
- Mesh grills need to be fitted to the tailboom vents, but without a brass set here is how this was achieved. Cut out panels for the side vents, RCVs and areas around the upper and lower vents. Make panels in front of the RCV from 5 thou and plugs for other vents from 40 thou, removing the

inner surfaces of the 40 thou pieces so that when they are attached and sanded to shape, the plastic around the mesh will be about 5 thou thick. Attach 60-grade mesh inside them then fit the panels and plugs and sand to shape
- A small bent pipe needs to be fitted just ahead of the fin's HF notch aerial panel on the starboard side
- The reserve UHF aerial needs to be made from 20 thou card sanded to an aerofoil section, with filler used for the base fairing and fitted under the rear fuselage on the port side of the front of the underfin. You need to make three of these aerials; the two main UHF aerials are fitted atop the fuselage behind the canopy

Underfin
- The underfin must be reprofiled as it should form a continuous line down from the rudder trailing edge to just above the IFF notch aerial
- New underfin radar altimeter aerial panel needs creating from 5 thou card

Airbrake
- The airbrake bay needs to be shortened, with framework detail being added using 20 thou card and scrap to replace part 134
- A new airbrake should be cut to length, and re-profiled internally using card and filler, with hinge and jack detail being added from rod and HSP with raised rivet detail being added

Wings
- A new wing fillet rear extension profile needs to be made from card and filler with sharper ledges along the fuselage side, using 5 thou card for the raised stepped panel at the side of the fillet
- New mainplane trailing edges needed improved definition, here's how:

Cut back the trailing edges to enable a 20 thou blank to be fitted along the span of each wing, having packed the gap between upper and lower surfaces with scrap, then sand the blank flush. Make new trailing edges in aileron/flap length sections to get the prominent 'steps' (which are different for the upper and lower surface aileron/flap joints) from 10 thou card and microstrip. The sections are then fitted slightly proud of the wing surface and sanded flush, any gaps being filled and sanded down

- Flaps and ailerons should be remodelled with sharpened trailing edges, undersurface hinge detail and the correct profile on the flap around and under the fuel vent pipe.
- Fuel jettison pipes should be constructed from drilled out rod and scrap
- Wingtip trailing edges need to be sharpened and the tips sanded to the correct under-cambered profile
- Upper RCVs and wingtip lights need cutting out
- Reaction Control Valves need detailing, the lower set using a similar process to that for the rear fuselage sides; for the uppers use 10 thou card boxes to fill the holes, and 10 thou card and strip for the details
- Wingtip lights: the bulbs can be made from clear heat

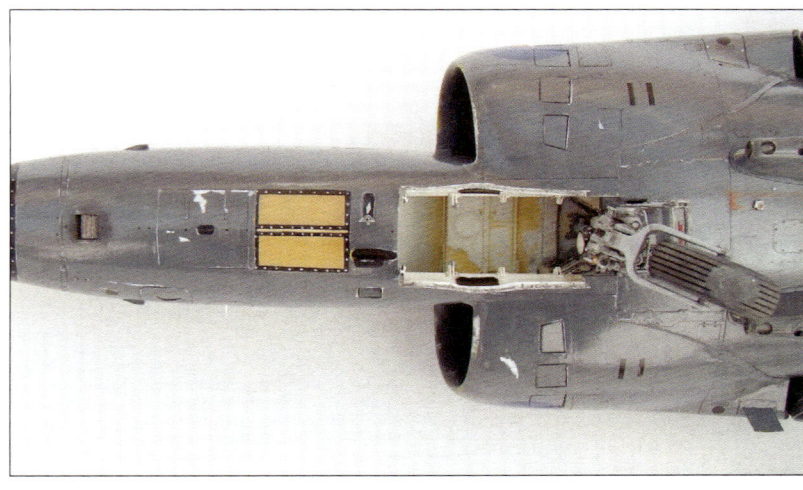

stretched sprue with the red and green light covers from stage-lighting acetate, tacked in place with PVA then secured with thin super glue

- Create new wing fences and brackets from 10 and 5 thou card, including those on the outrigger fairings
- Vortex generators need to be created with 10 thou card uppers and 5 thou card flanges, with the flanges always outboard
- All access panels and fastenings should be re-engraved

Fuselage – intakes to wings, above and under wings

- The upper engine cover panels should be detailed using 5 thou strip for overlaps onto the wings; sanding smooth into the engine cover panels where needed
- 5 thou card should be used for the angular slightly raised panels at the front lower corners of the upper engine bay

Looking at the Doppler panel and the detailed nosewheel bay

The centreline pylon with added details

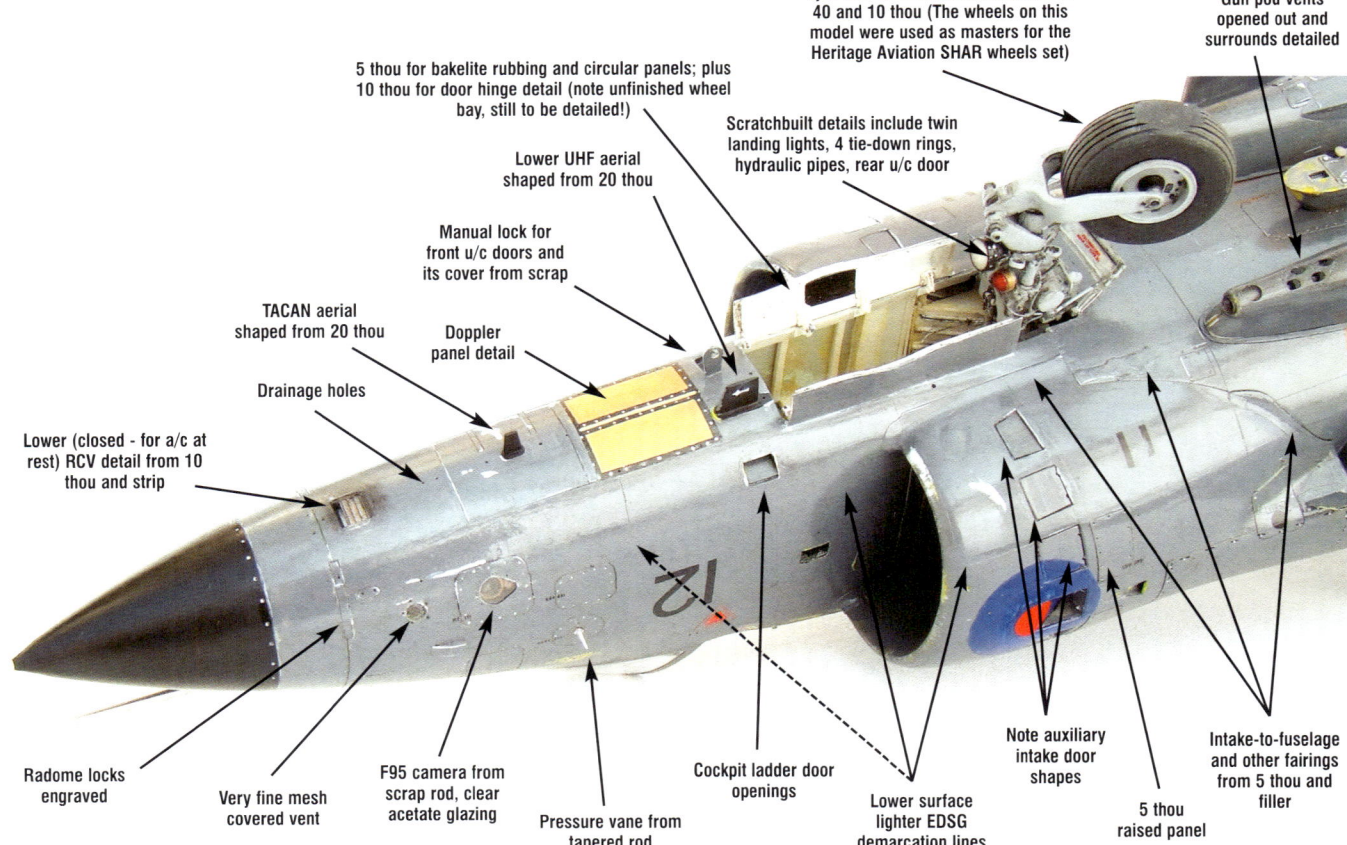

Kit hub detailed with rod, fitted with tyre sanded from laminated discs of 40 and 10 thou (The wheels on this model were used as masters for the Heritage Aviation SHAR wheels set)

Gun pod vents opened out and surrounds detailed

5 thou for bakelite rubbing and circular panels; plus 10 thou for door hinge detail (note unfinished wheel bay, still to be detailed!)

Scratchbuilt details include twin landing lights, 4 tie-down rings, hydraulic pipes, rear u/c door

Lower UHF aerial shaped from 20 thou

Manual lock for front u/c doors and its cover from scrap

TACAN aerial shaped from 20 thou

Doppler panel detail

Drainage holes

Lower (closed - for a/c at rest) RCV detail from 10 thou and strip

Radome locks engraved

Very fine mesh covered vent

F95 camera from scrap rod, clear acetate glazing

Pressure vane from tapered rod

Cockpit ladder door openings

Lower surface lighter EDSG demarcation lines

Note auxiliary intake door shapes

5 thou raised panel

Intake-to-fuselage and other fairings from 5 thou and filler

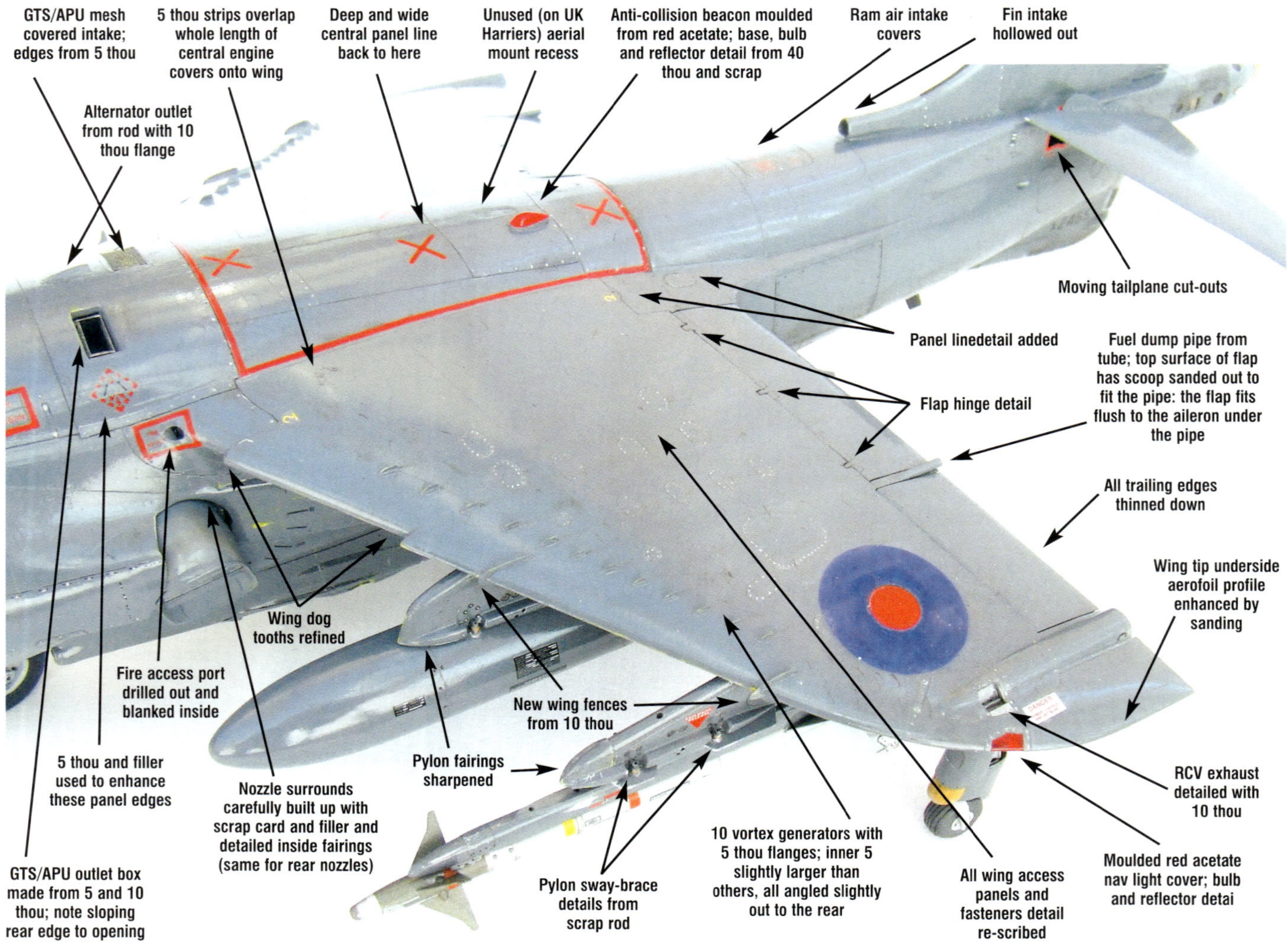

GTS/APU mesh covered intake; edges from 5 thou

5 thou strips overlap whole length of central engine covers onto wing

Deep and wide central panel line back to here

Unused (on UK Harriers) aerial mount recess

Anti-collision beacon moulded from red acetate; base, bulb and reflector detail from 40 thou and scrap

Ram air intake covers

Fin intake hollowed out

Alternator outlet from rod with 10 thou flange

Moving tailplane cut-outs

Panel linedetail added

Fuel dump pipe from tube; top surface of flap has scoop sanded out to fit the pipe: the flap fits flush to the aileron under the pipe

Flap hinge detail

All trailing edges thinned down

Wing tip underside aerofoil profile enhanced by sanding

Wing dog tooths refined

Fire access port drilled out and blanked inside

New wing fences from 10 thou

Pylon fairings sharpened

5 thou and filler used to enhance these panel edges

Nozzle surrounds carefully built up with scrap card and filler and detailed inside fairings (same for rear nozzles)

10 vortex generators with 5 thou flanges; inner 5 slightly larger than others, all angled slightly out to the rear

All wing access panels and fasteners detail re-scribed

RCV exhaust detailed with 10 thou

GTS/APU outlet box made from 5 and 10 thou; note sloping rear edge to opening

Pylon sway-brace details from scrap rod

Moulded red acetate nav light cover; bulb and reflector detai

Underfuselage tail section

covers
- The prominent underside intake/front nozzle fairing contours need to be sanded in as these are missing on the kit
- The kit's anti-collision beacon should be used as a mould to form two new ones from red acetate. The ACB mountings are made from 40 thou card, painted silver, and note that on the upper surface the mounting is higher at the back than the front
- 5 thou card can be used for the GTS/APU intake and exhaust surrounds, and the alternator outlet fairing flange with a new fairing being fashioned from hollowed out rod
- The GTS/APU exhaust outlet needs detail added, effectively an angled rectangular open box with 60 grade mesh used for the GTS/APU intake cover
- Fit the already made pair of two new UHF aerials

Port under-wing

- Two 10 thou card circles are used for the louvered outlets of the air-conditioning system sited by the UHF aerials
- The air-conditioning systems ram intakes behind the uppermost blow-in doors need to be reshaped from the kit parts and given 5 thou card flanges
- New rear nozzle heat shield /deflector plates need to be made from 10 and 5 thou card and micro-strip, with bracing detail being added
- All nozzles need to be remodelled and detailed
- Internal details to the nozzle fairings and the nozzle openings need to be made from card and filler to ensure the kit's massive gap around each nozzle is closed

Major work on the intakes:
- A big issue is siting the front of the Pegasus engine correctly in relation to the engine hatch, as the front of the turbine blades should align with the front of the removable forward

engine panel, as in the kit this is too far back

- Make new turbine compressor blades, which should be built over the kit part – new blades from 10 thou card are twisted to the correct shape and notched for the outer ring between the blades which is made from two laminations of 10 thou strip formed around a 60 thou disc of the correct diameter, with two laminations of 40 thou strip used for the central disc
- Using part of a spares-box bomb make the central fairing over the turbine hub, with 10 thou card flanges, fitting this over two 40 thou pieces to fill the gap between the kit fuselage and the front of the repositioned engine
- Fit a 60 thou card bulkhead behind the blow-in doors, fairing this into the front of the fan surround using scrap 40 thou card and filler
- Completely remove the blow-in doors, leaving the spacers between them over-size and reprofile the inner edges of the intakes to a more open shape than the kit parts. The inner

portion should stop on a line roughly 1/3 of the front to back depth of the blow-in doors
- After fitting the intakes, use an acetate template to mark the correct position of the door apertures, keying on the three central doors and their adjacent panel lines, then cutting the spacers to shape use scrap and filler to adjust the fronts of each opening
- Next make the spacers between each pair of doors point inwards into the intake using 10 thou card pieces cut individually to shape to meet the fairing
- Use some scrap strip for the door stops on the bulkhead.
- Finally, using filler and 5 thou card create the intake-to-fuselage attachment fairing shapes above and below each intake

Main undercarriage and outriggers

- For some ultra detailing make new tyres from laminated discs of 40 and 10 thou card, the latter being 1.5mm smaller

The mainwheel doors are shown slightly open

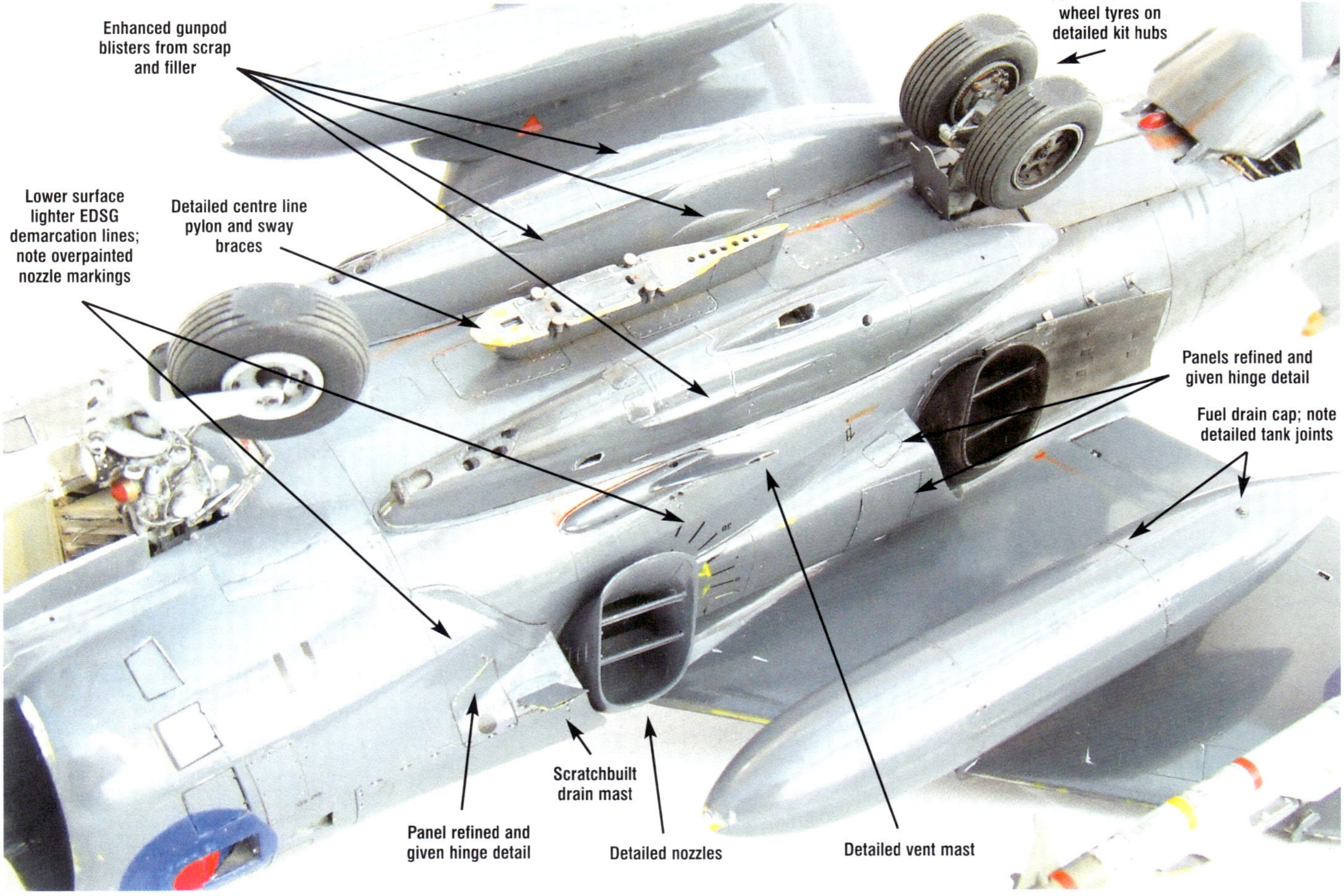

Enhanced gunpod blisters from scrap and filler

Lower surface lighter EDSG demarcation lines; note overpainted nozzle markings

Detailed centre line pylon and sway braces

Scratchbuilt main wheel tyres on detailed kit hubs

Panels refined and given hinge detail

Fuel drain cap; note detailed tank joints

Panel refined and given hinge detail

Scratchbuilt drain mast

Detailed nozzles

Detailed vent mast

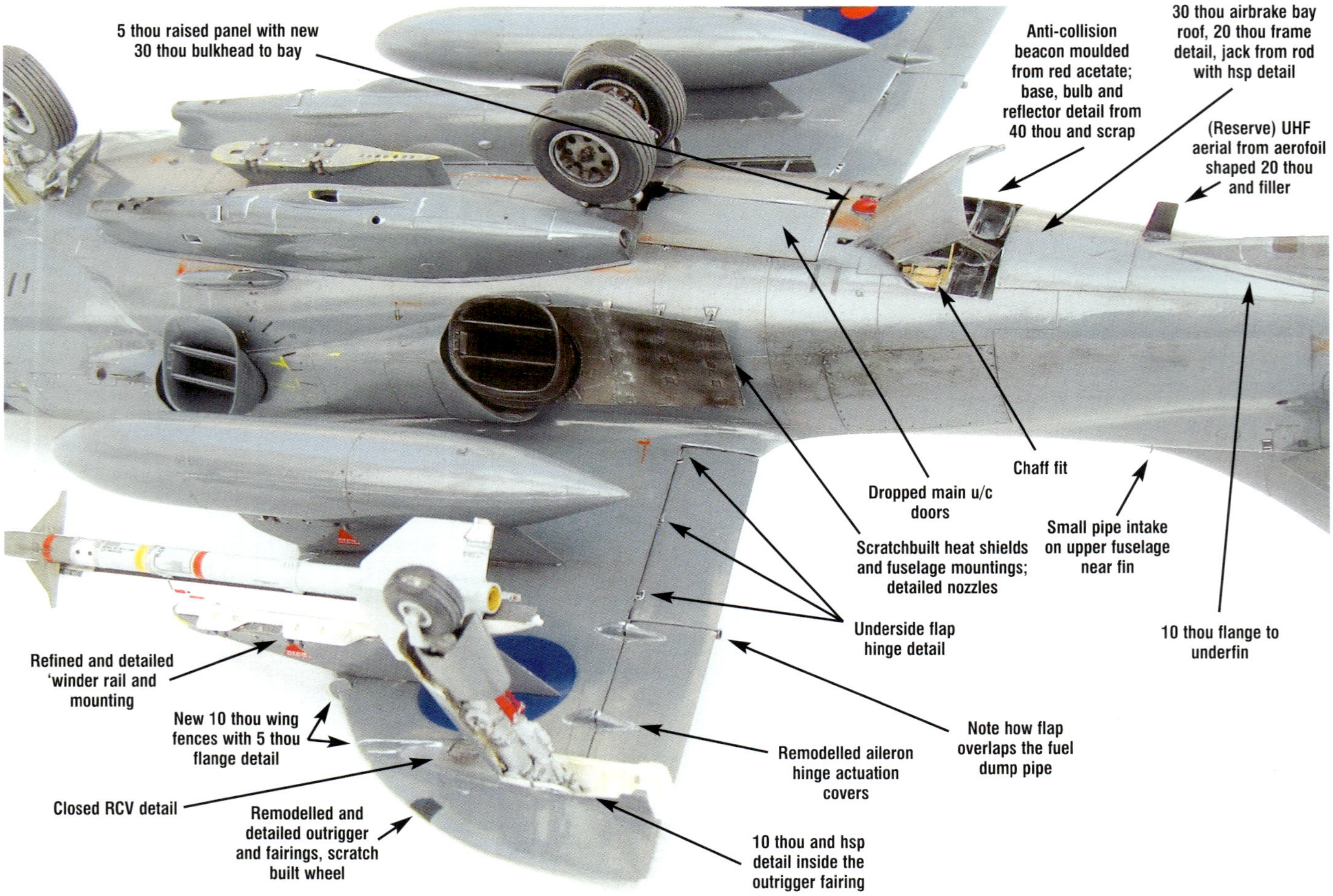

5 thou raised panel with new
30 thou bulkhead to bay

Anti-collision
beacon moulded
from red acetate;
base, bulb and
reflector detail from
40 thou and scrap

30 thou airbrake bay
roof, 20 thou frame
detail, jack from rod
with hsp detail

(Reserve) UHF
aerial from aerofoil
shaped 20 thou
and filler

Chaff fit

Dropped main u/c
doors

Small pipe intake
on upper fuselage
near fin

Scratchbuilt heat shields
and fuselage mountings;
detailed nozzles

Underside flap
hinge detail

10 thou flange to
underfin

Refined and detailed
'winder rail and
mounting

Note how flap
overlaps the fuel
dump pipe

New 10 thou wing
fences with 5 thou
flange detail

Remodelled aileron
hinge actuation
covers

Closed RCV detail

Remodelled and
detailed outrigger
and fairings, scratch
built wheel

10 thou and hsp
detail inside the
outrigger fairing

The unique 'Hermes Fit'
stuffing chaff into the airbrake
bay is detailed in the text and
shown here

Side view of the airbrake

in diameter to give the tread pattern
- Mainwheels. Each needs 6x 40 thou, 5x 10 thou discs, sandwiched alternately together, with 2 outer 40 thou discs being added one to each side, these being 1mm smaller in diameter than the 10 thou discs
- 2x 15 thou laminates are then added to the lower third of each tyre for the under-weight bulges, and faired in with filler
- The whole tyre is then sanded to shape for the outer and inner hub profiles, bulges and flats
- Sand the inner profiles and scribe the sidewall rings before fitting to detailed kit hubs
- Outrigger Wheels. Each needs 6x 40 thou, 5x 10 thou discs, sandwiched alternately together, again with 15 thou each side for the bulge. The hubs are engraved and hollowed out from the discs

- Rear mainwheel hubs: the outers are detailed for cooling holes, with bolts and valve detail from rod and the inners should be detailed around the brake discs and the toothed brake vents around the rim
- For the toothed vents make a microstrip ladder from 2x 10 thou square rungs and 15x10 thou sides. Cut it in two, trim back the rungs and fit one to each hub
- Brake cable details should be added to the hub inners and rear main undercarriage leg
- Front main wheel hub: rod is again used for the bolts and valves
- The main landing light is glazed using the kit part, the upper red light being moulded once more from red acetate
- A new rear wheel bay front door was made from 10 thou card with microstrip detailing to the inner surface for the framework, rod being used again for the links to the leg
- The main doors were all detailed by reducing their overall dimensions 1.5mm all round and reskinning them with 10 thou card to the original dimensions. The rubber seal around the front cut-out was shaped from 20 thou card and

thin rod was used for the sealing strip between the doors

- The front doors are similarly remodelled and detailed. However, as these doors will be open 5 thou card should be used for the circular panel inside the front of the port door and the black rubbing plates on both door interiors, which are slightly different shapes. The inside lips of the front bay are lined with strip with more hinge detailing to enable the doors to be fitted
- The outrigger bay/aileron walls are made from 10 thou card, the internal formers being constructed from 15 thou card with microstrip detailing; the kit's mounting for the legs should be removed and replaced with 60 thou card blocks using 20 thou card and scrap
- For the outrigger details suspension links should be made from 10 thou card and microstrip, the retraction mechanism being detailed with rod and hsp. The tie-down rings should be made from tubing and microstrip, with 5 thou strips also being used to detail the main strut
- The kit's outrigger doors should be thinned down internally and fitted with 10 thou card covers cut to the correct shape after fitting

Fuselage – forward of intakes

- The nose RCV is detailed in the same way as that on the tail boom underside, the outer edges of the opening being detailed with 10 thou strip sanded to shape
- A new pitot mount should be constructed from tube, scrap and filler, with 10 thou card used for the mounting plate
- A new pitot tube should be made from rod carefully sanded down to the complex tapering and arrowhead profile of the original
- New aerials, cockpit ram air intake, vanes, camera and camera port, and partially opened ladder attachment doors can also be added
- The whole under-canopy area at the rear of the cockpit

should be detailed for the boundary layer spiller duct outlets, canopy rails and the cockpit seal

Cockpit and canopy

- The cockpit's rear bulkhead needs more detail; this should be some 8mm aft of its kit position as it forms the wrap-around back of the canopy rails. The entire cockpit and seat is scratch-built
- A Sea Harrier's overall cockpit interior colour is Dark Admiralty Grey, not Medium Sea Grey. Weathering is pale grey, zinc primer and matt aluminium
- The HUD coaming needs detailing with careful reference to photographs. The kit part should be used as a basis for a corrected coaming with de-misting strips added around its junction with the windscreen from flattened rod
- The kit windscreen is detailed with an internal framework

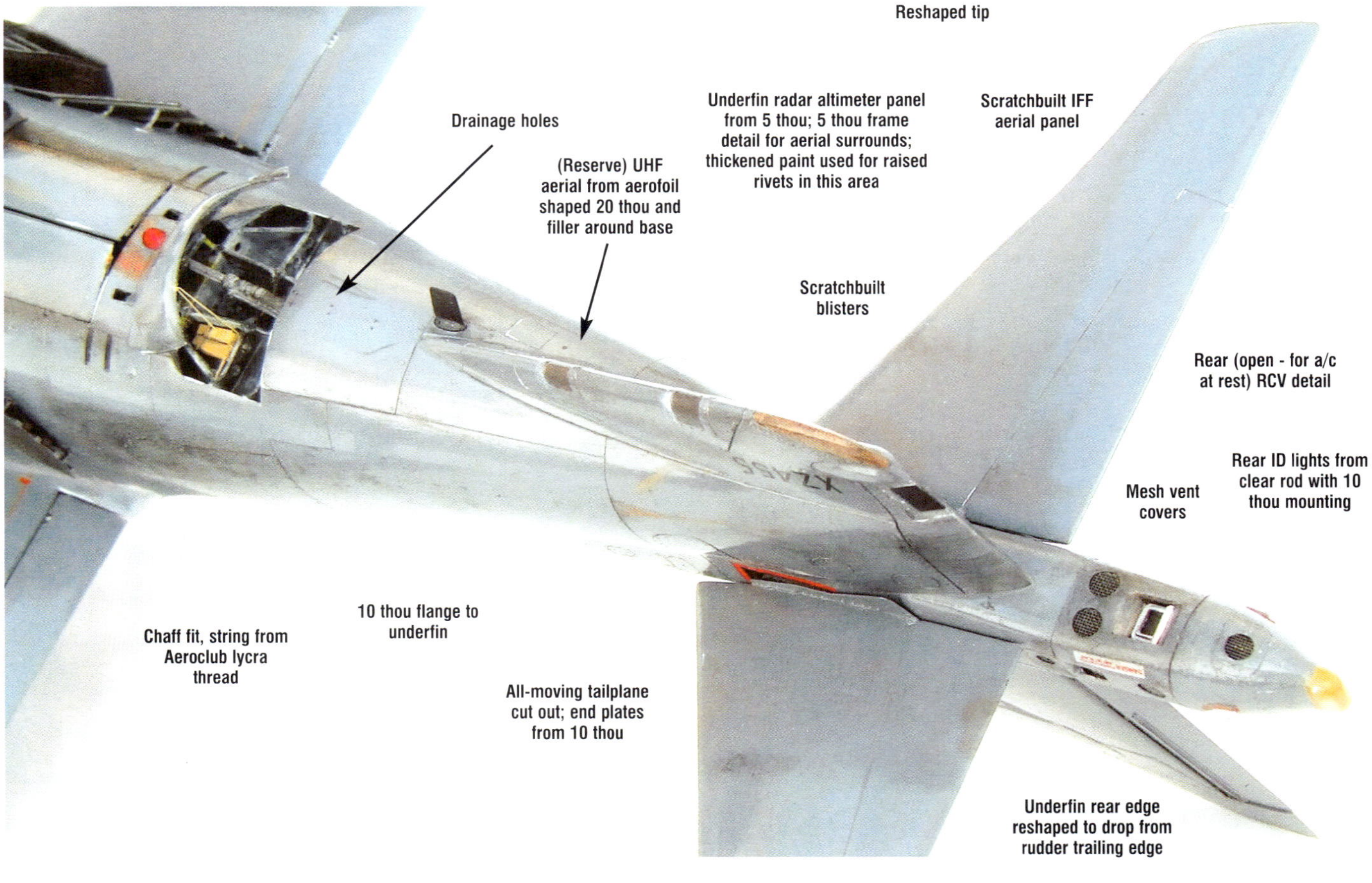

Tail details, note the overpainted markings

Reshaped tip

Drainage holes

Underfin radar altimeter panel from 5 thou; 5 thou frame detail for aerial surrounds; thickened paint used for raised rivets in this area

Scratchbuilt IFF aerial panel

(Reserve) UHF aerial from aerofoil shaped 20 thou and filler around base

Scratchbuilt blisters

Rear (open - for a/c at rest) RCV detail

Rear ID lights from clear rod with 10 thou mounting

Mesh vent covers

Chaff fit, string from Aeroclub lycra thread

10 thou flange to underfin

All-moving tailplane cut out; end plates from 10 thou

Underfin rear edge reshaped to drop from rudder trailing edge

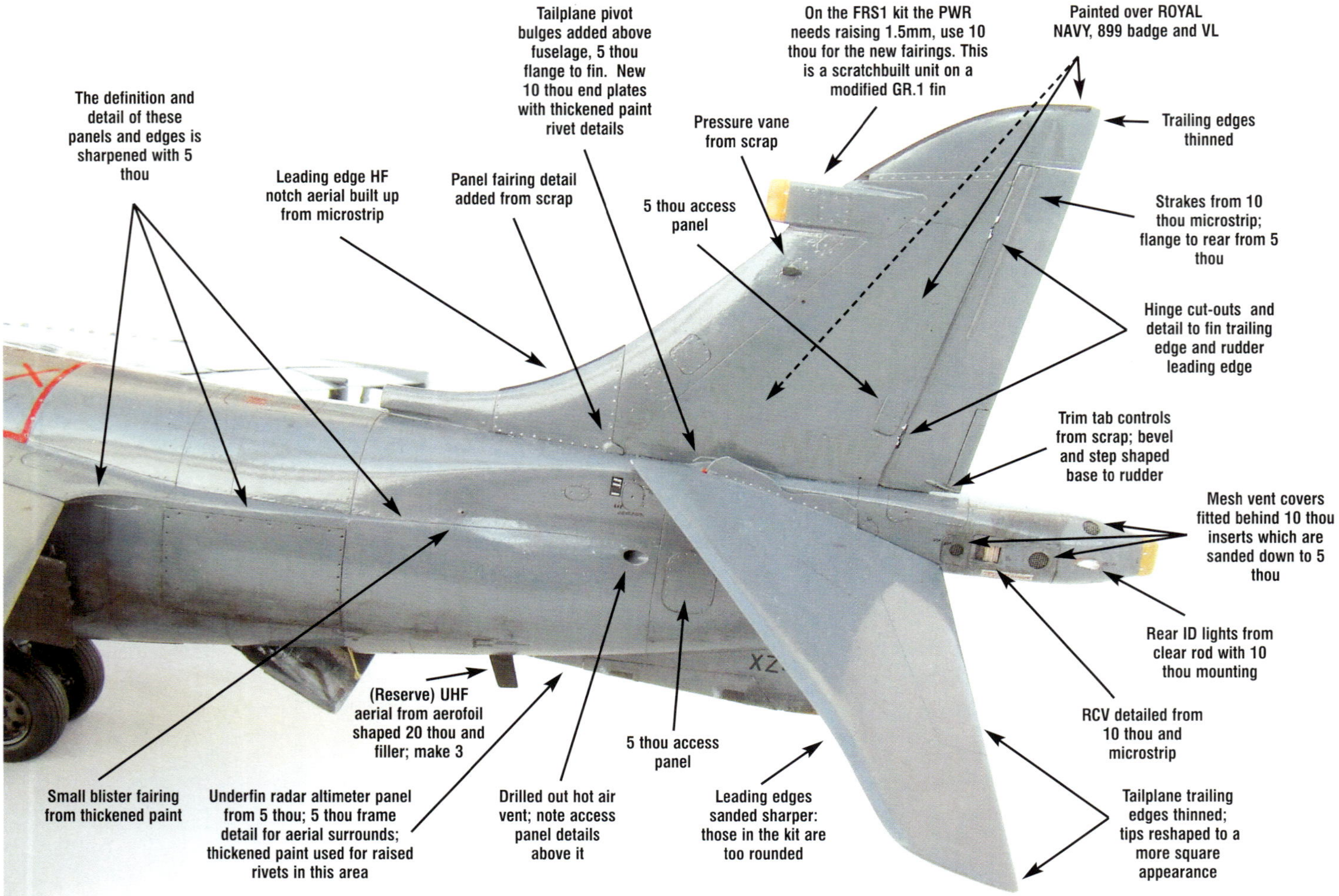

The definition and detail of these panels and edges is sharpened with 5 thou

Leading edge HF notch aerial built up from microstrip

Panel fairing detail added from scrap

Tailplane pivot bulges added above fuselage, 5 thou flange to fin. New 10 thou end plates with thickened paint rivet details

Pressure vane from scrap

On the FRS1 kit the PWR needs raising 1.5mm, use 10 thou for the new fairings. This is a scratchbuilt unit on a modified GR.1 fin

Painted over ROYAL NAVY, 899 badge and VL

5 thou access panel

Trailing edges thinned

Strakes from 10 thou microstrip; flange to rear from 5 thou

Hinge cut-outs and detail to fin trailing edge and rudder leading edge

Trim tab controls from scrap; bevel and step shaped base to rudder

Mesh vent covers fitted behind 10 thou inserts which are sanded down to 5 thou

Rear ID lights from clear rod with 10 thou mounting

RCV detailed from 10 thou and microstrip

(Reserve) UHF aerial from aerofoil shaped 20 thou and filler; make 3

Small blister fairing from thickened paint

Underfin radar altimeter panel from 5 thou; 5 thou frame detail for aerial surrounds; thickened paint used for raised rivets in this area

Drilled out hot air vent; note access panel details above it

5 thou access panel

Leading edges sanded sharper: those in the kit are too rounded

Tailplane trailing edges thinned; tips reshaped to a more square appearance

Superb Sidewinder missiles, scratch built as described in the text

adding a new wiper from microstrip with the wiper housing being reprofiled with filler. Once fitted the internal frame is faired into the cockpit rails and the canopy guides and locking detail added

· The sliding canopy was made using the Heritage Aviation transparency attached to the tidied-up scratch-built frame made from various thicknesses of plasticard

· The frame was detailed using thin rod/hsp for the Miniature Detonation Cord recessed along the upper frames and ledges, and bent rod was used for the cockpit air-conditioning outlets, using scrap and strip for the locking. To complete the canopy a mirror was made from scrap strip and rod

Ordnance and accessories

Pylons:

· The front portion of the crutch fairing needs sanding to a more pointed profile than the almost semi-circular shape of the kit parts

· The rear portion of these fairings should be shaped to the

same length as the front

· Sway braces can be made from plastic rod, with very fine cuts being used for the explosive release unit contact pads

· Centreline – this needs shortening and six 6 holes drilling out at the rear underneath. Two 2 sets of five ERU bolts need detailing between the crutch fairing gaps and holes should be drilled out on both sides with bolt heads being added from rod on the left

· Inner – new pylon front fairings should be built up from card and filler; again with two sets of five ERU bolts detailed between the crutch fairing

· Outer – once more the two sets of five ERU bolts needed

Sidewinder rail detailing:

· Assemble the kit rails with a piece of 20 thou card inserted between their halves to bulk the rails to their correct width and sand to shape

· The rails should then be sanded down on their undersides along their whole length so they are flush with the rearmost step. 15 thou card strips should be used to make each rail's lower edge and these are then faired into the rest of the body with filler to get the correct cross section

- A curved piece of 10 thou card can be used for the heat shield under the rear step; the roll-bearing detail is made from scrap and added ahead of the front steps
- Panels and fastenings need to be engraved and holes drilled into the rail upper surfaces, two in front of the forward mounting point, one after it; a vent from drilled rod also needs to be fitted to the rear end of each rail

Sidewinder pylon mountings (single rail fit):
- The kit parts winglets should be removed and used as templates for new pieces of 15 thou card and fitted after each mounting is widened, by adding some 10 thou card to both sides
- Triangles of 10 thou also need to be fitted under each winglet – two under the smaller fronts and three under the larger rears and should be sanded to a curved shape

AIM-9L Sidewinders:
- These are made from 7/32" diameter plastic tube, the bands being from 10 thou, with join detail from scrap
- The front fins are two pieces of 5 thou with 5 thou rod sandwiched in between them to give the impression of the aerofoil profile.
- The main fins are from three laminations of 10 thou card, the inner core being smaller than the outer portions. Rod is used for the front fins' pivot points, its stubs being used to mount them into holes drilled in the bodies. The rear fin flanges are fashioned from 10 thou card, the fins then being fixed on top of these before they are mounted on the bodies
- The rolleron mountings are made from 40 thou card, with 5 thou card detail with scraps of rod being used for the rollerons themselves
- Tanks – panel line and section fastening details need to be engraved; add drainage caps from rod to the underneath at the tanks' lowest point after the tanks are fitted to the pylons.
- Gun pods – rescribe new panel lines, vent fairings, barrel and anti-flash apertures and link ejector chutes
- Chaff – the 'Hermes Fit' airbrake bay chaff fit was made up from scrap card for the chaff bundles, scrap rod for the welding rods used to hold it in place and some Aeroclub Lycra Thread for the string used to pull the bundles out when the airbrake was fully deployed

Painting and finishing

Xtracolor Extra Dark Sea Grey, which has a gloss finish, making it roundel friendly, was used to coat the entire model, and this was brush painted to simulate the effect on the real aircraft. On top of the EDSG Johnson's Klear was applied after the decaling was completed and prior to weathering. Thinned Xtracolor Roundel

Overall view on hand-made stand

Blue was used for the roundels. The white portions of each roundel were painted white before being painted blue, giving the effect of these areas showing paler as on the actual aircraft. All of the raised rivet detail was added using small dabs of old, thick EDSG paint, darkened with black. The edges of selected panels were highlighted using white, matt aluminium, zinc primer or light aircraft grey paint with the actual lines being emphasised using very sharp HB, 2B and 4B pencils. Dry brushing using matt red and matt black added more staining under the fuselage, with graphite dust and matt black being used around the rear fuselage RCVs and aft of the rear nozzles. Oil runs were simulated using very thin satin black. The rear nozzles and deflector plates were painted with a mix of gun metal, antique bronze, matt black and with additional staining applied using matt black and 4B pencil graphite dust on a cotton bud.

Parked SHARs on Hermes are often shown with their nozzles in the down position, as David Morgan explains "We were aware of the bearing wear caused by constantly windmilling engines. We dropped the nozzles (manually) after each sortie to reduce the airflow through the engines so that we could insert a broom handle (I kid you not) into the LP compressor blades to stop the engines rotating."

Finally the AIM-9L Sidewinder colours. The 9L bodies and main fins are FS.36375, the front fins and head are a metallic green, and the seeker head itself is a shade of gloss bronze, and the kit's decals are suitable for use on the missiles.

Airfix 1/24 FRS.1 'from the Box'

Chapter 19

XZ 493/001 'Sharky's' Machine

Pre-Falklands Sea Harrier

Modelled by Karl W Branson

Construction started with the cockpit. As I was going to use the Heritage replacement set I needed to make sure that it would align with the opening in the new front fuselage section. I installed a platform for the new tub to sit on to make the alignment easier, but getting the rear wall and the instrument panel and the coaming to align required quite a bit of filing and sanding. The new side panels were then fitted to the fuselage walls. The Heritage instrument panel looked better than the Airfix offering, but the dials were just blank circles. I quite liked the new Airfix dials that came with the kit, so I detached each of the dials from the clear kit part; I then drilled out the resin panel so it would accept the Airfix dials, which gave me a Heritage/Airfix hybrid instrument panel. When I was satisfied with the fit of the new tub, I fixed it in place with epoxy. The next phase was the construction of the fuselage. The Sea Harrier kit contains the original GR.1 fuselage and an additional new front fuselage section that replaces everything forward of the air intakes. This requires that the original front section is removed.

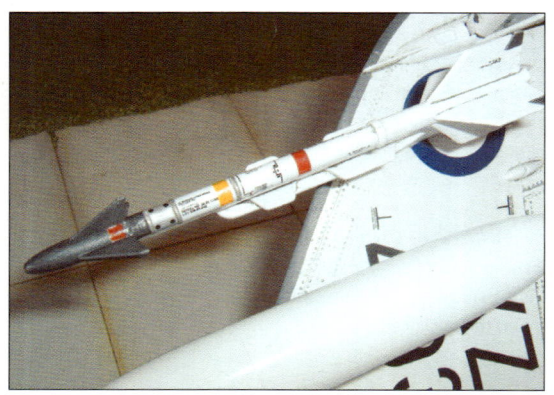

The remaining rear sections of the fuselage were joined together, incorporating the rear landing gear bay. The tail section and vertical fin were assembled and attached to the fuselage. The air intakes were another area that required a bit of re-modelling. The Airfix kit has the auxiliary intake doors moulded in the closed position, however, I wanted mine open. I marked out the position of the doors and drilled them out with my Dremel, squaring them off with a knife and a file. I made the intake doors out of styrene sheet, and attached them to the inside of the intake in the open position. The wing was constructed next. Next came a major filling job – the new front FRS.1 fuselage is nice and rivet free, however the old rear fuselage and wing are covered with them. Almost the entire fuselage and wing were coated in filler, which was then sanded right back to the plastic so as to just fill the rivet holes. The completed front section was then permanently attached to the

seal in the weathering. Finally the engine was fitted into its bay and the nozzles installed as were the landing gear, fuel tanks and Sidewinders. The ejection seat was slid in place and the canopy attached to complete the model. This is a very large model when complete and looks very impressive on display, even if it does take up a whole shelf!

rear fuselage, and any remaining joints filled. I sprayed the fuselage with Halfords grey primer to show up any surface imperfections and after some remedial work gave the fuselage/wing a final coat of primer. Additional parts such as the landing gear and the AIM-9D Sidewinders were assembled and painted ready for installation.

I chose to paint my Sea Harrier in its initial delivery colour scheme of Extra Dark Sea Grey over White. I sprayed the underside of the fuselage and wing Halfords appliance white; it's super white, very smooth and won't yellow. I then masked off the lower white section and airbrushed the upper fuselage with Extra Dark Sea Grey and when it was fully dry, I gave the upper surface a coat of Humbrol 'Clear Cote' Satin. Despite a few decal problems the markings presented no major issues and the whole airframe was given another application of Satin 'Clear Cote' to seal them in. Finally I did a little light weathering with a sludge wash which was daubed on and left to dry. The excess was then cleaned off and, when I was satisfied with the finish, I applied yet another 'Clear Cote' to

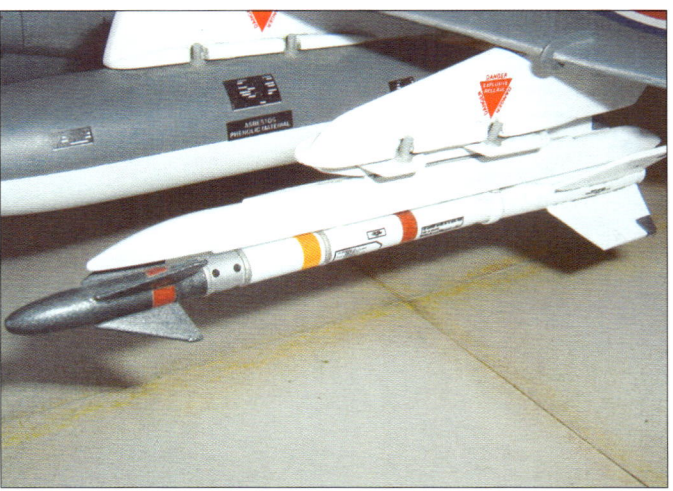

Quarter Scale Sea Harriers

As both of these kits share the same genesis, the detailing for the FRS.1 forms the basis for the F/A.2, adding the necessary detailing for the later marque as required.

The Sea Harrier FRS.1

Modelled by Nick Greenall

Airfix's 48th FRS.1 kit first appeared 20 years ago and many of the moulds are showing their age, and copious amounts of filler will be needed for the many moulding flaws. The raised panel lines on the wings and tailplanes can be virtually sanded off and not engraved back in place, as only the access panels are notable on the real aircraft. On the fuselage, the raised panel lines should only be used as a guide for engraving, but there are inaccuracies, such as the access panels on the nose and the prominent rectangular panels aft of the exhaust shields.

Pilot

Pilot colours: helmet 163 dark green (gloss) and g-suit (matt), olive green overalls; black oxygen mask, gloss visor and matt cloth visor cover over the top of the helmet; an aluminium reflective tape cross on top of the helmet; harness straps are matt sand and there should be small triangles of flesh at the side of oxygen mask, with dirty white gloves.

Cockpit and seat

Assemble the instrument panel and cockpit tub but do not fit the HUD or the seat until the final assembly. The cockpit interior should be Dark Sea Grey, not as in the instructions. If a pilot is not fitted, detail the cockpit from scratch or use an aftermarket item. Remove the harness clips on the side of the headbox and the side detail on the seat base to enable it to fit the cockpit tub.

Fan and bell-mouth

Paint the back of the bell-mouth – where the blades fit, and the blades themselves Aluminium. The bell-mouth is Extra Dark Sea Grey (EDSG), and remove the dome on kit part 9.

Basic fuselage assembly

Airfix have put the turbine blades too far back in the fuselage. The stage 5 assembly should fit in front of the two locating ridges so the blades are just behind the forward engine cover panels on the fuselage top. So this sub-assembly can fit without

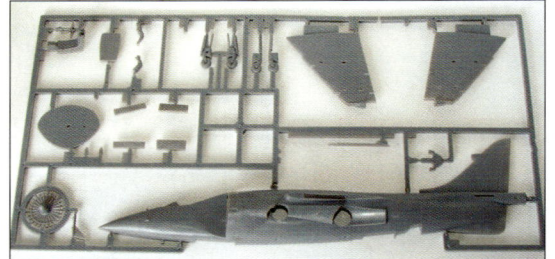

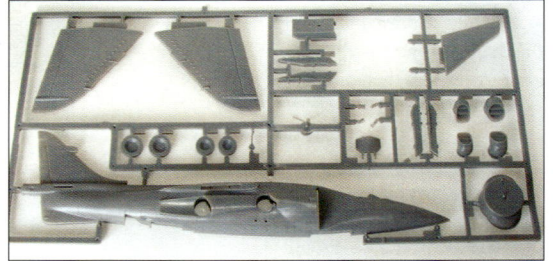

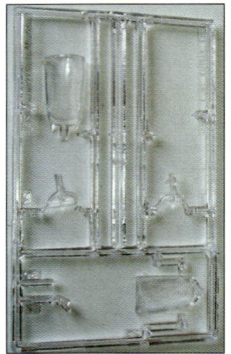

The Airfix FRS.1 kit parts

forcing the sides apart remove the top 4mm of part 11 and trim its ends. Part 10 needs its central top and bottom rims trimming back a few millimetres to enable it to fit in its new position. Then cut a line 2.5mm behind the engraved line on each fuselage half just inside where the intakes fit. Make two 90-degree cuts to this line and remove this area. Then fix the stage 5 assembly into place in one of the fuselage halves. Use an oblong piece of 30 thou plastic card to replace the removed piece. Curve it gently around a pencil and fix it in place to form one half of a

The kit has the turbine blades too far back and some surgery is required to give the correct look

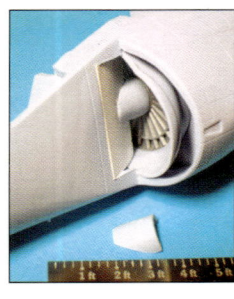

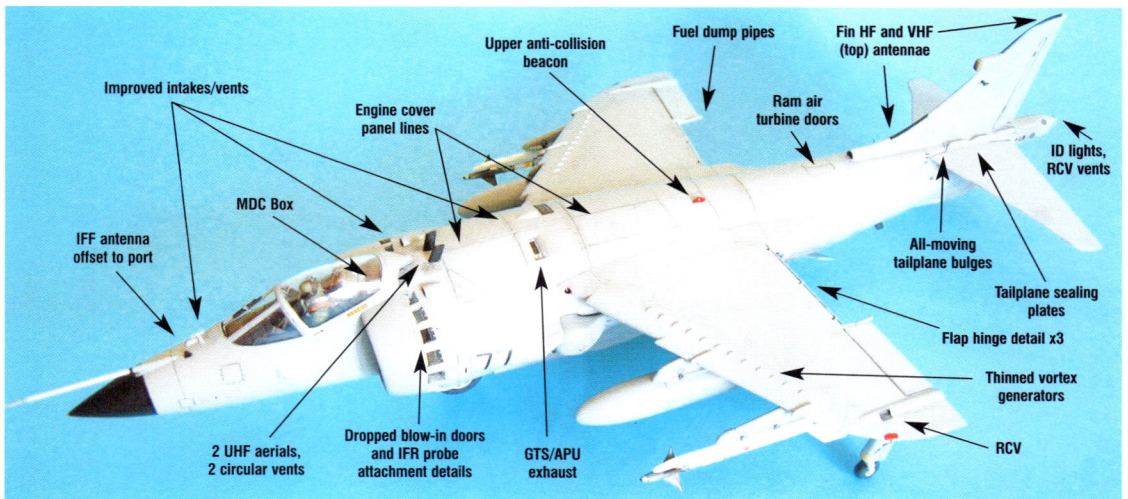

Improved intakes/vents · Engine cover panel lines · Upper anti-collision beacon · Fuel dump pipes · Fin HF and VHF (top) antennae · Ram air turbine doors · ID lights, RCV vents · All-moving tailplane bulges · Tailplane sealing plates · Flap hinge detail x3 · Thinned vortex generators · RCV · IFF antenna offset to port · MDC Box · 2 UHF aerials, 2 circular vents · Dropped blow-in doors and IFR probe attachment details · GTS/APU exhaust

gently curved V with its apex 3mm in front of the turbine blades on the fuselage centre-line. The area ahead of this pencil line will be removed from the bell-mouth so the intakes can be fitted. This gap is 2.5mm wide between the panel and cut lines. For the round fairing over the hub of the Pegasus use one of the kit's Sea Eagle halves, remove the ridge and sand it round. Cut two bevelled sections 9mm long and fix one to the card insert so it sits just off the fan blades overlapping the rear of the insert, then fix the cockpit bulkhead and tub into place. Hold the intakes in place while you draw lines inside them where they overlap this new assembly. Cut some card triangles to fill the gap between the new curved V and the intakes when they are fitted.

The kit nozzles can be improved by sanding off all mould lines before a scalpel is used to thin down the rims of the openings. The rear edge of the back nozzles should be squared off slightly and once done the finished nozzles can simply be pushed into place. The kit's heat shields are pretty hopeless and it would be better to make new heat shields from 5 thou plasticard, with microstrip to depict the lower three braces on the underside of the kit's moulded-in shields. Leave fitting the new shields until the final assembly stage to avoid damage. FRS.1 nozzle colours notes: before late 1984 all SHARs had their front (cold) nozzles painted in their upper surface colour. The rear (hot) nozzles have always been left natural metal. The instructions show the two 'grilles' of the gas turbine starter/auxiliary power intake and outlet unit as decal number

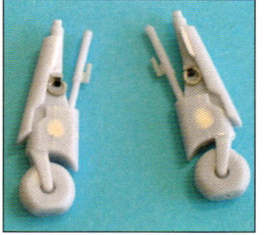 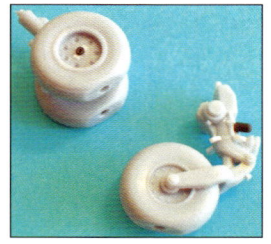

Adding detail to the outriggers

Adding detail to the main and nose wheels assemblies

76. The intake on the starboard side has a mesh grill, which can be better depicted by scoring cross-hatched lines with a scalpel. The same-sized outlet on the port side needs opening out with a scalpel. The rear edge of this opening is steeply bevelled, which can be achieved by paring it with a scalpel blade. Back the hole with card and fit a small piece of 10 thou scrap for the GTS/APU exhaust. In front of the GTS/APU intake a small fairing has been badly depicted in the kit. Remove this and replace it with a small section of rod sanded to shape. Before joining the fuselage halves, drill out the angled hot air outlet on either side of the rear fuselage just below the tailplane leading edges and back the holes with scrap black card. Rather than at stage 12, fit the closed undercarriage doors and airbrake now for an aircraft to be depicted in-flight or an on-the-deck with engine running SHAR. Most SHARs at rest have the forward undercarriage doors and airbrake down but the main doors closed, though very slightly dropped. Some filler is needed on the rear canopy

Making the airbrake bay look more accurate

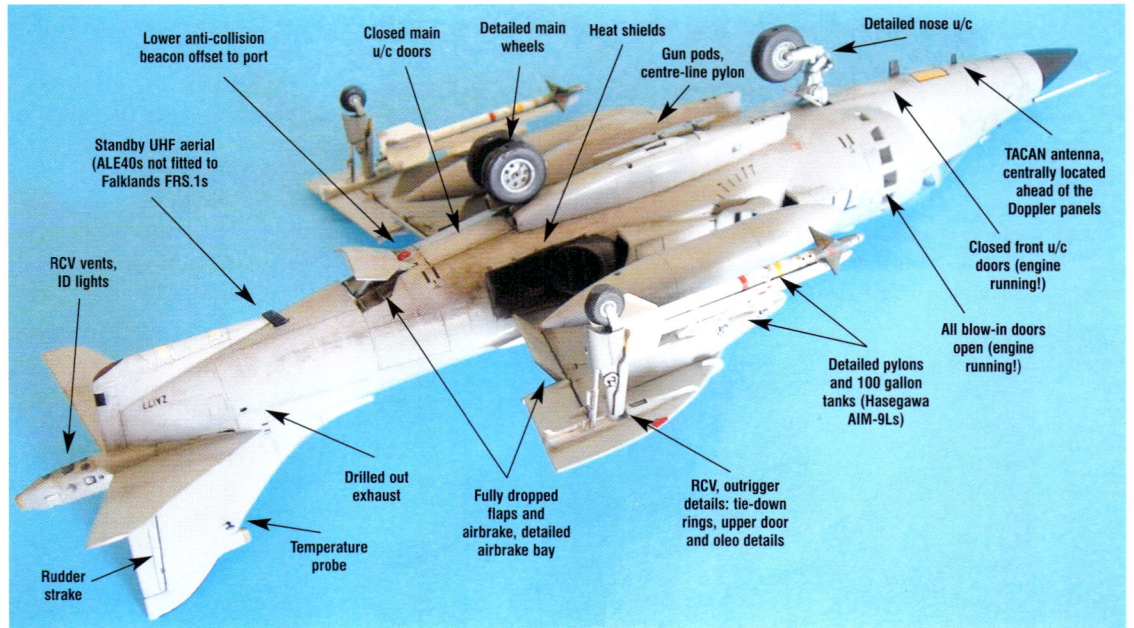

Lower anti-collision beacon offset to port · Closed main u/c doors · Detailed main wheels · Heat shields · Gun pods, centre-line pylon · Detailed nose u/c · Standby UHF aerial (ALE40s not fitted to Falklands FRS.1s · TACAN antenna, centrally located ahead of the Doppler panels · RCV vents, ID lights · Closed front u/c doors (engine running!) · All blow-in doors open (engine running!) · Detailed pylons and 100 gallon tanks (Hasegawa AIM-9Ls) · Drilled out exhaust · Fully dropped flaps and airbrake, detailed airbrake bay · RCV, outrigger details: tie-down rings, upper door and oleo details · Temperature probe · Rudder strake

Gun pod cooling slot details

100-gallon tank drain caps

Semi-circular vent to port of centre-line pylon

Standby UHF antenna

TACAN antenna and Doppler panels

Thinned down nozzle edges

Painted heat shield mounts

Reshaped outrigger fairing ends

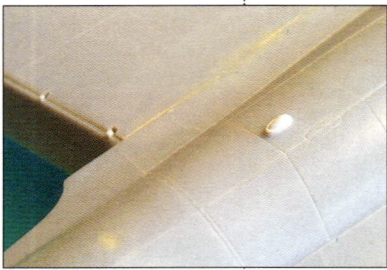

above left: Reshaping the upper anti-collision beacon and adding the wing fuel vent pipe

above right: Removing the sink mark from the airbrake and adding detail

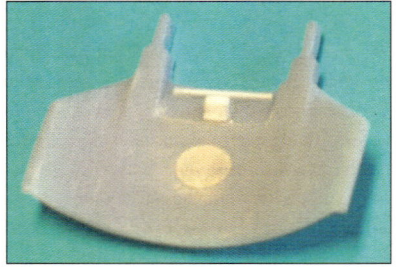

The blow in doors require work to depict an aircraft at rest

decking, the sunken areas around the airbrake and mainwheel bays and on top of the rear fuselage, plus areas around the front undercarriage doors. Reinstate all fuselage panels, undercarriage door and airbrake outlines.

Main component assembly and upper fuselage details

Filler is needed in the gaps under the wings when the upper and lower surfaces are glued together, and use a scalpel to thin down the vortex generators by half. Cut out the upper and lower Reaction Control Valve (RCV) nozzles in the wingtips and outrigger fairings, paring out small sections at a time to make the openings. Sand off the incorrect raised panel lines around the wingtip navigation lights; the lights are best just painted on later. Fill then redrill out the fire access ports in the wing root leading edges. Partly dropping the flaps on an in-flight model does give it more interest, however, when on deck SHARs can be seen with flaps both up and down, most usually up. Fit the wings using the angle templates given in the instructions as a

guide. The gaps on both upper and lower surfaces' joints will need filling and sanding down; those on the top will need quite a bit of filler over an area both sides of the joint. Filler will be needed for the tailcone joint and small pieces of trimmed rod are best used for the two rear ID lights on the tailcone. Use a thin razor saw to separate the top and bottom of the rudder from the fin and fuselage, and 16mm long strakes should be added to each side of the rudder. They are positioned one third of the way back from the leading edge at the top of the rudder. Also add small triangular wedges of plasticard to form the rudder control links on the starboard side and the rudder trim tab controls on the port. A 'T' of microstrip should be used for the temperature probe on the port side of the fin, and use a scalpel to open out the intake at its base

The instrument panel coaming is detailed with 10 thou card and add a further two 1.5mm strips of 10 thou to the windscreen sill to represent the de-mister units, with two triangles of 10 thou above these to alter the angle of the coaming at its rear. The whole coaming is painted toned-down matt black. Before joining it to the canopy use 30 thou card to make the canopy Miniature Detonating Cord (MDC) activator cover box that's missing from the kit part, adding detail with thin rod and scrap. Paint all internal windscreen and canopy frames and the bulkhead 164 Dark Sea Grey, with yellow and red detail on the MDC detonator cover.

For an on-the-deck SHAR it's easy, though time-consuming, to modify the intakes and drop the auxiliary doors. For a static SHAR the top 4 doors on both sides will be dropped and the central door may be partially open or shut; gravity keeps the

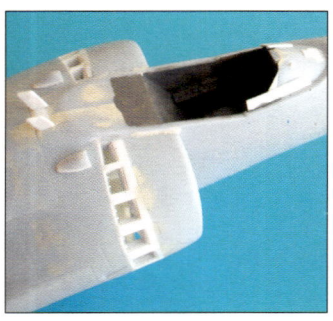

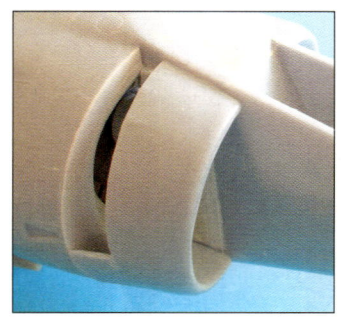

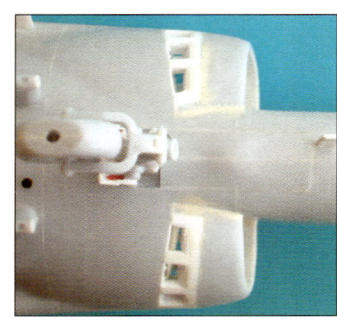

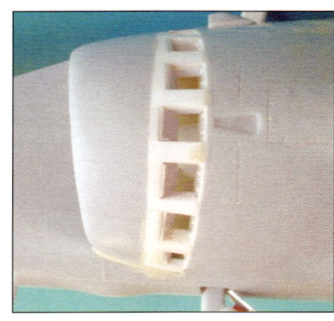

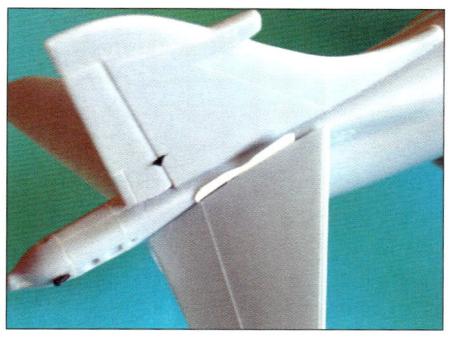

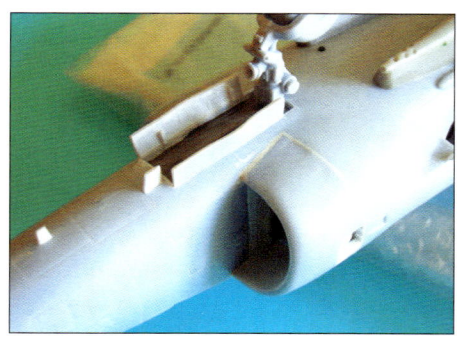

lower three doors closed. Mark out where the intake fronts will fit on the fuselage before using a razor saw to cut through the outer and inner surfaces of the intakes, cutting the inner surfaces so that they will end where the dropped doors sit. 10 thou is used for the bulkhead between the bell-mouth and fuselage. Fit the intakes to the fuselage aligning them with the marks made earlier. Once set, with reference to the fuselage panels, fit scrap pieces of plasticard to make the segments between the doors; they are all different in shape! The doors themselves are cut from 10 thou card and simply stuck in place at the required angles.

Undercarriage fitting options

For an in-flight SHAR the undercarriage doors and airbrake will already have been fitted in their closed positions and liberal layers of filler applied to smooth everything out and remove the sink marks under the fuselage. The outriggers are improved by rounding off the tyre profiles, which are too square, and the square edges of the wheel yokes. Cut off the yokes and wheels to do this, reducing the gap between the tyre and the cover to 1mm when refitting them. Again filler will be needed on and around the outrigger/wing joints and to fill sink marks and gaps. For a non-flying SHAR the kit outriggers are poor compared to the Tamiya items and at least need the obvious sink marks filling. The tyres and wheel yokes are rounded off as above. The tie-down rings are made from tube and scrap. On the wings, the rear of the outrigger openings should be square and not aligned to the trailing edge, the cutback going outboard. The rears of the openings need carving out. The main bay doors are often closed when a SHAR is parked. The kit's nosewheel leg needs some work. Firstly, it's too long, so reduce the angle of the yoke to the

vertical. Also take a couple of mm off the top of the leg. Use some clear sprue to make the two landing lights, the smaller upper one on SHARs being red. Plastic off-cuts are used for the tie-down rings. The upper leg has lots of piping, which is best made from copper wire, superglued into fine holes drilled in the leg. The interiors of the u/c doors are satin white and the nose gear doors have rectangular black rubbing plates inside them around their bulge. The last bit of detailing is to make a new front bay rear door and its arms from 10 thou card and strip, to replace the kit part.

Fuselage details

Small pieces of card sanded to shape are used for the upper and lower anti-collision beacons, the one moulded on part 52 being cut off and replaced. Both are offset from centre on the port side. The cockpit conditioning system ram air intakes need beefing-up by mounting on some 15 thou card. The UHF antenna parts need replacing and a further scratch-built UHF antenna needs to be on the lower fuselage offset to port at the front of the underfin. The fresh-air ram intake on the fuselage in front of the windscreen wiper fairing is poorly depicted and should be removed and replaced with one cut and sanded to shape from

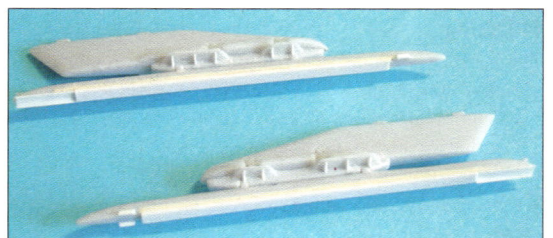

above left: Tailplane plates added

above middle: The interior of the airbrake detailed

above right: Antennae added to the underside

Detailing the wing pylons and launch rails

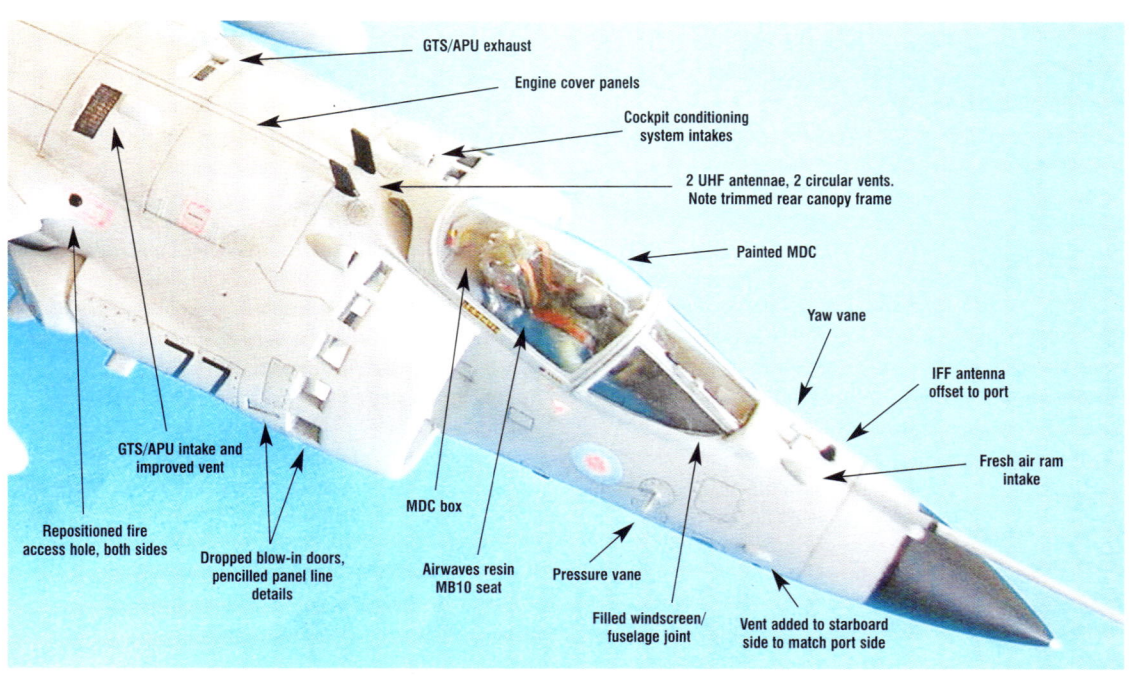

GTS/APU exhaust

Engine cover panels

Cockpit conditioning system intakes

2 UHF antennae, 2 circular vents. Note trimmed rear canopy frame

Painted MDC

Yaw vane

IFF antenna offset to port

Fresh air ram intake

GTS/APU intake and improved vent

Repositioned fire access hole, both sides

Dropped blow-in doors, pencilled panel line details

MDC box

Airwaves resin MB10 seat

Pressure vane

Filled windscreen/ fuselage joint

Vent added to starboard side to match port side

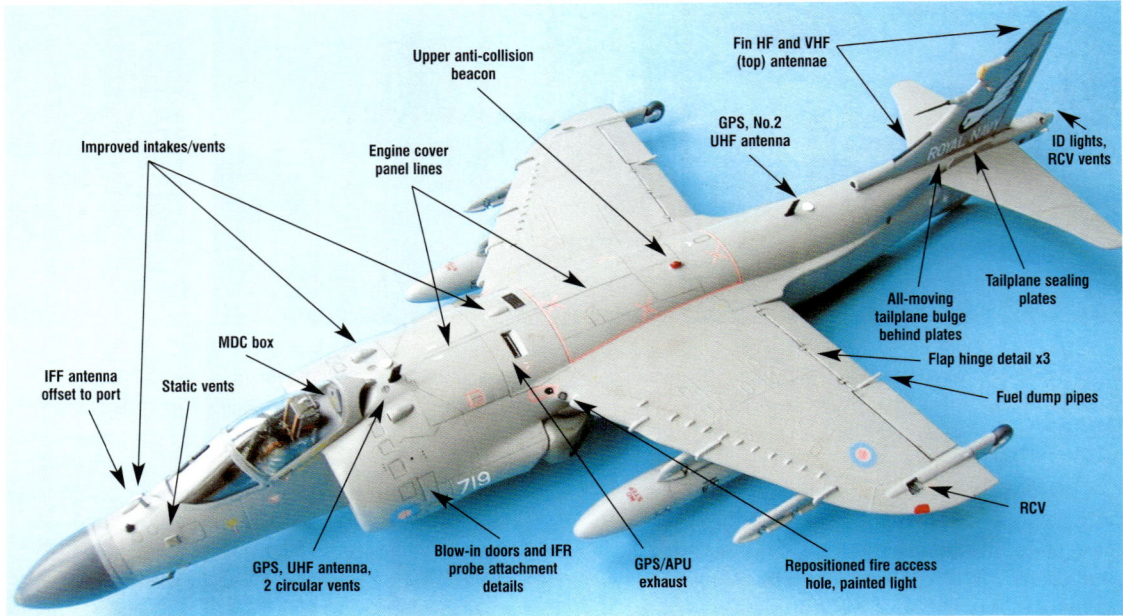

Labels on image (clockwise):
- Upper anti-collision beacon
- Fin HF and VHF (top) antennae
- GPS, No.2 UHF antenna
- ID lights, RCV vents
- Improved intakes/vents
- Engine cover panel lines
- Tailplane sealing plates
- All-moving tailplane bulge behind plates
- Flap hinge detail x3
- Fuel dump pipes
- RCV
- Repositioned fire access hole, painted light
- GPS/APU exhaust
- Blow-in doors and IFR probe attachment details
- GPS, UHF antenna, 2 circular vents
- Static vents
- MDC box
- IFF antenna offset to port

rod. A new IFF antenna should also be made from 15 thou and fitted offset to port ahead of the windscreen. 15 thou should also be used for the I-band transponder antenna fitted centrally on the panel in front of the Doppler panel.

Gunpods, pylons, AIM-9L Sidewinders and tanks

Detail the pylons by cutting off the kit's weapon mounting lugs and use small pieces of rod for each of the sway braces, which should protrude about 1mm from the undersides. Engrave the explosive release bolts on both sides with a small drill bit or burr. The gunpods will need some work to improve their shape and detail.

Finishing

The following painting notes clarify the kit instructions and apply to Falklands-era FRS.1s.

- All undercarriage legs and wheel hubs: Satin Blue Grey 127
- Fin and tailcone RWR covers: Tan 94
- All UHF, IFF, I-Band antennae: Matt Black 33
- Two underfin radar altimeter aerials: Matt Black or Tan 33 or 94
- Underfin rear IFF notch aerial and bumper: Matt Black 33
- Fin VHF and HF notch antennae: Matt Black 33
- RCVs and meshed vents, fin pressure head: Gunmetal 56
- Lights: Tailcone IDs – 2x silver; anti-collision beacons and port wing – red 19 + clear red; starboard wing – green 3 + clear green

Decaling

For Falklands War Extra Dark Sea Grey SHARs the kit decals and instructions (option C) are fairly comprehensive. XZ455, an ex-899 aircraft, was with 800/899 NAS on HMS Hermes during the war as black 12, transferring to 801 NAS on HMS Invincible before Hermes sailed for the UK. The kit's decal quality is variable – in some the register is spot on, in others the white appears to one side of the red walkway markings and Xs. A steady hand easily rectifies this. Leave adding decals 57 and 58 until the canopy has been fitted and painted.

As ever a little patience, care and consulting references will pay handsome dividends producing an excellent replica in quarter scale.

The Sea Harrier F/A.2

Modelled by Nick Greenall

As already noted as the Airfix FRS.1 and F/A.2 share the same manufacturing heritage, and the equivalent basic modelling techniques described in building the FRS.1 hold true for the F/A.2; the latter's nuances are described here.

As with the FRS.1 kit many of the moulds are also used in the F/A.2, however the F/A.2 kit features a wholly new fuselage complete with engraved panel lines. For an 'on-the-deck' SHAR, you can now add airbrake bay detail using microstrip, having first smoothed out the join line inside the bay. Detailing the airbrake is straightforward, with the actuating jack being made from rod. Leave fitting the brake until final assembly.

Also for an F/A.2 the second outboard wing vortex generator needs to be removed, and also, using a sharp scalpel thin down the other vortex generators by half. From 2002 a twin GPS antennae fit replaced the under-nose Doppler panel and to represent the GPS discs, a 1mm high 2.5mm diameter disc should be added centrally on the ram turbine doors, with

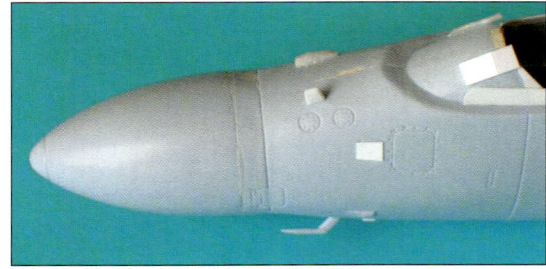

another similar disc on the starboard upper fuselage beside the forward UHF aerial. A new IFF antenna is also needed and can be made from 15 thou plasticard and fitted offset to port. Replace the fin-mounted pressure probe (if it's not become detached already!) with a pin cut down to size.

On any Medium Sea Grey FA.2 both inner and outer pylons will be needed but the new Heritage Aviation resin 190-gallon tanks should be used to replace the kit's 100-gallon tanks as the latter have been the standard fit on SHARs since the mid-80s. The F/A.2 kit decals are also correct for the 190 tanks.

If fitting AIM-9L Sidewinders, either drill or acquisition rounds, to the outer pylons, you'll need to modify the kit's launcher rails to the current standard. If fitting AIM-120

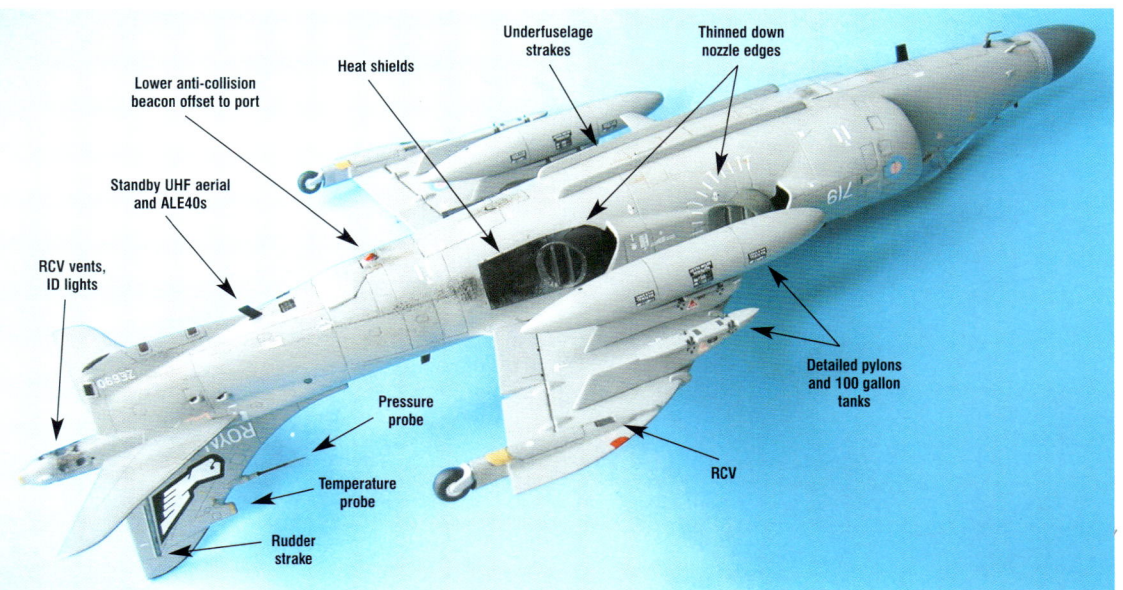

Lower anti-collision
beacon offset to port

Heat shields

Underfuselage
strakes

Thinned down
nozzle edges

Standby UHF aerial
and ALE40s

RCV vents,
ID lights

Detailed pylons
and 100 gallon
tanks

Pressure
probe

Temperature
probe

RCV

Rudder
strake

Finishing

The following painting notes clarify the kit instructions,
applying to MSG F/A.2s.

- Radome: Extra Dark Sea Grey 123
- Band at rear of radome: Medium/Dark Sea Grey mix 165/164
- Radome tip: A gloss 50:50 mix of 94/164
- GPS disc aerials: White 130
- Main and outrigger wheel hubs: White 130
- All U/C legs and outrigger wheel yoke: Satin Blue Grey 127

AMRAAMs to the outer pylons then you will need to make the
launch rails from scratch. Note that AMRAAMs fitted to these
pylons do not have the semi-circular ejector clasp on them that
pushes them away from the fuselage pylons, so cut these off the
missile bodies. After 800 NAS decommissioned it was very rare
to see an F/A.2 carrying gunpods, and strakes were fitted
instead. For the strakes use either the new Heritage Aviation
items, some salvaged from a Tamiya FRS.1 kit, or fashion new
ones made from 20 thou card. Alternatively, the kit's AMRAAM
pylons or gun pods can be fitted.

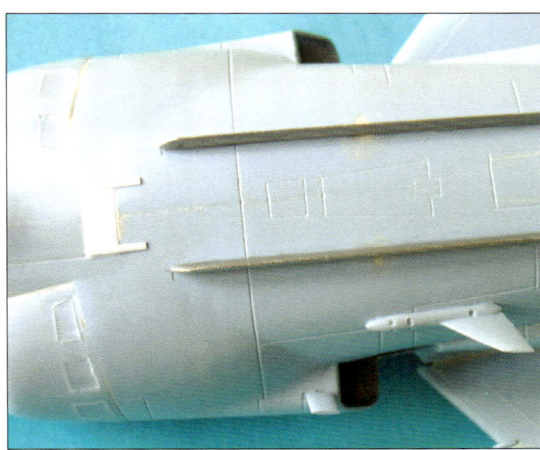

Antennae added and airbrake
filled in

Rear of the nose wheel door
has additional detailing
added. The hole is for a
mounting stand for display
purposes

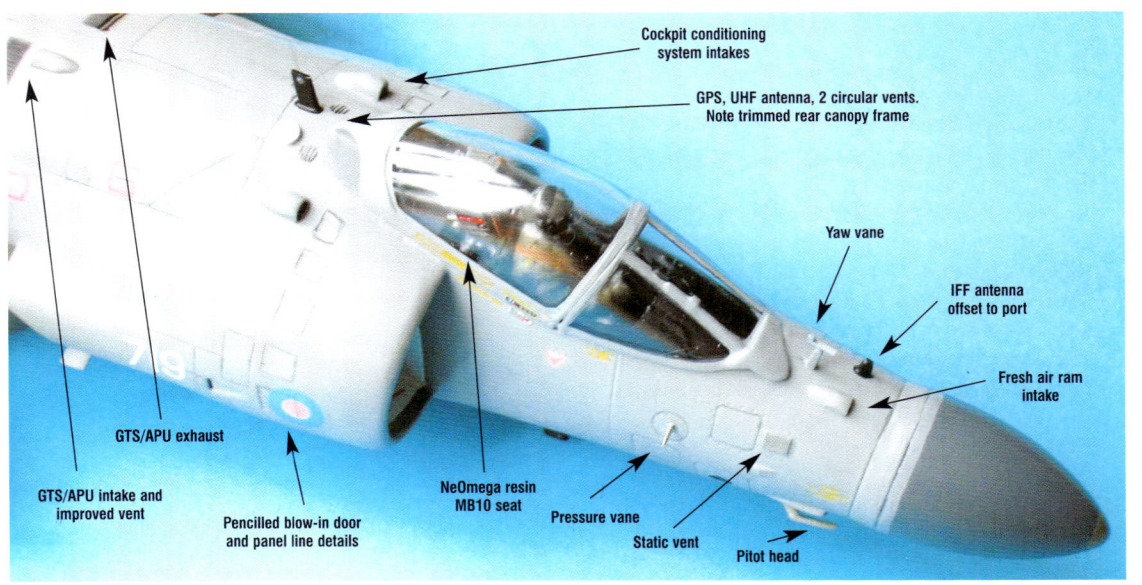

Cockpit conditioning
system intakes

GPS, UHF antenna, 2 circular vents.
Note trimmed rear canopy frame

Yaw vane

IFF antenna
offset to port

Fresh air ram
intake

GTS/APU exhaust

GTS/APU intake and
improved vent

Pencilled blow-in door
and panel line details

NeOmega resin
MB10 seat

Pressure vane

Static vent

Pitot head

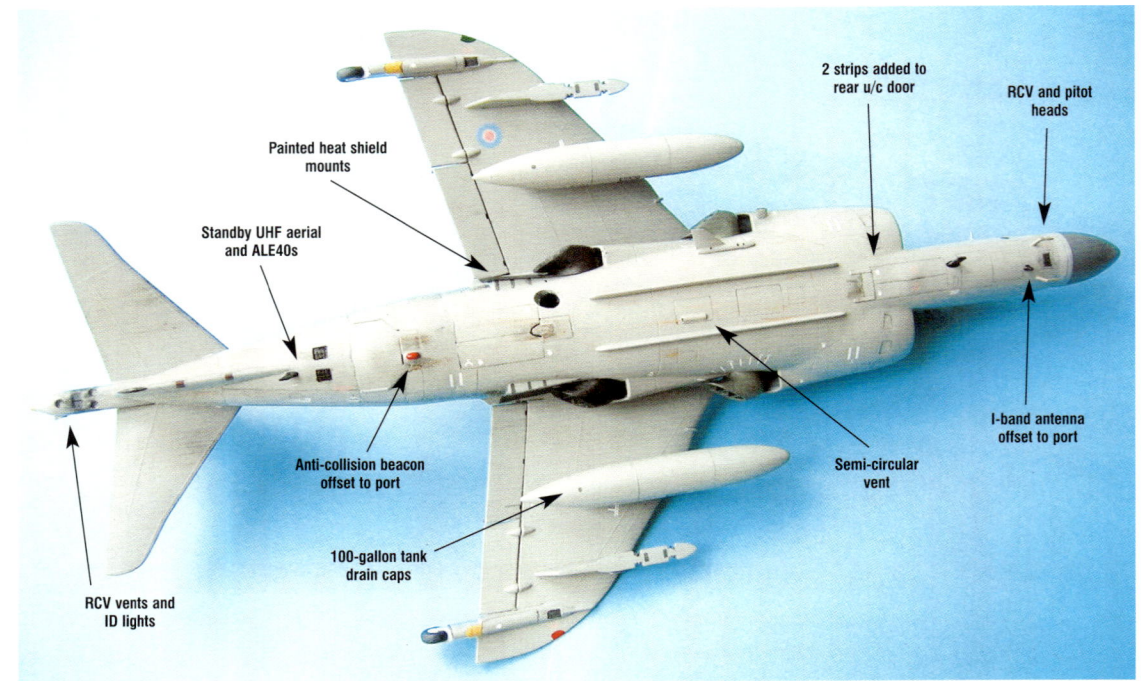

Painted heat shield mounts

2 strips added to rear u/c door

RCV and pitot heads

Standby UHF aerial and ALE40s

Anti-collision beacon offset to port

RCV vents and ID lights

100-gallon tank drain caps

Semi-circular vent

I-band antenna offset to port

Lower fuselage showing areas requiring filler. The hole is for a display stand to show the aircraft in flight

Upper fuselage areas showing where filler is required and the work done to the vortex generators on the wings

use are 42 and 43. By 2004-5 all SHARs had GPS fitted meaning the Doppler panels under the nose was removed, so kit decal 72 is not required. Some SHARs still retain the stencilling around the bay, so if possible refer to photos of the aircraft you are modelling.

Here we see an 899 Squadron F/A-2 built as an in-flight model. Note the white GPS antennae on the upper fuselage

- Fin and tailcone RWR covers: Tan 94
- All UHF, IFF, I-Band antennae: Matt Black 33
- Two underfin radar altimeter aerials: Matt Red Wine 73
- Underfin rear IFF notch aerial and bumper: Matt Black 33
- Fin VHF and HF notch antennae: Matt Black 33
  This runs along the top of the fin panel in front of where the RN logo sits and should be just over1mm wide. The fin tip leading edge antenna is of similar width
- Fin mounted pitot – rear 2/3rds: Satin Black 85
- RCVs and meshed vents, fin pressure head: Gunmetal 56
- Nose pitots and static vents: A 50:50 mix of 56/54
- Lights: Tailcone IDs – 2x silver; anti-collision beacons and port wing – red 19 + clear red; starboard wing – green 3 + clear green.

ZD613, the 800 Squadron decommissioning jet in 1:48 scale

Decaling

For MSG SHARs the kit decals and instructions are very comprehensive. For a 2004-6 period SHAR the style options to

ZH809 the 899 in the Anniversary Scheme, the so called 'Admirals Barge'

ZH803 in the markings of the final days of No.801 Squadron

Kits

The kits and accessories listed below represent only a small fraction of the many items released over the years that relate to this most popular of subjects. Present are a selection of those most current or most readily available, and as space precludes a more comprehensive selection it is the intention of this appendix to point the modeller towards those manufacturers most likely to be of help in this field, rather than to act as a definitive guide to available products.

DESCRIPTION	MANUFACTURER	KIT NUMBER	OPTIONS / NOTES
1/24			
Sea Harrier FRS.1	Airfix	20001	700A OEU; 800 + 801 NAS - pre-Falklands; 809 Phoenix; 899 DSG; 300 Sqn Ind Navy. Twin AIM-9s; Matra Magics. Notes: basic seat, poor fin RWR shape
1/48			
Sea Harrier FRS.1	Airfix	5101	XZ454/250 800 NAS, 1980; XZ455/000 801 NAS post Falklands, Sept 1982; ZE691/713 899 NAS 50th Anniversary Scheme. Notes: poor flap/aileron sizes and RWR fairings, raised panel lines, and innaccurate in parts – such as the nose panels. However, has the correct RN 2 rocket pods
Sea Harrier FRS.1	Hobby Craft	1571	Notes: not a particularly good kit but has nice undercarriage
Sea Harrier FRS.1	Tamiya	61026	800 Squadron markings. Notes: poor intake shape, overlarge vortex generators
Sea Harrier F/A.2	Airfix	6100	Markings for all units included. Notes: good overall shape but lacks upper anti-collision light and has suspect flap/aileron sizes
T4 Harrier	Maintrack / Heritage		
1/72			
Sea Harrier FRS.1	Hasegawa		XV457/104 899 NAS; XZ495/003 801 NAS; XZ457/14 800 NAS; ZA194/251 809 NAS. Notes: nose about 1 scale foot too short
Sea Harrier FRS.1	Hasegawa	235	899 50th Anniversary markings. Notes: Nose about 1 scale foot too short
Sea Harrier FRS.1	Matchbox	PK37 - 1st issue	XZ493/001 801 NAS / 300 Squadron Indian Navy. Notes: based on GR.1 kit – very basic detail, and the only current source of Indian decals in 1/72
Sea Harrier FRS.1	Matchbox	PK52 - 2nd issue	XZ493/001801 NAS (EDSG/white) and ZD614/124 800 NAS (DSG). Notes: as above
Sea Harrier FRS.1	Matchbox	40064 Revell issue	(Black box release) – XZ454/250 800 NAS (EDSG/White), XZ499/99809 NAS (MSG). Notes: Based on GR1 kit – crude detail, nice decals
Sea Harrier FRS.1	Italeri (Esci)	1236	700A NAS, 800NAS, Indian Navy. Notes: best FRS.1 in 1:72
Sea Harrier FRS.1	Fujimi		Original release had all EDSG/White schemes. Current (Japan only) release has 800 NAS Falklands markings
Sea Harrier FRS.1	Revell (Fujimi moulds)	4344	XZ500/127, 800 NAS, DSG
Harrier T.2/T.4	Heritage Aviation	HACK72006	Resin/white metal/vacform
Harrier T.4	Humbrol/Heller/Bobcat		XW269 4 Sqdn RAF Snap together kit available in 2 versions, later release has Matra pods and tanks. Notes: has erroneous ferry wingtips, no strakes/airbrake, has a tall fin with RWR, no RWR on tailboom and an indistinct windscreen
1/144			
Sea Harrier FRS.1	Crown/Revell		
Sea Harrier FRS.1	Minicraft	14425	

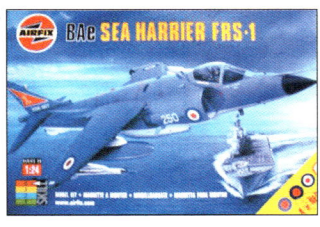

Accessories & Conversions Appendix **II**

DESCRIPTION	MANUFACTURER	REFERENCE	OPTIONS / DETAILS
1/24 SCALE CONVERSION & DETAIL SETS			
Sea Harrier FRS.1 detail set	Flightpath	FHP24005	Etched brass frets with resin cockpit, seats, AIM-9s, aeials, wing fences, airbrake details, undercarriage legs, wheels, ladder, chocks, canopy and screen
Harrier Intakes with dropped doors	Heritage Aviation	HAAC24001	
Harrier Wheels	Heritage Aviation	HAAC24002	Treaded tyres, handed mainwheels, all shown as under load
AMRAAM Missiles	Heritage Aviation	HAAC24004	
SHAR 190 Gallon Drop Tanks	Heritage Aviation	HAAC24005	
Sea Harrier FRS.1 cockpit set	Heritage Aviation	HAAC24006	
Sea Harrier FRS.1 conversion set	Heritage Aviation	HACV24000	
Sea Harrier F/A.2 conversion set	Heritage Aviation	HACV24001	
1/32 SCALE CONVERSION SET			
Sea Harrier FRS.1	John Wilkes		Basic outlines only will need engraving
1/48 SCALE CONVERSION & DETAIL SETS			
Sea Harrier FRS.1 detail set	Eduard	EDFE165	Etched parts for Tamiya kit – cockpit details – all panels, consoles and seat
Sea Harrier FRS.1 detail set	Eduard	48214	For the Airfix kit
Sea Harrier FRS.1 detail set	Flightpath	48068	Twin AIM-9 launchers and a fantastic cockpit
Sea Harrier FRS.1 / GR.3 detail set	Airwaves	SC48084	Etched brass parts – for Airfix kit
Sea Harrier F/A.2 detail set	Airwaves	SC48091	Etched brass parts for Airfix FA.2 including cockpit set, aerials, AIM-9 fins, tailplane sealing plates, tie-down rings, mesh covers
Harrier / Sea Harrier Nozzles	Airwaves	SC48102	Superb representations
Sea Harrier Ejector Seats	Airwaves	AES48027	Resin Seats
Sea Harrier F/A.2 detail & weapons	Flightpath	48069	Again an excellent cockpit
Sea Harrier FRS.1 Cockpit Set	NeOmega	C34	A beautiful set for Airfix kit which has everything
Harrier Intakes with dropped doors	Heritage Aviation	HAAC48001	
Harrier detail set	Heritage Aviation	HAAC48002	Intakes, nozzles, tailplanes, 190gal tanks
Sea Harrier Tanks	Heritage Aviation		2x 190 Gallon Wing Tanks
Intakes and Nozzles Set	Pavla Models	PAVU4820	Resin replacements
Control Surfaces	Pavla Models	PAVU4821	
T.2/4/8 conversion set	Heritage Aviation	HACV48010	For the Airfix GR.3 kit with resin, photo-etch, white metal and decals
Martin-Baker Mk 10 seat	NeOmega	E16-48	Superb resin seat
Martin-Baker Mk 10 seat	Airwaves	SC48027	Very nice FRS.1 and F/A.2 resin seat but needs the canopy breakers removing and sides of headrest modifying
1:72 SCALE CONVERSION & DETAIL SETS			
Sea Harrier FRS.1 detail set	Airwaves	72005	Etched parts
Sea Harrier F/A.2 detail set	Maintrack Models	7235	Resin set for Hasegawa Sea Harrier.
Sea Harrier F/A.2 conversion set	Model Alliance	CS-25	Decals included
Martin-Baker Mk10	Aeroclub	EJ011	2 FRS.1 and F/A.2 white-metal seats

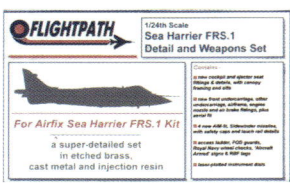
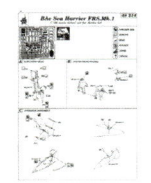

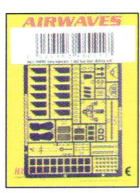

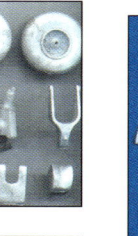
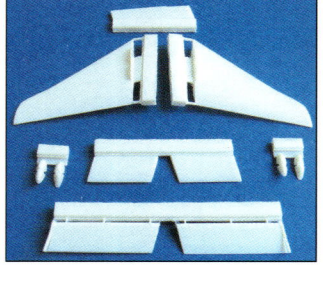
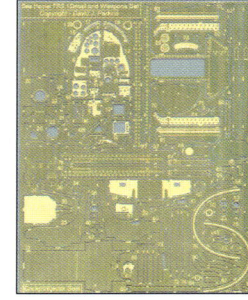

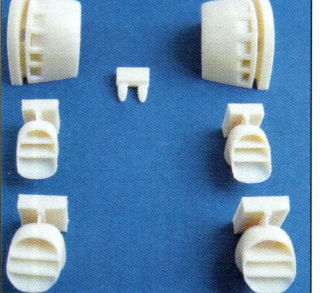

Decals

DESCRIPTION	MANUFACTURER	REFERENCE	OPTIONS / DETAILS	GENERAL COMMENTS
1/24				
Sea Harrier FRS.1	JumpJet	JJ24001	Post-Falklands schemes 800 and 801	
1/48				
Sea Harrier FRS.1	Aeromaster	48450	Pre-Falklands 700A OEU; 800, 801 and 899 Indian Navy	
Sea Harrier FRS.1	JumpJet	JJ48001	Post-Falklands schemes 800 and 801	
Sea Harrier FRS.1	SkyDecal	SKY4802	899 and 800 Squadron part of Multi-Harrier sheet	
Harrier T.8N	Model Alliance	MA48130	Black Harrier T.8N. Part of RAF/RN Trainers sheet	
Sea Harrier F/A.2	Model Alliance	MA48137	801 Squadron Omega Tail part of UK Air Arm Update Sheet	
Sea Harrier F/A.2	Model Alliance	MAS489007	800 Squadron Decommissioning Scheme	
Sea Harrier F/A.2	Model Alliance	MAS489008	899 Anniversary Scheme	
Sea Harrier F/A.2 & FRS.2	Model Alliance	MA72004	All Squadrons including Development Aircraft and AMRAAM Trials	
Falklands War	FCM	48MF	Hermes and Invincible Sea Harriers as part of Falklands Sheet	
1/72				
Sea Harrier FRS.1 Falklands 1982	Modeldecal	MD067		
Sea Harriers 800 / 801 / 899 NAS 1982/3	Modeldecal	MD070	Post-Falklands colours	
Sea Harriers 809 NAS 1982	Modeldecal	MD071	Illustrious deployment colours, part of Vulcan B.2 set	
809 NAS Sea Harrier Names	Modeldecal	MD075	Light Grey Harrier T.4N Sea Harrier names part of 15 + 16 Sqn Tornado set	
Sea Harrier FRS.1	Fineline	2005a	899 Squadron Anniversary aircraft	
Harrier T.8N	Model Alliance	MA72130	Black Harrier T.8N. Part of RAF/RN Trainers sheet	
Sea Harrier F/A.2	Model Alliance	MA72137	801 Squadron Omega Tail part of UK Air Arm Update Sheet	
Sea Harrier F/A.2	Model Alliance	MAS729007	800 Squadron Decommissioning Scheme	
Sea Harrier FRS.1s	Superscale	72393	XZ451 700A IFTU; XZ454 800 NAS; XZ457 899 NAS; XZ498 801 NAS	
Sea Harrier FA.2	Model Alliance	MA-017	801 NAS ZD613/002	
Sea Harrier FRS.1	JumpJet	JJ72001	Post-Falklands schemes 800 and 801	
Sea Harrier FRS.1	Condor	72005	Part of Multi-Falklands sheet	
Sea Harrier F/A.2	Model Alliance	MAS729008	899 Anniversary Scheme	
Sea Harrier F/A.2 & FRS.2	Model Alliance	MA72004	All Squadrons including Development Aircraft and AMRAAM Trials	
Falklands War	FCM	48MF	Hermes and Invincible Sea Harriers as part of Falklands set	

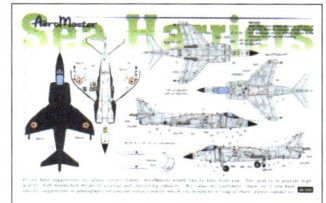
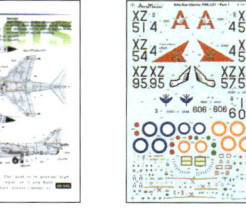

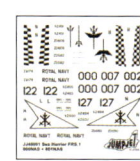

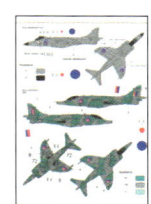
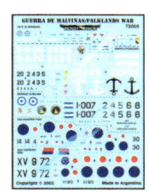

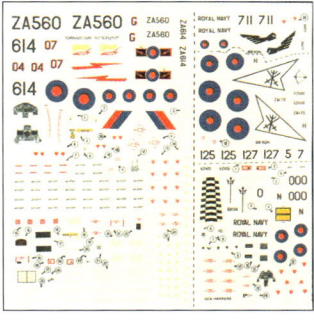
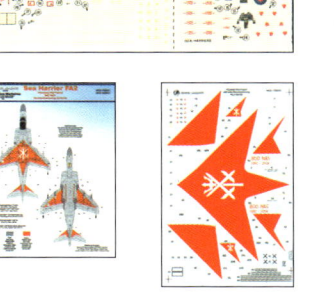
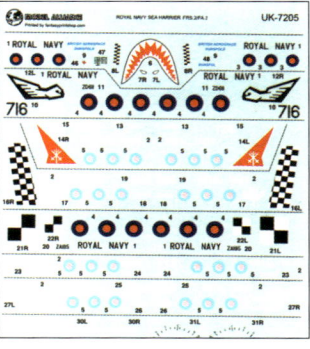
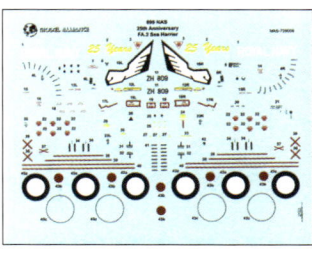
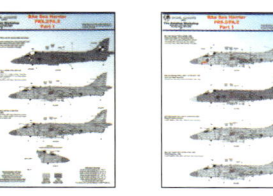

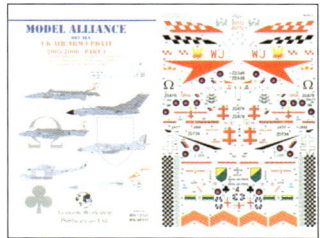

Harrier Histories

Single-seaters

Serial	Type	c/n	1st flight

XZ438   FRS.1   41H-912001   30/12/78

BAe & A&AEE development aircraft. Delivered to 809 NAS 19 Apr 1982. Crashed at Yeovilton 17 May 1982 while trialling 330 gallon drop tanks due to fuel imbalance on taking off from ski jump. Lt Cdr Poole ejected successfully.

XZ439   F/A.2   41H-912002/DB2   30/3/79

BAe & A&AEE development aircraft. First aircraft to ramp launch at sea on 30 Oct 1980. Delivered to RN 19 Apr 1982. Converted to FRS.2 in Oct 1989 as second development aircraft. Shot down three QF-106 drones during AMRAAM trials in 1993. Departed St Athan by road 11 Nov 2004 to Everett Aero at Sproughton. Has been sold to Art Nallis who plans to fly the aircraft in the USA. Shipped from Seaforth Docks during Feb 2006. Allocated US civil registration N94422.

XZ440   F/A.2   41H-912003/P34   6/6/79

BAe & A&AEE development aircraft. Delivered 03 Jun 1982. Conversion to service 27 May 1988. Fuel system over-pressurized 29 Oct 1989. Converted to F/A.2 and damage repaired 1991. Delivered to SFDO Culdrose 14 Feb 2006.

XZ450   FRS.1   41H-912004   20/8/78

BAe & A&AEE development aircraft for Sea Eagle. Shot down by AAA 04 May 1982 over Goose Green, Falkland Islands. Pilot Lt Taylor was killed.

XZ451   FRS.1   41H-912005   25/5/79

First production aircraft; delivered 18 Jun 1979. Three confirmed kills during Falklands campaign. Crashed 01 Dec 1989 near Sardinia following control failure. Pilot Lt Auckland ejected successfully.

XZ452   FRS.1   41H-912006   17/8/79

Delivered 12 Oct 1979. One confirmed kill during Falklands campaign. Lost 06 May 1982 in suspected collision with XZ453 while on CAP over Falklands. Pilot Lt Cdr Eyton-Jones was killed.

XZ453   FRS.1   41H-912007   5/12/79

Delivered 31 Jan 1980. One confirmed kill over Falklands. Lost 06 May 1982 in suspected collision with XZ452 while on CAP over Falklands. Pilot Lt Curtis of 801 NAS was killed.

XZ454   FRS.1   41H-912008   12/12/79

Delivered 15 Feb 1980. Crashed in English Channel off Lizard Point on 01 Dec 1980 after striking top of ramp on HMS Invincible during a flypast. Pilot Lt Cdr Blissett ejected successfully.

XZ455   F/A.2   41H-912009/P8   9/10/79

Delivered 09 Oct 1979. Two confirmed kills during Falklands campaign. Converted to FA.2 Feb 1994. Crashed in Adriatic Sea 50km off Bosnia 14 Feb 1996. Pilot Lt Phillips ejected successfully. Wreck stored at Everett Aero, Sproughton.

XZ456   FRS.1   41H-912010   9/11/79

Delivered 04 Jan 1980. No kills during Falklands conflict. Crashed near Port Stanley on 01 Jun 1982 after being hit by Roland SAM.

XZ457   F/A.2   41H-912011/P10   15/12/79

Delivered 31 Jan 1980. Four confirmed kills during Falklands campaign. Converted to F/A.2 in Feb 1994. Crashed at Yeovilton 20 Oct 1995 after engine exploded on takeoff. The airframe now in the Boscombe Down Aviation Collection.

XZ458   FRS.1   41H-912012   10/1/80

Delivered 22 Feb 1980. No kills during Falklands conflict. Crashed near Fort William, Scotland 01 Dec 1984 after low-level birdstrike caused engine failure. Pilot Lt Collier ejected successfully.

XZ459   F/A.2   41H-912013/P18   21/3/80

Delivered 15 May 1980. No kills during Falklands conflict. Converted to F/A.2 1994. In storage at St Athan 11 Apr 2002. Gone to Aerospace Logistics Charlwood.

XZ460   FRS.1   41H-912014   10/4/80

Delivered to RN 29 May 1980. No kills during Falklands conflict. Crashed off Sardinia 08 May 1990 - flew into sea after taking off from HMS Invincible. Lt Holmes of 800 NAS was killed.

XZ491   FRS.1   41H-912015   20/6/80

Delivered to RN 14 Apr 1982. No kills during Falklands conflict. Crashed off Benbecula on 16 Apr 1986 after running out of fuel. Pilot Lt Sinclair ejected successfully.

XZ492   F/A.2   41H-912016/P20   25/10/80

Delivered 29 Dec 1980. One confirmed kill during Falklands campaign. Converted to F/A.2 1994. Crashed in Mediterranean Sea 10 Dec 1996 after engine failure. Pilot ejected. Wreckage stored at Faygate.

XZ493   FRS.1   41H-912017   26/11/80

Delivered 06 Jan 1981. No kills during Falklands conflict. Ditched in Adriatic Sea 15 Dec 1994 after control failure during hover. Pilot Lt Kistruck ejected successfully. On display at FAA Museum Yeovilton (restored using parts from XV760).

XZ494   F/A.2   41H-912018/P30   24/10/80

Delivered 05 Dec 1980. Led first attack on Port Stanley during Falklands campaign on 01 May 1982. Converted to F/A.2 1995. Stored at Everett Aero, Sproughton.

XZ495   F/A.2   41H-912019/P4   3/2/81

Delivered 01 Mar 1981. Converted to FA.2 Oct 1993. Crashed in Bristol Channel 05 Jan 1994 after engine failure. Pilot Lt Wilson ejected successfully.

XZ496   FRS.1   41H-912020   9/12/80

Delivered 11 Feb 1981. One confirmed kill over Falklands. Ditched in the North Sea off Norway 16 Mar 1984 after engine failure.

XZ497   F/A.2   41H-912021/P1   2/4/82

Delivered 22 Apr 1982. Converted to F/A.2 Mar 1993 (first production conversion). Seen at Aerospace Logistics, Charlwood late Mar 2005.

XZ498   FRS.1   41H-912022   26/3/81

Delivered 13 May 1981. Shot down over Gorazde, Bosnia, on 16 Apr 1994 by Bosnian Serb SAM. Pilot Lt Richardson ejected successfully.

XZ499   F/A.2   41H-912023/P32   12/6/81

Delivered to RN 22 Jul 1981. One confirmed kill during Falklands campaign. Converted to F/A.2 1995. Del to FAAM store at Cobham Hall (Yeovilton) 13 Nov 2002.

XZ500   FRS.1   41H-912024   28/5/81

Delivered to RN 05 Aug 1981. One confirmed kill during Falklands conflict. Crashed in Bay of Biscay 15 Jun 1983 after control failure during inverted spin. Pilot Lt Hargreaves ejected successfully.

ZA174   FRS.1   41H-912025   15/9/81

Delivered to RN 16 Nov 1981. Written off 29 May 1982 in south Atlantic near Falkland Is. Slid off HMS Invincible in heavy seas. Pilot Lt Broadwater ejected successfully.

ZA175   F/A.2   41H-912026/P23   28/10/81

Delivered to RN 07 Dec 1981. One confirmed kill during Falklands conflict. Converted to F/A.2 1996. Arrived Norfolk and Suffolk Aviation Museum, Flixton, 22 Jul 2004.

ZA176   F/A.2   41H-912027/P6   29/1/81

Delivered to RN 16 Nov 1981. No kills during Falklands conflict. Landed on Spanish freighter after NAVHARS failure 07 Jun 1983. Converted to F/A.2 Nov 1993. Arrived Newark Air Museum on 21 Jul 2004. See a more extensive service history.

ZA177   FRS.1   41H-912028   5/12/81

Delivered to RN 06 Jan 1982. Two confirmed kills during Falklands conflict. Crashed at Cattistock, Dorset 21 Jan 1983 after failing to recover from spin. Pilot Lt Fox ejected successfully.

ZA190   FRS.1   41H-912029   5/11/81

Delivered to RN 07 Dec 1981. Two confirmed kills during Falklands conflict. Crashed in Atlantic Ocean NW of Ireland on 15 Oct 1987 after bird strike.

ZA191   FRS.1   41H-912030   4/12/81

Delivered to RN 05 Jan 1982. One shared kill during Falklands conflict. Crashed in English Channel off Lyme Regis 04 Oct 1989 after hitting HMS Ark Royal's mast during flypast. Pilot Lt Simmonds-Short NAS ejected successfully.

ZA192   FRS.1   41H-912031   29/1/82

Delivered 03 Mar 1982. Three shared kills during Falklands campaign. Flew 23 operational sorties. Crashed in south Atlantic 23 May 1982 after engine exploded on take-off from HMS Hermes near the Falklands. Lt Cdr Batt was killed.

ZA193   FRS.1   41H-912032   13/1/82

Delivered Feb 1982. One confirmed kill during Falklands campaign. Ditched in Mediterranean Sea off Cyprus 28 May 1992 after losing a nozzle. Pilot Lt Watson of ejected successfully.

ZA194   FRS.1   41H-912033   23/4/82

Delivered 28 Apr 1982. One confirmed kill during Falklands campaign. Crashed West Knighton, Dorset on 20 Oct 1983 after loss of control. Pilot Maj O'Hara (USMC) ejected successfully.

ZA195   F/A.2   41H-912034/DB1   9/9/83

BAE and A&AEE development aircraft. Delivered 25 Jan 1984. F/A.2 conversion prototype. To FAST Farnborough 09 Mar 2006 for display.

ZD578   F/A.2   41H-912041/P22   7/3/85

Delivered to RN 27 Mar 1985. Converted to F/A.2 1994. Placed at the gate at the Pyle Lane entrance to RNAS Yeovilton on 04 Dec 2002. The aircraft carries markings from both 800 and 801 NAS.

ZD579   F/A.2   41H-912042/P14   9/4/85

Delivered 20 May 1985. Converted to F/A.2 1993. To Shawbury for storage 10 Jan 2006.

Sailing out from Portsmouth, the crowded flight deck of HMS Hermes
(© FAA Museum)

ZD580 F/A.2 41H-912043/P17 19/6/85

Delivered 10 Jul 1985. Converted to F/A.2 1994. Stored at Everett Aero, Sproughton.

ZD581 F/A.2 41H-912044/P31 14/6/85

Delivered 29 Aug 1985. Converted to F/A.2 1994. To RN Fire School Predannack 01 Sep 2004.

ZD582 F/A.2 41H-912045/P5 10/8/85

Delivered 07 October 1985. Converted to F/A.2 1995. Stored at Shawbury 15 June 2005. Now sold to private owner.

ZD607 F/A.2 41H-912046/P25 12/8/85

Delivered 06 Nov 1985. Converted to F/A.2 1995. St Athan BDRT 08 Jul 02. Delivered to HMS Sultan 27 May 2005 for disposal.

ZD608 F/A.2 41H-912047/P13 20/9/85

Delivered 17 Oct 1985. Converted to F/A.2 Aug 1994. To St Athan as spares source 19 Nov 2002. Delivered to Aerospace Logistics Charlwood 02 Nov 2005.

ZD609 FRS.1 41H-912048 19/10/85

Delivered 11 Dec 1985. Crashed near Chepstow on 10 May 1991 after control failure. Pilot Lt Mitchell ejected but sustained serious injuries.

ZD610 F/A.2 41H-912049/P27 5/11/85

Delivered 11 Dec 1985. Converted to F/A.2 1996. To Dunsfold for preservation 11 Oct 2005.

ZD611 F/A.2 41H-912050/P15 15/11/85

Delivered 11 Dec 1982. Converted to F/A.2 1994. At SFDO Culdrose.

ZD612 F/A.2 41H-912051/P7 6/12/85

Delivered 09 Jan 1986. Converted to F/A.2 1993. Assigned to ground instruction at RNAS Yeovilton. Now at Topsham near Exeter.

ZD613 F/A.2 41H-912052/P16 17/12/85

Delivered 04 Nov 19865. Converted to F/A.2 Nov 1994. 800 Decommissioning markings. In storage at Shawbury June 2005. Sold to to WSV Metals, Nov 2005.

ZD614 F/A.2 41H-912053/P26 14/3/86

Delivered 07 Apr 1986. Converted to F/A.2 1995. Crashed into the River Yeo after a landing accident at RNAS Yeovilton on 08 Oct 2001. Pilot ejected. Aircraft deemed not repairable; taken to St Athan dump 25 Jun 02. Departed St Athan 08 Oct 2002 for Everett Aero, Sproughton.

ZD615 F/A.2 41H-912054/P3 15/5/86

Delivered 19 Jun 1986. Converted to F/A.2 Aug 1993. To St Athan for storage 04 Apr 2002. To Aerospace Logistics Charlwood 01 Nov 2005.

ZE690 F/A.2 B49/P12

Delivered 13 Nov 1987. Converted to F/A.2 1994. Delivered to SFDO Culdrose 29 Mar 2006.

ZE691 F/A.2 B50/P19

Delivered 23 Nov 1987. Converted to F/A.2 1994. Stored Everett Aero, Sproughton.

ZE692 F/A.2 B51/P21

Delivered 08 Dec 1987. Converted to F/A.2 Aug 1995. Del to SFDO Culdrose 23 Feb 2006.

ZE693 F/A.2 B52/P24

Delivered 05 Jan 1988. Converted to F/A.2 1995. Withdrawn from use 2005. Now in the grounds of the Snipe Inn at Duckinfield, Cheshire.

ZE694 F/A.2 B53/P28

Delivered 08 Mar 1988. Converted to F/A.2 1996. Now in Midland Air Museum Baginton.

ZE695 F/A.2 B54/P2

Delivered 02 Feb 1988. Second F/A.2 conversion in Apr 1993. Never saw service as an FRS.1. Crashed on landing at RNAS Yeovilton 26 Jul 2000. Front end of aircraft burnt, CAT.4/5 damage. Stored Everett Aero, Sproughton.

ZE696 F/A.2 B55/P9

Delivered 06 April 1988. Converted to F/A.2 1994. Stored at Shawbury 2005 sold to Witham Specialist Vehicles.

ZE697 F/A.2 B56/P11 25/3/88

Delivered 13 May 1988. Converted to F/A.2 1993. Stored at St Athan. Del to Aerospace Logistics Charlwood 19 Oct 2005.

ZE698 F/A.2 B57/P29

Delivered 16 Aug 1988. Flew last operational FRS.1 sortie on 18 Feb 1995. Converted to F/A.2 1995. Noted at Aerospace Logistics, Charlwood, Mar 2005.

ZH796 F/A.2 NB01

Delivered 20 Oct 1995. To Shawbury 29 Mar 2006.

Seen post-Falklands, the all-over warpaint has transformed the aircraft, and gone are the flamboyant markings
(© Denis Calvert)

ZH797 F/A.2 NB02

Delivered 14 Dec 1995. Del to SFDO Culdrose 23 Feb 2006.

ZH798 F/A.2 NB03

Delivered13 Mar 1996. To Shawbury 13 Dec 2005 for storage.

ZH799 F/A.2 NB04

Delivered 19 Mar 1996. Arr St Athan from Warton 16 May 2002 for storage. Sold to Everett Aero. Now at Cold War Museum, Bentwaters.

ZH800 F/A.2 NB05

Delivered 05 Jun 1996. Marked as ZH801/001 for display at RAF Cottesmore.

ZH801 F/A.2 NB06

Marked as ZH800/123 for display at RAF Cottesmore. Dep Yeovilton 28 Mar 2006.

ZH802 F/A.2 NB07

Delivered to RN 01 Oct 1996. Withdrawn from use 2005. Del to SFDO Culdrose as fire/rescue trainer, 21 Feb 2006.

ZH803 F/A.2 NB08

Delivered to RN 08 Nov 1996. To Shawbury 29 Mar 2006.

ZH804 F/A.2 NB09

Delivered to RN 18 Dec 1997. To Shawbury 29 Mar 2006.

ZH805 F/A.2 NB10

Delivered to RN 29 Jan 1997. Crashed into the Bristol Channel 11 Jun 2003 while on an air test. Pilot Lt Cdr Schwab ejected having failed to recover the aircraft from an uncontrollable spin.

ZH806 F/A.2 NB11

Del to Shawbury for storage 28 Jul 2005. Del to Everett Aero at Bentwaters 02 Feb 2006. At Cold War Museum at Bentwaters.

ZH807 F/A.2 NB12

Suffered CAT.4/5 damage at Yeovilton on 01 May 2002 when its undercarriage retracted on the ground. Stored at St Athan. Delivered to GJD Services, Farnborough 01 Sep 2005. Cockpit is with a private owner at Newport, IOW.

ZH808 F/A.2 NB13 30/10/97

Delivered 18 Dec 1997. Made emergency landing at RAF Akrotiri Cyprus March 2005 after fuel leak caught fire. Now at Chorio near Larnaca after being sold to local scrap merchant.

ZH809 F/A.2 NB14

Delivered 02 Feb 1998. Carried special 25th anniversary colour scheme in 2004/5. Withdrawn from use 2005. Del to SFDO Culdrose 07 Mar 2006.

ZH810 F/A.2 NB15

Placed in open storage at Yeovilton 15 Dec 04. Sold to Everett Aero, Sproughton.

ZH811 F/A.2 NB16

Delivered 17 Sep 1998. To Shawbury 29 Mar 2006.

ZH812 F/A.2 NB17

Delivered 12 Nov 1998. To Shawbury 29 Mar 2006.

ZH813 F/A.2 NB18

Delivered 18 Jan 1999. To Shawbury by 10 Mar 2006.

Two-seaters

Serial	Type	c/n	1st flight
XZ445	T.4A(N)	41H-212031	12/3/79

Delivered 10 Jul 1987. Crashed on landing 09 May 1990 and was repaired. Crashed 23 Feb 1996 at Leigh Hill near Taunton. Lt Cdr Auckland and passenger CPO Brooks were killed.

ZB603	T.8	41H-212035/T4	11/5/83

Built as T.4 for the RAF. To 899 NAS 29 Oct 1991. Heavy landing 02 May 1995, subsequently repaired and upgraded to T.8. To SFDO Culdrose 06 Mar 2006.

ZB604	T.8	41H-212036/T5	8/8/83

Built as T.4N and delivered 21 May 1983. Fifth T.8 upgrade. Withdrawn Apr 2005. Departed Shawbury 09 Mar 2006 by road for display at RAF Wittering.

ZB605	T.8	41H-212037/T1	7/10/83

Built as T.4N and delivered 09 Nov 1983. First flew on 27 Jul 1994 as T.8 and redelivered Oct 1994. Crashed on takeoff at RAF Wittering 05 Dec 2002. Instructor pilot Lt Cdr 'Jak' London was killed.

ZB606	T.4N	41H-212038	26/11/83

Delivered Jan 1984. Crashed 07 Feb 1985. Pilot Lt Cdr George and passenger Midshipman Norman were both killed.

ZD990	T.8	212043	19/5/87

Delivered 25 Mar 1997 as a T.8. To SFDO Culdrose 15 Mar 2006.

ZD991	T.8	41H-212044	13/5/87

Delivered 09 June 1997 after conversion to T.8. Written off 24 Jun 1997 after engine exploded on take-off. Stored Everett Aero, Sproughton.

ZD992	T.8	41H-212045/T2	9/7/87

Delivered 13 Mar 1996 after T.8 conversion. Repaired after wheels-up landing on 11 Jul 1997. Crashed on takeoff from ramp at RNAS Yeovilton 16 Nov 2000. Lt Walsh and Lt Blackmore both ejected successfully.

ZD993	T.8	41H-212046/T3	13/7/87

Delivered 01 Nov 1994. Suffered heavy landing mid-June 2001. Made last T.8 movement from Yeovilton 20 Mar 2006.

Falklands Sea Harriers

Guide to Camouflage and Markings

Carrier Group - Sqn Serial (size and location)	Conflict scheme	Fin/Side Codes and colours *800/899 wore 12", *801 wore 16"			Fin Emblem on departure Royal Navy	Airbrake Code	Outrigger Code 801 only
		Departure	Conflict	Return			
Hermes - 800 NAS		**(White)**	**(Black or Roundel Blue)**			**12"**	
XZ492	EDSG	H / 123	23	23	800	3	
XZ459	EDSG	H / 125	25	25	800	5	
XZ460	EDSG	H / 126	26	26	800	6	
XZ496	EDSG	H / 127	27	27	800	7	
XZ500	EDSG	H / 130	30	30	800	0	
XZ450	EDSG	50 (fin)	50	Lost	None	None	
ZA192	EDSG	None	92	Lost	None	None	
ZA193	EDSG	None	93	93	None	None	
Hermes - 899 NAS		**(White)**				**12"**	
XZ455	EDSG	VL / 712	12	000	899	2	
XZ457	EDSG	VL / 714	14	14	899	4	
XZ494	EDSG	None / 716	16	008	899	None	
ZA191	EDSG	None / 718	18	18	None	8	
Hermes - 809 NAS							
XZ499 (3" fuselage)	MSG/BG	None	99	99	809	None	
ZA176 (4" ventral fin)	MSG/BG	None	76	76	809	None	
ZA177 (3" fuselage)	MSG/BG	None	77	77	809	None	
ZA194 (4" ventral fin)	MSG/BG	None	94	94	809	None	
Invincible - 801 NAS		**(White)**				**16"**	**(Black/White)**
XZ493	EDSG	N / 001	001	001	801	1	1
XZ495	EDSG	N / 003	003	003	801	3	3
ZA175	EDSG	N / 004	004	004	801	4	4
XZ498	EDSG	N / 005	005	005	801	5	5
Invincible - 899 NAS		**(White)**				**16"**	
XZ451	EDSG	VL / 710	006	006	899	6	None / 6
XZ452	EDSG	VL / 711	007	Lost	899	7	None > 7
XZ456	EDSG	None / 713	008	Lost	899	8	None > 8
XZ453	EDSG	VL / 715	009	Lost	899	9	None > 9
Invincible - 809 NAS		**Pale Blue**				**16"**	**(White)**
ZA174 (3" fuselage)	MSG/BG	None	000	Lost	809	0	None > 0
XZ491 (3" fuselage)	MSG/BG	None	002	N/A*	809	2	None > 2
XZ458 (3" fuselage)	MSG/BG	None	007	N/A*	809	7	None >7
ZA190 (3" fuselage)	MSG/BG	None	009	009	809	9	None >9

EDSG - Extra Dark Sea Grey BS381C:640; MSG - Medium Sea Grey BS381C:637; BG - Barley Grey BS4800:18B.21; Roundel Blue BS381C:110; Roundel Red BS381C:538
EDSG - EDSG overall aircraft - the original white undersurfaces, whether brush painted - Hermes, or sprayed - Invincible, appear slightly lighter than the original uppersurfaces; squadron markings and RN titles show as lighter too; underside stencils often overpainted except for trestle marking bars. White portions of roundels were overpainted with Roundel Blue, which shows lighter in photos. 4" high black serials in standard position on ventral fin.
MSG/BG aircraft - the overpainted fin markings - 809 Sqn emblem and RN titles - appear a slightly darker shade of MSG on both Air Groups' SHARs. Intake interiors were satin white, but on return to UK ZA190's were MSG.

Red red X alignment	Actions (*Damaged, **Shared)	Pilot's Name on departure	Other markings
		(White, both sides)	
Centre-line	21-May, Skyhawk, Lt Cdr Neill Thomas	LT Cdr AD Auld	
Aircraft beacon		Lt Cdr GJ Ramsay	Retained underwing serials
Centre-line			White strips either side of front u/c doors
Aircraft beacon	21-May, Skyhawk, Lt Cdr Mike Blissett		Yellow wing stripe
Centre-line	21-May, Skyhawk, Flt Lt John Leeming	Lt M Hale	
Centre-line			
Aircraft beacon	23-May, Puma, A-109A**, Flt Lt David Morgan		
Aircraft beacon	24-May, Dagger, Lt Dave Smith"		Retained R/W/B underwing roundels
Aircraft beacon			
Aircraft beacon	01-May, Dagger, Flt Lt Robert Penfold;		899 zap on nose, white strips as XZ460
	21-May, Dagger, Lt Cdr Rod Frederiksen		
Centre-line	21-May, 2x Skyhawk(1*), Lt Clive Morrell;		
	21-May, 2x Dagger, Lt Cdr Andy Auld		
Centre-line		Maj W McAtee USMC	899 zap on nose
Aircraft beacon	23-May, A-109A**, Flt Lt John Leeming		
N/A	08-Jun, Skyhawk, Lt Dave Smith		
N/A			
N/A	08-Jun, 2x Skyhawk, Flt Lt David Morgan		
N/A	23-May, Dagger, Lt Mike Hale		Carried standard black underwing serials
		(White, starboard only)	
Centre-line		Lt Cdr ND Ward	
Centre-line			
Aircraft beacon	01-May, Canberra*, Lt Cdr Mike Broadwater;		
	21-May, Dagger, Lt Cdr 'Sharkey' Ward		
Aircraft beacon			Yellow wing stripe
Aircraft beacon		**(White, starboard only)**	
Aircraft beacon	01-May, Canberra, Lt Alan Curtis;		Top 5 angle nozzle markings white
	21-May, Pucara, Lt Cdr 'Sharkey' Ward;		
	01-Jun, Hercules, Lt Cdr 'Sharkey' Ward		
Aircraft beacon	01-May, Mirage, Flt Lt Paul Barton	Flt Lt PC Barton	Yellow wing stripe
Aircraft beacon			
Aircraft beacon	01-May, Mirage*, Lt Steve Thomas		899 zap on nose, 3 Sqn zap stbd fuse
N/A			
N/A			*Transferred direct to 809NAS on Illustrious
N/A			*Transferred direct to 809NAS on Illustrious
N/A	21-May, 2x Dagger, Lt Steve Thomas		MSG intakes on return to UK

Sea Harrier Bibliography

Books

Hostile Skies
David Morgan
Orion Publishing
ISBN 297846450

A Maverick at War – Sea Harrier over the Falklands
Nigel 'Sharkey' Ward
Phoenix
ISBN 304355429

Falklands Air War
Chris Hobson
Midland
ISBN 1857801261

Aeroguide No.3 Sea Harrier FRS.1
Roger Chesnau
Linewrights

Aeroguide No.32 Sea Harrier
Roger Chesnau
Ad Hoc Publications
ISBN 946958440

The Sharp End
Neil Mercer
Airlife
ISBN 1853105449

Sea Harrier The Last All-British Fighter
Jamie Hunter
Midland
ISBN 1857802071

Harrier – The Vertical Reality
Roy Brabrook
RAFBF
ISBN 189980840

Ski-Jump to Victory
John Godden
Brasseys
ISBN 8311679

World Air Power Journal
Various
Aerospace Publishing

Aircraft Illustrated Special – Harrier
Dennis J Calvert
Ian Allan
ISBN 711018863

The Fleet Air Arm
Neil Mercer
Airlife

Sea Harrier & AV-8B
Robert Jackson
Blandford Press

Harrier at War
Alfred Price
Ian Allan

The Harrier Story
Anthony Thornborough & Peter Davies
NI Press

Battle for the Falklands 3 Air Forces
Roy Braybrook
Osprey

Yeovilton – Defenders of the Fleet
Mike Verrier
Osprey Superbase 22

Bae/McDonnel Douglas Harrier
Andy Evans
Crowood Press
ISBN 1861261055

Harrier
Francis K Mason
PSL

Harrier & Sea Harrier
Roy Brabrook
Osprey Air Combat

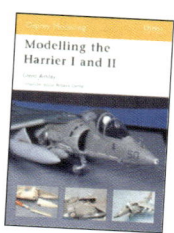

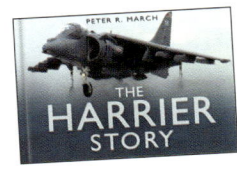

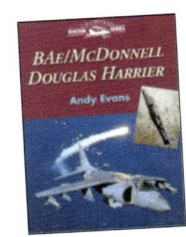

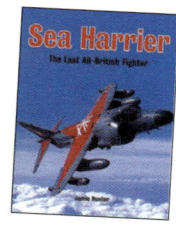

Magazine Articles

Sea Harrier Specials
Dick Ward
Scale Models International
February 1983

Scale Models International
March 1983

Bae Sea Harrier FRS.1 & F/A.2
Andy Evans
Scale Aircraft Modelling August 2002

War In the Falklands
Paul Jackson
Scale Aircraft Modelling December 1982

SHAR Scoreboard
Keith A Saunders
Scale Aircraft Modelling September 2000

Bae Sea Harrier F/A.2
Andy Evans
Model Aircraft Monthly August 2002

Flight Deck – Falklands Edition
Fleet Air Arm
FAA Publication 1982

Sea Harrier School
Mike Gaines
Flight International October 1985

Sea Harrier Operations in the Falklands
George Baldwin
Air Pictorial December 1982

Sea Harrier Train ing
T. Malcolm English
Air Pictorial October 1986

Index

Please note: this index does not reference appendices, walkarounds or tables.

In the shadow of its replacement, the Harrier GR.9 an F/A.2 gets airborne
(© Royal Navy)

With its Phoenix markings removed an 809 Harrier prepares for a CAP
(© BAE Systems)

Sunset on the SHAR!
(© Royal Navy)

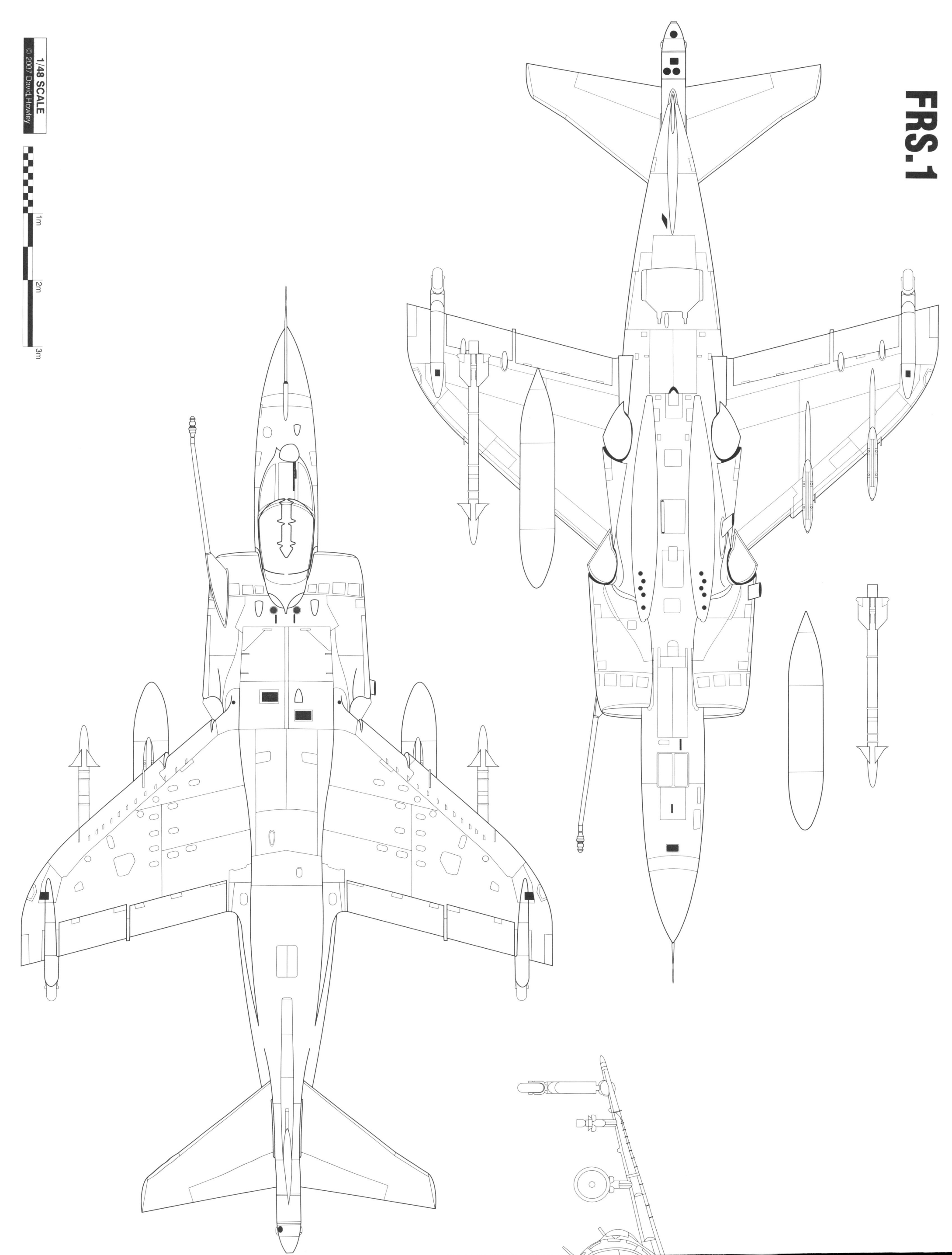

1m
2m
3m

FRS.1

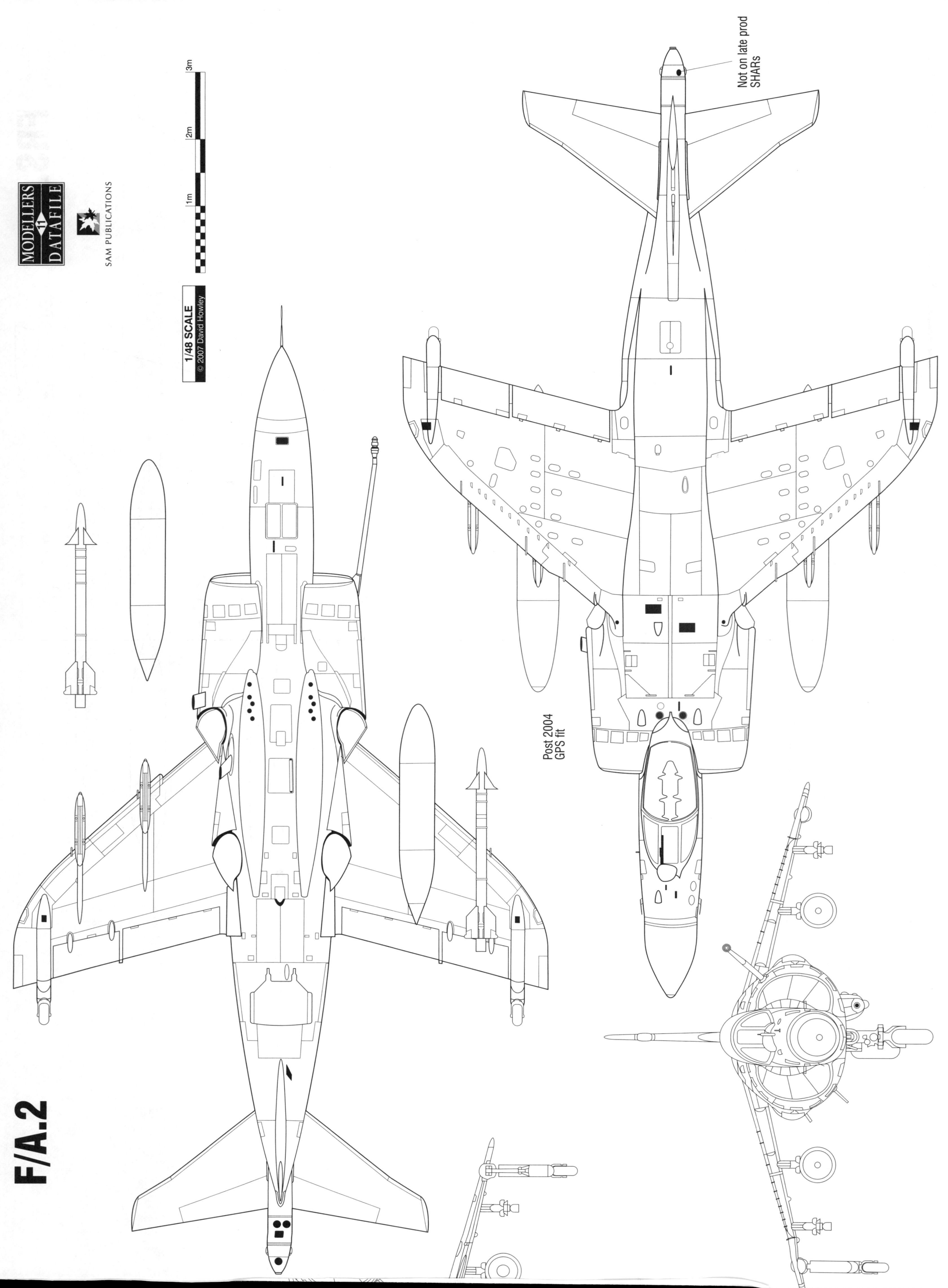

F/A.2

3m

2m

1m

1/48 SCALE
© 2007 David Howley

Not on late prod
SHARs

Post 2004
GPS fit

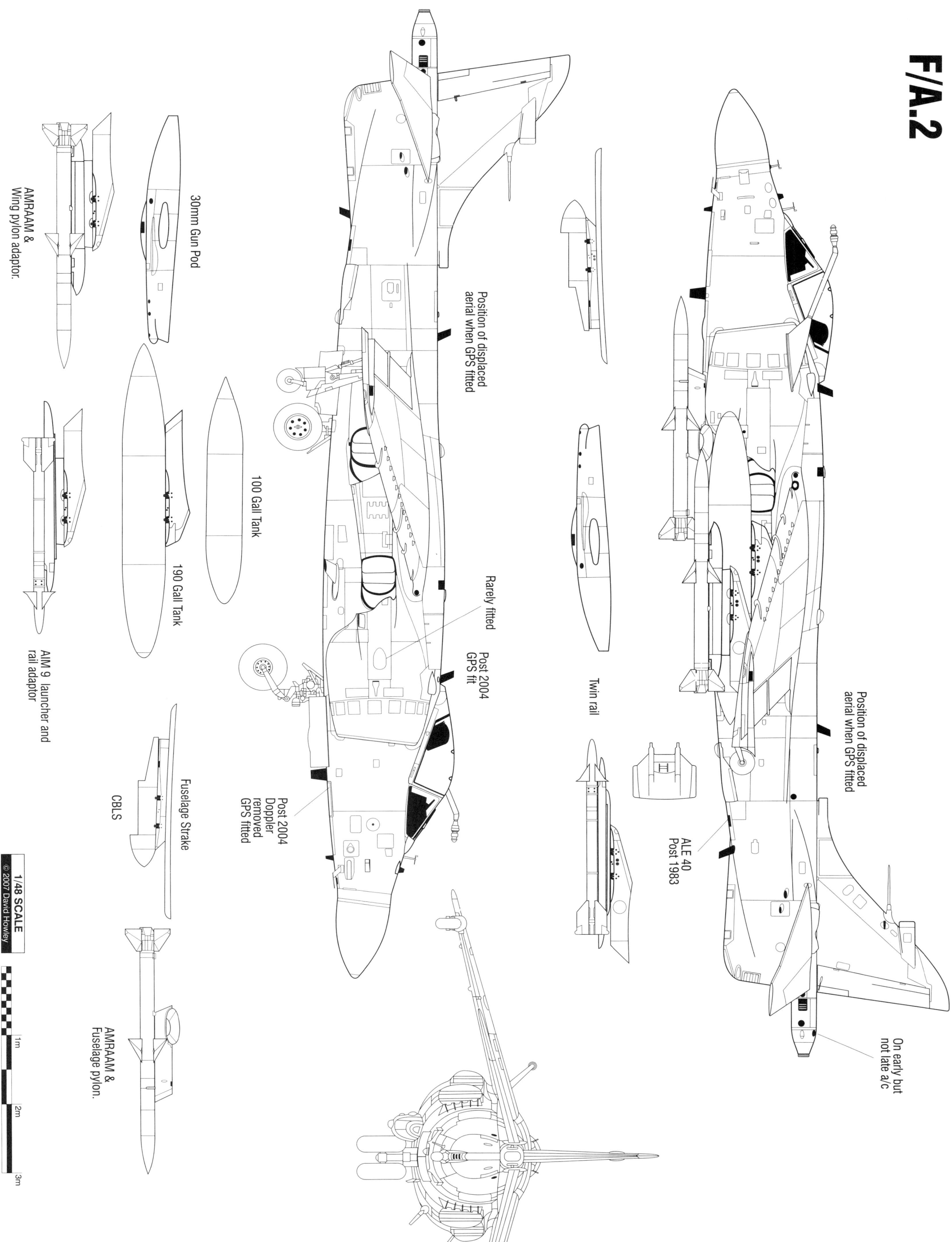

F/A.2

AMRAAM &
Wing pylon adaptor.

30mm Gun Pod

100 Gall Tank

190 Gall Tank

AIM 9 launcher and
rail adaptor

CBLS

Fuselage Strake

AMRAAM &
Fuselage pylon.

Position of displaced
aerial when GPS fitted

Rarely fitted

Post 2004
GPS fit

Post 2004
Doppler
removed
GPS fitted

Twin rail

ALE 40
Post 1983

Position of displaced
aerial when GPS fitted

On early but
not late a/c

1m

2m

3m

FRS.1

Vent fairing
late FRS1

ALE 40
Post 1983

AIM-9L

Initial production
100 Gall Tank
with fins.

AIM-9G

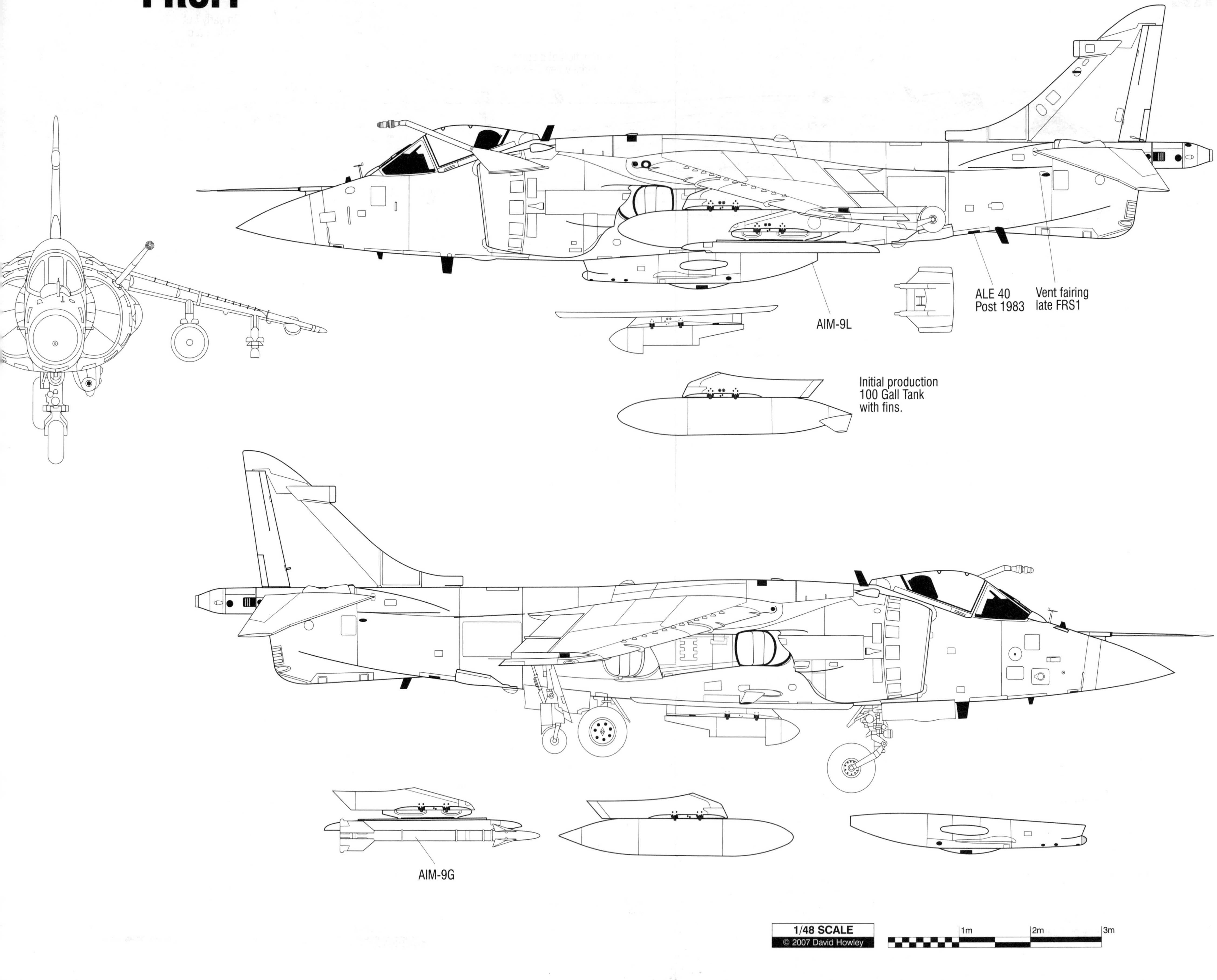

1/48 SCALE

© 2007 David Howley

1m   2m   3m